THE ANTI-JACOBINS, 1798–1800

The Anti-Jacobins 1798–1800

The Early Contributors to the
Anti-Jacobin Review

EMILY LORRAINE de MONTLUZIN

Professor of History
Francis Marion College, Florence, South Carolina

MACMILLAN
PRESS

First published 1988

Published by
THE MACMILLAN PRESS LTD
Houndmills, Basingstoke, Hampshire RG21 2XS
and London
Companies and representatives
throughout the world

Typeset by Wessex Typesetters
(Division of The Eastern Press Ltd)
Frome, Somerset

Printed in Hong Kong

British Library Cataloguing in Publication Data
De Montluzin, Emily Lorraine
The Anti-Jacobins, 1798–1800: the early contributors
to the *Anti-Jacobin Review*.
1. *Anti-Jacobin Review and Magazine*
2. Pamphleteers – Great Britain –
Biography
I. Title
320'.05   PN5130.A5
ISBN 0–333–44137–0

To E. de M. and the memory of R. de M.

Contents

Preface

This study of the early contributors to the *Anti-Jacobin Review* grew indirectly out of research for a doctoral dissertation at Duke University, North Carolina, concerning the role played by several late eighteenth- and early nineteenth-century British periodicals in the conservative press's war of words against the French Revolution. While engaged in my preliminary research, I was repeatedly surprised to find that precious little material existed concerning the *Anti-Jacobin Review*, one of the most militant champions of the counter-revolutionary cause the age had produced. In fact, grudging references of five or six lines in general histories of the periodicals seemed to be the standard treatment meted out to the *Review*, while many studies of the periodical press omitted even that. Later, when I sat under the dome of the British Library Reading Room, copying out the handwritten names of the otherwise anonymous contributors of articles listed in the office copy of the *Anti-Jacobin*, I speculated idly that something should be done to make the list of *Anti-Jacobin* reviewers available in print to students of the periodicals at large. That vague speculation eventually matured into a more ambitious idea, namely, not only to publish a complete cross-reference of articles and known contributors to the *Review* but also to assemble biographical data concerning the contributors themselves – seventy men who ran the gamut from fame to near-total anonymity. More than most publications a literary review is the sum of its parts, or, in this case, the sum of the writers contributing articles to it. Only if light could be shed on those writers themselves, with their individual backgrounds, attitudes, and motivations, would it be possible, I felt, to lift the *Anti-Jacobin* out of its undeserved obscurity and facilitate a better appreciation of this important Church-and-King review in the setting of late eighteenth-century counter-revolutionary thought. The following volume is the result of that project.

In the researching and writing of any undertaking such as this, great debts of gratitude are invariably incurred. I should like to express my deep appreciation to the Francis Marion College Foundation, whose generous subsidy helped make the publication of this book possible, and to Thomas C. Stanton, William C. Moran, and James A. Rogers at Francis Marion College for their enthusiastic support of the project. Part of the initial research for this book was undertaken with the aid of a travel grant from the Department of History at Duke University in 1973. In addition I have been privileged to receive grants on three occasions from the Faculty Research Committee at Francis Marion College. I am most grateful to the Department of Printed Books at the British Library, which allowed me to make use of the office copy of the *Anti-Jacobin Review*, and to the reference personnel at the various other libraries where I gathered information concerning the *Anti-Jacobin* and its contributors, particularly the staffs of the Library of Congress, the Public Record Office, the Duke University Library, and the James A. Rogers Library at Francis Marion College, with special thanks to Neal A. Martin and Roger K. Hux at the last-named institution. I am particularly grateful to Gayle T. Pendleton, who drew upon her formidable knowledge of the press war between Church-and-King and Radical pamphleteers in England in the 1790s and made many incisive suggestions for improvements in the manuscript. I would like to thank Mrs Jacob Kaplan and Patricia A. McDaniel for typing the manuscript, and the editors of the Macmillan Press, especially T. M. Farmiloe and Pauline Snelson, for their decisive support and assistance. Finally I would like to express my special appreciation to Lewis Patton and Charles R. Young of Duke University for their valued suggestions, their ready advice, and their continued interest and friendship.

E. L. de M.

List of Abbreviated Titles

Alumni Cantab.	*Alumni Cantabrigienses*, edited by John Venn and J. A. Venn, 10 vols (Cambridge: Cambridge University Press, 1922–54)
Alumni Oxon.	*Alumni Oxonienses: The Members of the University of Oxford, 1715–1886*, edited by Joseph Foster, 4 vols (London: Joseph Foster [vols I and II] and Parker [vols III and IV], 1887–8)
AJ	*Anti-Jacobin Review*
BLGC	British Library, *General Catalogue of Printed Books*, 263 vols, photolithographic edn to 1955 (London: Trustees of the British Museum, 1959–66)
DNB	*Dictionary of National Biography*, 1st edn (1885–1901)
English Catalogue	*The English Catalogue of Books (Including the Original 'London' Catalogue)* . . . , *1801–1836*, edited by Robert Alexander Peddie and Quintin Waddington (London: Publishers' Circular, 1914)
GM	*Gentleman's Magazine*
Index Eccles.	*Index Ecclesiasticus; or, Alphabetical Lists of all Ecclesiastical Dignitaries in England and Wales since the Reformation*, edited by Joseph Foster (Oxford: Parker, 1890)
Upcott, *Biog. Dict.*	Upcott, William, *A Biographical Dictionary of the Living Authors of Great Britain and Ireland* (London: Henry Colburn, 1816)
Watt, *Biblio. Brit.*	Watt, Robert, *Bibliotheca Britannica*, 2 vols (Edinburgh: Archibald Constable, 1824)

Introduction

In the closing days of 1800 one of the conductors of the Tory *British Critic* paused in his duties for a last look back at the turbulent events of the 1790s and the role he had played in that critical decade in English history. 'At the time of gloom and apprehension,' he wrote, 'when Faction and Impiety had grown insolent and menacing, and those principles which our Church and Constitution support . . . had scarcely any public advocates; . . . duty bid us quit our private walk to do our utmost for the general cause.' The battle was not yet won, however, and 'the season of gloom is not yet past! Britain, after exhausting her strength to support the liberties of Europe . . . [is still menaced]. The storm lowers on every side; and the power that wages war against all duties, human and divine, is daily gaining strength by victories.' Britain's fate, said the writer, was in God's hands. Meanwhile, 'our office is clearly marked. It is, to wield the arms that we are competent to use, in defence of a pure church and wisely ordered state.'[1]

The *British Critic*'s analysis of the situation was eminently typical of conservative[2] thought in the 1790s, especially among the army of thousands of Church-and-King defenders making up the counter-revolutionary, anti-Jacobin wing of the British periodical press. In the first place, the writer portrayed the dangers threatening Britain as the products of a grand conspiracy against Church and State. In the second place, he cast the struggle in literary terms. Britain was endangered by enemy principles even more than by enemy arms – principles spread by the publication of seditious and corrupting writings. Hence it was necessary for the defenders of political and religious orthodoxy to take up their opponents' weapons and mount a literary counter-attack. For many clergy and laymen of a journalistic bent, 'wielding the arms that they were competent to use' meant the creation or rededication of a powerful conservative press – a press charged with the duties of circulating conservative viewpoints on politics, religion, morality, and the social system, encouraging and popularising those writers who supported those principles, exposing those who did not, and keeping an Argus-eyed watch over the literary renegades – the Paines and Priestleys, the Wollstonecrafts and Godwins, the Holcrofts and Kotzebues – that the Tories feared so much. It was, as the *British Critic* succinctly put it, 'a state of literary warfare', in which all supporters of the established order, and especially the conservative periodicals, were duty-bound 'to wield the pen, and shed the ink'.[3]

The *Anti-Jacobin Review* (1798–1821) was one such combatant in the conservative British press's literary war against Jacobin revolution. A latecomer to the counter-revolutionary scene, it has suffered unmerited scholarly neglect – a sin of omission that this study hopes to correct. Just why historians of the British periodical press of the 1790s and early 1800s have chosen to overlook the *Anti-Jacobin Review* is difficult to determine. Certainly the *Anti-Jacobin* ranks among the leading conservative propaganda organs of the revolutionary epoch, on an equal footing with such periodicals as the *British Critic*, the *Gentleman's Magazine*, and (on the Radical side) the *Analytical*, *Monthly*, and *Critical* reviews. Born in 1798 into an epoch of violent revolution, conflicting ideologies, and fundamental changes, the *Anti-Jacobin* not only reflected the anxieties and uncertainties of its day; it also took an active part in the impassioned and often rabid propaganda war then raging for the allegiance of British subjects. Clearly, therefore, it was a publication of importance and influence, a significant development in the history of the British press.

On the strength of its team of contributors and the works they reviewed, the *Anti-Jacobin* likewise merits consideration. Though its staff lacked celebrities of the calibre of the *Analytical Review*'s stable of contributors,[4] the *Anti-Jacobin* enjoyed the support of a number of capable writers, including a few of some fame: John Reeves of the Crown and Anchor Association; John Bowles, the Tory pamphleteer; William Jones of Nayland and William Stevens, leading shapers of the destiny of the High-Church party; J. J. Mounier, erstwhile president of the French Constituent Assembly; John Giffard of Dublin and John Taylor, important figures in the contemporary newspaper scene; Jonathan Boucher, celebrated Tory loyalist and exile from revolutionary America; John Gifford and John Whitaker, both well-known historians; Richard Polwhele, the Cornish poet and author of *The Unsex'd Females*; William Cobbett, the Tory 'Peter Porcupine' and future Radical editor of the *Political Register*, soon to emerge as a giant of the nineteenth-century newspaper press. As for the writers whose publications the *Anti-Jacobin* reviewed or otherwise discussed over the years, the list could well serve as a roster of the leading and lesser figures of the literary age, including in its number Wordsworth and Coleridge, Thomas Paine, Joseph

Priestley, Thomas Moore, Charles Lamb and Charles Lloyd, Thomas Holcroft, Southey, Kotzebue, Gibbon, Goethe, Schiller, Herder, Kant, 'Monk' Lewis, Ann Radcliffe, Mary Wollstonecraft, William Godwin, Madame de Staël, Maria Edgeworth, Fanny Burney, Amelia Opie, Charlotte Smith, Isaac D'Israeli, Thomas Campbell, Hannah More, Leigh Hunt, Walter Scott, William Hazlitt, Shelley, and Byron.

The single major deterrent to scholarly study of the *Anti-Jacobin Review* in the past has no doubt been the paucity of manuscript sources available. The conductors of the *Anti-Jacobin* left no cohesive collection of staff correspondence for researchers to draw upon – nothing comparable to the Murray papers for the *Quarterly Review* or the massive collection of manuscript materials relating to the history of *Blackwood's Magazine*, for example. Thanks to the *Anti-Jacobin*'s records of contributors, however, scholarly opportunities are brighter. The British Library Reading Room is fortunate in possessing the office copy of the first six volumes of the *Anti-Jacobin Review* (minus several numbers),[5] bearing handwritten identifications of the otherwise anonymous contributors of most of the articles that appeared during the *Review*'s earliest years of existence, when its influence was greatest and its anti-Jacobinical passion ran highest. The primary aim of the present study has been to make available for the first time in print a complete listing of the authors of the approximately 700 articles, letters, and poems that appear in the British Library copy of those first six volumes, covering the period from July 1798 to August 1800. Wherever possible, the authors of articles contained in numbers missing from the annotated office copy have been identified as well (and appear marked with an asterisk in the general table of articles – see p. 169). As a comprehensive listing of the contributors of pieces appearing in the early numbers of the *Anti-Jacobin Review*, this volume thus follows in the tradition of similar reference works dealing with the authorship of other eighteenth- and nineteenth-century periodicals, notably Hill Shine and Helen Chadwick Shine's *The 'Quarterly Review' Under Gifford: Identification of Contributors, 1809–1824* (Chapel Hill: University of North Carolina Press, 1949); George L. Nesbitt's *Benthamite Reviewing: The First Twelve Years of 'The Westminster Review', 1824–1836* (New York: Columbia University Press, 1934); Alan Lang Strout's *A Bibliography of Articles in 'Blackwood's Magazine', 1817–1825* (Lubbock, Texas: Texas Tech Press, 1959); Benjamin Christie Nangle's *The 'Monthly Review', First Series, 1749–1789:*

Indexes of Contributors and Articles (Oxford: Clarendon Press, 1934) and *The 'Monthly Review', Second Series, 1790–1815: Indexes of Contributors and Articles* (Oxford: Clarendon Press, 1955); James M. Kuist's *The Nichols File of 'The Gentleman's Magazine'* (Madison: University of Wisconsin Press, 1982); and *The Wellesley Index to Victorian Periodicals, 1824–1900*, ed. by Walter E. Houghton (3 vols; n.p.: University of Toronto Press, 1966–78). Of course, by its very nature a periodical publication is the work of many hands, and its outlook – political, philosophical, and literary – is the aggregate of the opinions of its editor and staff. Accordingly a second purpose of this study has been to gather together information, often from obscure sources, concerning the seventy known contributors[6] to volumes I–VI of the *Anti-Jacobin Review* and, wherever possible, to provide a short biography of each contributor, together with a brief consideration of his political outlook.[7] Thus, although lists of reviewers are unfortunately non-existent for the subsequent volumes, in this way it should be possible to construct a profile of the *Anti-Jacobin Review* during its early, formative years.

In every conceivable way the *Anti-Jacobin Review* was the product of its place and time, a place and time dominated, inspired, and overshadowed by the terrifying reality of the French Revolution. To Tory pamphleteer John Bowles, writing for the *Anti-Jacobin* in 1798, the French Revolution was quite simply 'the most dangerous enemy which ever disturbed the peace of the world',[8] a view shared by virtually every Church-and-King conservative in the British Isles. For in the opinion of Bowles and his friends the events across the Channel signalled not just the fall of a government but, quite correctly, an assault upon a social order, an economic structure, a philosophical and religious world view, a civilisation. In the reaction of Britain's Tories toward the developments in revolutionary France there is almost an echo of the horror of an Augustine or a Possidius learning of the Visigothic sack of Rome. In fact, political writers in the 1790s frequently drew analogies between the barbarian invasions and recent events in France. 'Europe,' said the *Gentleman's Magazine* in 1793, 'since the period when it was overrun by the Goths and Vandals, has never experienced more alarm and danger than at the present moment – Religion, Manners, Literature, and the Arts, are all equally menaced by a foe, whose characteristick is a compound of impetuosity, ignorance, and crime.'[9] For English conservatives the destruction of France by the revolution became, like the fall of Rome itself, an awful example of the collapse of a nation that had become rotten at the core through irreligion, immorality, and corruption – a terrible warning to Britain to reform itself while there was still time.[10]

It was not, though, the spectacle of revolution and bloodshed abroad *per se* that most horrified English conservatives. What frightened men like Bowles the most was the conviction that the French were engaged in a campaign to export their radical ideology – in a word, revolutionary Jacobinism – to Britain and the rest of Europe. In the 1792 Propaganda Decrees the French revolutionary regime had intimated that Jacobinism was in fact a commodity for export. Accordingly British Tories soon came to regard France's 'proselytising dexterity'[11] as the number-one threat to European order – a threat beside which military dangers paled. In the European wars spawned by the Jacobin takeover of the revolution French arms were triumphing, but as one anonymous conservative saw it, Britain had considerably more to fear than armies:

> [T]he French . . . know [he wrote] that much more certain dependence may be placed in the efficacy of seduction and corruption. Before they attempt to invade a country, they constantly endeavour to weaken it, by destroying the principles of the people, by instilling into their minds a mistrust or hatred of their rulers, by raising dissentions, and fomenting parties in *their* favour; which done, they become easy conquests.[12]

John Bowles spoke for all the Church-and-King alarmists when he warned against 'that *moral* – that *revolutionary* force, which has enabled France to set at nought all the rules of military tactics'. The generals of the Coalition powers had miscalculated, he said. '[T]hey considered only the physical force of France, and they neglected to take any precautions against those revolutionary resources, which constituted her strength, and which produced their weakness. They contended with her armies, but it seems never to have entered their thoughts to oppose her principles.'[13]

The medical imagery with which the conservatives so often referred to Jacobinism further demonstrates their overriding conception of the movement as a source of contamination threatening to pollute European political thought. Jacobinism was a 'pestilence', as widespread as a medieval plague and as fatal to thousands of unsuspecting victims. It was an 'infection' that ran through the European body politic, a 'contagion' that corrupted healthy members and left feverish discontent in the place of Pope's universal harmony. It was a 'scourge' divinely sent to chastise sinful England and win her back to a state of holiness by the sobering spectacle of an overrun Continent. Given their fear of a French Jacobin effort to export the revolution abroad, it is easy to see why the Church-and-King camp viewed Britain's political unrest during the 1790s with alarm. Unrest and discontent, the conservatives realised, constituted a perfect incubator for the spread of the Jacobin disease to Britain. In addition the very presence of so much Radical activity seemed to conservatives proof positive that their worst fears were realised – that the infection was indeed already stalking the land.

The grounds for concern were certainly real enough. Britain during the decade of the 1790s endured one of the most turbulent periods in its history, both on the domestic and the international fronts. The situation first became dangerous in 1792, when British Radicals, inspired by the course of events in France, set about establishing or reactivating societies in favour of sweeping political reforms at home. One of the first to organise was master cobbler Thomas Hardy's London Corresponding Society (LCS), a Radical club with a mass artisan membership, an organisation similar to that of the revolutionary *sections* in Paris, and an avowed aim of securing annual parliaments, universal manhood suffrage, and the abolition of rotten boroughs. By the early summer of 1792 the LCS had been joined in the cause of reform by two other Radical societies, both representing predominantly gentlemanly, propertied interests – the Society for Constitutional Information (SCI; founded some years earlier and recently revived) and the Society of Friends of the People (established in the spring of 1792 as an association in favour of parliamentary reform). Despite a Royal Proclamation against Seditious Writings and Publications (issued in May), Radicalism spread rapidly in Britain during 1792, spurred by the massive distribution of Thomas Paine's anti-monarchy, anti-property *Rights of Man, Part II*, to the working classes by the LCS.[14] By the fall of the year events across the Channel had taken a violent turn with the build-up of power in Paris by the Jacobin Club's republican extremists, the bloodshed of the September Massacres, the abolition of the French monarchy, and the defeat of the counter-revolutionary expeditionary force dispatched to France by the First Coalition governments. Meanwhile in Britain the situation was equally critical with mass meetings of Radicals convening, the funds in a slump, France seemingly on the brink of war with Britain, London filled with French *émigrés* (some of whom were certainly French operatives of some sort), and rumours flying of supposed plots by the English Radical societies to stage an insurrection in co-operation with a French invasion of the country. It was in response to one such rumoured conspiracy that Pitt in December 1792 mobilised the militia and called Parliament into special session[15] – actions that followed hard on the heels of the establishment of a Treasury-controlled propaganda mouthpiece (the *Sun* newspaper), the initiation of simultaneous prosecutions of writers, printers, and sellers of seditious literature nationwide (climaxing in the conviction and outlawing of Thomas Paine for seditious libel), and the founding (with government aid and approval) of the counter-revolutionary Crown and Anchor Association.

The Crown and Anchor Association, established 20 November 1792 by John Reeves, an eminent legal historian, civil servant, and future *Anti-Jacobin* contributor, was without doubt one of the most important single elements in the campaign to suppress British Radicalism. Its widespread success is also clear evidence of just how serious the Radical threat was perceived to be by propertied elements in Britain. According to the *Gentleman's Magazine*, Reeves, returning to the country after a tour of duty as Chief Justice of Newfoundland, was appalled to find

the public mind much agitated by the revolutionary scenes then acting in France, and by the practices of democrats and incendiaries at home, and the minds of many well-meaning persons desponding at the gloomy prospect then exhibited to the world. To counteract the destructive designs then meditated, and to diffuse confidence into the well-intentioned, he summoned to the Crown and Anchor Tavern, on the 20th Nov. 1792, a set of respectable persons,[16] who placed Mr. Reeves in the chair, and formed themselves into an 'Association for preserving Liberty and Property against Levellers and Republicans,' announcing the following as the objects for which they met: 1. 'for discouraging and suppressing seditious publications, tending to disturb the peace of this kingdom, and for supporting a due execution of the laws made for the protection of persons and property;' 2. 'to use its best endeavours occasionally to explain those topics of public discussion which have been so perverted by evil-designing men . . . ;'   3. 'to recommend to all those who are friends to the established laws and to peaceable society, to form themselves, in their several neighbourhoods, into similar societies.'[17]

The degree of government support enjoyed by the Association for Preserving Liberty and Property (APLP), or the Crown and Anchor Association, as it is frequently called, has been the subject of much argument. Eugene Charlton Black, for example, has contended that the Association was from its inception an arm of Pitt's late-1792 repressive measures, organised with government support and filled with government placemen, its very appearance on the scene timed to coincide with Pitt's call-up of the militia, summoning of Parliament, and orders for nationwide grand jury proceedings against seditionists.[18] The charge, however, is open to serious challenge. Reeves himself denied that the Ministry had any advance warning of the establishment of the Association,[19] and contemporary accounts by Reeves's Church-and-King associates claim that Pitt in fact had to be persuaded to allow the Association to organise, as he preferred a government ban on all political meetings of whatever stripe.[20] There is little dispute, however, concerning the spectacular success of the movement Reeves initiated. Within weeks the nation was dotted with local Associations, perhaps nearly 1500,[21] chiefly composed of parsons, squires, and other propertied men of all types (but containing some recruits from the tenantry),[22] all protesting their loyalty to the Constitution and pledging themselves to assist the government in ferreting out sedition.[23] In addition the Crown and Anchor Association threw itself into the production of a series of loyalist pamphlets, aimed at both middle-class and working-class readers and designed specifically to counteract Radical propaganda and to mould public opinion in favour of the established order.[24] Printed by the Association and shipped with official Post Office assistance throughout the kingdom to local Associations for distribution, the pamphlets soon found their way to taverns and coffee-houses, cottages and parish churches, mines and dockyards.[25] By early 1793, chiefly thanks to the Association's efforts, the majority of the nation was welded into a thoroughly frightened but determined phalanx of order and property,[26] while the Radical minority was left in a dangerous state of discontent and isolation.

Though 1792 was clearly the crisis point for the government, the next few years saw a continued, substantial Radical threat, both from the activities of the British Jacobins and from the danger of French military intervention. The year 1793 brought the French declaration of war against England and the assemblage in Edinburgh of representatives from English and Scottish Radical societies as the British Convention of the Delegates of the People, the members vowing to fight until death for universal suffrage and annual parliaments[27] and dating their notes the 'first year of British liberty, one and indivisible, by the appointment of the rabble of sans culottes'.[28] The following year, 1794, saw renewed calls for a Radical convention from both the LCS and the SCI, a round of intemperate, inflammatory speeches and published addresses by the Radical societies, the publication of Paine's Deistical *Age of Reason, Pt. I*, with its vicious attack upon the Established Church and Christianity in general, and Robert Watt's abortive conspiracy of armed insurrection. Once again the government's response was swift. Habeas Corpus was suspended; the LCS was severely weakened (and the SCI and Scottish Societies of Friends of the People smashed) by the prosecution of the Radical leaders in the State Trials of 1794;[29] the Volunteer Corps was organised as a home defence reserve in the event of invasion;[30] and the Two Acts of 1795 were drafted to tighten the net of repression around Radical activity: the Treasonable Practices Act broadening the definition of treason and the Seditious Meetings Act clamping fresh restrictions on public meetings and lecture halls.

Far more serious were the developments across the Irish Sea, however, where the United Irish (which had organised in 1790 in support of parliamentary reform) had grown by the mid-1790s into a secret underground extremist group, its members dedicated to turning Ireland into a republic by force, its ranks swollen by untold thousands of armed Catholic irregulars (the Defenders), and its leaders in treasonous contact with the French revolutionary government. The year 1796 brought an unsuccessful French attempt to invade Ireland, involving 45 ships and nearly 15,000 French troops and orchestrated in co-operation with the United Irish. By 1797, a year marked by the mutiny of the British fleets at Spithead and the Nore,[31] United Irish operatives were infiltrating LCS groups in London and Lancashire and successfully luring the LCS into an undeniably treasonous plot to subvert the army, assassinate political leaders, stage insurrections at strategic locations around the country, and assist a French invasion force in capturing London. The date of the *Anti-Jacobin Review*'s founding – 1798 – saw the bloody Irish insurrection of that year, coupled with three more abortive French invasions of Ireland (all of them small scale) and the very real danger of a French military invasion of Britain itself.[32] Finally the end of the decade brought one of the most turbulent epochs in the modern history of Britain to a close with a further suspension of Habeas Corpus, the official suppression of the United Irish and the LCS, and the passage of the Combination Acts of 1799 and 1800 in restraint of strikes among British workers.

In such highly charged circumstances it was natural enough for conservatives to exaggerate the influence of French Jacobins upon the activities of their British Radical counterparts. Likewise it is understandable that conservatives should leap to the conclusion that the sudden spate of Radical activity in Britain was not a spontaneous occurrence but rather the result of deliberate design. How else, they asked, could one explain the eruption of Jacobin Radicalism, with its assaults upon Church and King and Constitution, in a nation as stable and politically advanced as Britain? Thus, quite naturally, Jacobinism to many minds took on the aura of a plot – a conspiracy of atheists, Deists, and Radicals on both sides of the Channel in league to effect a wholesale revolution in Great Britain and Ireland. An extremely important element in that assumption was the broadness of the Jacobin threat, for in Tory minds the alleged 'plot' soon came to encompass far more than the political sphere alone. Church-and-King extremists began to see Jacobinism as a four-pronged conspiracy against political orthodoxy, religion, morality, and established social conventions. 'Jacobinism' became an omnibus catchword for subversion in all its forms – disaffection, sedition, immorality, irreligion, levelling, contempt for the Constitution, scorn of hierarchy. The *British Critic* in 1797 offered a good example of this loose definition. 'A Jacobin . . . ,' said its anonymous contributor, 'is the result and combination of . . . [various types of dissent]. Of Deism, or Atheism, as the particular enemy of religion; of the hatred of monarchy; and, finally, of the hatred of all social order, and moral restraint upon the passions of men.'[33] A Jacobin was in short a deviant from political, moral, social, and religious norms – the more dangerous in Tory eyes because he was also a subversive, committed to imposing his ideology upon an orthodox Britain. So important is this quadripartite definition for an understanding of the anti-Jacobin mind-set that it merits examination in some detail.

First, there was the Jacobin threat to the political structure, the assault upon the Constitution. To understand conservative fears on that score, it is necessary of course to have a clear perception of what the anti-Jacobin Church-and-King camp believed the word 'Constitution' to mean. One may safely say that most anti-Jacobins in Britain in the 1790s ascribed to the post-1660 mainstream interpretation of the English Constitution, as articulated by Burke. That is to say, they believed in a Constitution resting on tradition, flexibility, caution, establishment, order, property, Christian Providence, and benevolent minority rule – the hallmarks, *par excellence*, of Burkean conservatism. They believed, with Burke and with their eighteenth-century forebears, that the British Constitution was to be held in reverence as a priceless legacy, 'an *entailed inheritance* derived to us from our forefathers, and to be transmitted to our posterity',[34] as Burke's *Reflections* put it. Theirs was a Constitution that was traditional while maintaining flexibility, a Constitution based on the wisdom and experience of the past and yet open to new ideas, an historical partnership of the dead, the living, and the unborn. Hence British anti-Jacobins were for the most part not reactionaries, clinging blindly to the past. At least theoretically they were willing to countenance change, if the times were not disturbed and if change were implemented with due caution. While they certainly did not believe that change necessarily meant progress, especially when it came quickly or on a drastic scale, they acknowledged the need for gradual and prudent reforms, timely repairs to the castle of the Constitution, as Burke expressed it.[35] Of course, however, British anti-Jacobins would add as with one voice the proviso that in troubled times – like their epoch of the 1790s – reforms must be temporarily shelved, for the body politic was then in so precarious a state of health that any drugs would be dangerous.

Beside the watchwords of tradition, flexibility, and caution the anti-Jacobins placed the idea of establishments. Obviously they believed in an established monarchy, though limited and bound by legislative power, independent courts, prescriptive rights, and fundamental law. Though most anti-Jacobins of the 1790s made allegiance to Church and King the centrepiece of their political philosophy, they were unequivocally 1688 Whigs (in the specific sense of the word)[36] and firm believers in the concept of limited monarchy, with nothing but disdain for the royal absolutism of the French *ancien régime* and little patience for Filmerean nostalgia.[37] With an established monarchy went an Established Church, for religion, in the anti-Jacobins' view, was inextricably intertwined with politics and morality and thus formed the very underpinning of the state and of civil society. In addition they believed in a class system surmounted by an established aristocracy, privileged but obligated in return to set an example of morality, duty, benevolence, and rectitude. Finally, the anti-Jacobins, again like Burke, added to their constitutional principles an insistence upon order as an absolute necessity for the smooth functioning of society; a belief in the inalienable right to property; a view of history that rested firmly on the Christian creed, revealed religion, and the unfolding of Divine Providence; and a reliance on benevolent minority rule, 'a political order in which the minority exercised power as a trust for the protection of the liberty and property of all people'.[38]

How, therefore, did the British Church-and-King party envisage the political face of quadripartite Jacobinism? Quite obviously, to such men Jacobinism in France or England represented a destructive force of mammoth proportions, a tidal wave of unchecked innovation, capable of sweeping away all the accumulated wisdom and institutions of centuries and ushering in either anarchy or dictatorship. In what, asked one conservative, does Jacobinism consist if not 'in the open display of contempt for all legitimate authority, . . . in a studied subversion of all ancient orders, and existing institutions, [and] in the encouragement of resistance and rebellion against lawful governments'?[39] Accordingly all Radical political activity of any type whatsoever met the standards of Jacobinism and qualified under the umbrella of subversion. There were the republican demands of Paine and the United Irish – an open assault upon established monarchy. There was the oft-repeated Radical cry for a convention of the 'people', empowered by popular will to secure their 'rights' – clearly in anti-Jacobin eyes a subversive notion that smacked of the Tennis Court Oath and was an affront to parliamentary power. As for the matter of public order, *that* (the anti-Jacobins believed) was endangered by every Radical society and every reformist meeting, not to mention physical force plots, active rebellion in Ireland, and conspiracies to collaborate with invading French troops. In particular, however, British conservatives looked with horror upon the drastic, Radical parliamentary reform programme of the LCS, the SCI, and the

Society of Friends of the People, with its twin demands of annual parliaments and universal manhood suffrage. Such activities in anti-Jacobin eyes were nothing less than a 'breaking in upon the Constitution', an offence of the greatest magnitude against tradition and political caution and the principle of minority rule. 'Reform', the anti-Jacobins warned, was a beguiling word, connoting amelioration of abuses, purification of established institutions, and the restoration of venerated principles in pristine form. But reform was too often the first step toward ruin. It was the excuse for tampering with a Constitution that was widely regarded as the best yet devised by the hand of man. It was the crack in the dyke that would bring revolution flooding through. 'The enemy', said one anxious Tory, 'bawls out *reform*, that by so specious a pretext he may change, and ultimately destroy, our whole constitution.'[40] Hence reformers of whatever stripe were to be considered suspect as seditionists, and needed constitutional changes were to be held rigorously in abeyance until less dangerous times.

Second, there was the Jacobin conspiracy's threat to conventional morality, a threat which *Anti-Jacobin* contributors and their brother reviewers never ceased to point out. The *British Critic* found such moral Jacobinism evident in 'the writers of France, as well as of Germany, whose design was to conciliate the attention by interesting narratives, . . . [while] poison[ing] the sources of piety and morality'.[41] The *Gentleman's Magazine* also detected the Jacobin plot at work in the vice and 'specious . . . liberality' which filled contemporary literature and threatened to undermine the character of the young.[42] The *Anti-Jacobin Review* echoed its colleagues' sentiments, declaring that literature 'has . . . been rendered by the sceptical, schismatical, and disaffected writers of the age, a vehicle for the promulgation of every false, bad, and vicious principle, that can corrupt the heart or contaminate the mind of the present and of the rising generation'.[43] Thus in the conservatives' minds the sentimental novels that poured from French presses were part of the Jacobin plot, as they lured hapless English readers away from wholesome tracts and homilies and exposed them to scenes of vice. Thus the waltz was a tool of Jacobin subversion, as it required partners to embrace – an act which broke down the barriers of propriety and led to moral collapse. Thus Mary Wollstonecraft, with her feminism and her unorthodox lifestyle, was the very epitome of 'JACOBIN MORALITY',[44] a threat to the virtue and domesticity of every English woman and, ultimately, to the moral fibre of England itself.

The *Anti-Jacobin* was clearly correct: 'It require[d], indeed, the eyes of Argus to watch and detect the multifarious channels through which . . . [Jacobinical] poison . . . [was] attempted to be infused into the minds of the people of this realm.'[45]

Third, the Jacobin conspiracy threatened the British conception of a hierarchical society of classes and orders resting on the inalienable right to property. A host of subversive authors, the conservatives believed, were 'now very earnestly at work [in Britain] to render the nobility . . . of this country odious to the people'.[46] 'Jacobin' writers in Britain fostered insubordination and 'conspired . . . to substitute the jargon of licentious philosophy and the follies of an imaginary equality, for the rules of social government'.[47] Following the example of their French masters, they launched 'daring, atrocious, and systematic attempts' to destroy rank and property, as they had been destroyed in France,[48] to ridicule magistrates and denounce powerful nobles, and to paint the ruling class from the community level to the Palace of Westminster in the blackest possible colours. Such alarmist fears were only natural. For years propertied Britons had looked on with horror at the unfolding plight of their aristocratic and propertied counterparts in France. They had witnessed through newspaper descriptions the wholesale killing of aristocrats in the September Massacres and in the Terror. They had pored over Burke's shocked account of the 'violation' of Versailles, 'the most splendid palace in the world', by revolutionary mobs.[49] They had read the French Jacobin toasts: 'May the blood of the aristocrats flow, and democracy swim upon the stream . . . may the heads of the aristocrats form stepping stones for the rise of the democrats.'[50] No wonder that in the view of Britain's propertied classes Jacobinism behaved like a sort of Grendel on the loose, smashing up the mead halls and gobbling the thegns.

Finally, the Jacobin conspiracy threatened the Established Church and the Christian community in general. One Church-and-King supporter perceived organised forces plotting to try to stamp out the Christian religion world-wide,[51] and others warned of the existence of secret societies formed to circulate irreligious literature to the lower orders.[52] To most conservatives the Jacobin plot against religion was epitomised by Thomas Paine, whose blatantly anti-Christian *Age of Reason* was in fact sponsored in a cheap edition by the LCS.[53] To the Church-and-King party the implications of such an action were obvious. As the *British Critic* noted, '[I]t has come accidentally under our certain knowledge that the publication of

Paine's wretched book . . . was part of an extensive plan for subverting religion in this country, as had been practised before in France, by corrupting the lower orders of the people; and that large sums were employed, and probably still are, for the purpose of promoting its circulation.'[54] Worse, the circulation of Paine's *Age of Reason* in Britain was perceived to be only a part of the whole – a conspiracy supposedly organised in France and adopted abroad by the Jacobins of other lands to strike at religion everywhere. Indeed to one *Gentleman's Magazine* contributor the entire French Revolution might be seen as 'a deep and deliberate plan' by the irreligious – 'a plan laid for some time, originating in a most obstinate enmity to Christianity, working in darkness . . . to inculcate Atheism, to propagate vice'.[55]

In short, to the way of thinking of the Church-and-King party, orthodox British conservatism was not unlike the military square. It stood as a unit against attack, each of its four flanks protecting and drawing strength from the others. Moreover, its defenders knew that a breach in any one side would automatically imperil the other three. A weakening of religious orthodoxy, for example, would endanger conservative moral standards; a falling off in the acceptance of the class structure and one's place in society would shake the political Constitution. The four faces of conservatism – political, religious, moral, and social – offered the possibility of a number of alliances within conservative ranks and mergers of assets against the common danger posed by Jacobinism. Conversely the Jacobin counterparts of quadripartite conservatism could unite to form various double threats to the Tory defences. It is for this reason that Church-and-King defenders were not content to attack political Jacobinism alone. They recognised that religious, moral, and social aberrations from the orthodox norm must be met with equal force if the whole of the conservative canon were to be preserved intact. Thus an anti-Jacobin defender on whatever front would say, with Donne, that a loss on any flank diminished him – diminished his effectiveness in beating back the Jacobins' arguments, diminished the safety of his own position itself.

One of the most dangerous of the Jacobin combined assaults was that uniting political and religious Jacobinism. Conservatives were not likely to forget Diderot's notorious wish, and the Radicals' drinking toast, that the last king should be strangled with the bowels of the last priest. On this score conservatives who saw danger in the symbiotic relationship between religious and political

Jacobinism found their strongest support in the 1797 *Mémoires pour servir à l'histoire du Jacobinisme* by the Abbé Barruel. Barruel, an *émigré* cleric and historian, was the leading early exponent of what might be called the conspiratorial theory of the origins of the French Revolution.[56] Barruel's thesis, as his 'Preliminary Discourse' outlined it, argued that the entire train of events comprising the revolution was the result of a conspiracy, or, to be more precise, 'a triple conspiracy, in which, long before the revolution, the overthrow of the altar, the ruin of the throne, and the dissolution of all civil society had been debated and resolved on'.[57] As Barruel perceived it, the preparation of the French Revolution could best be seen in terms of a step-by-step subversion of the principles of the *ancien régime*, a progressive and deliberate destruction of France's religious, political, and social fabric:

> 1st.   Many years before the French Revolution men who styled themselves Philosophers conspired against the God of the Gospel, against Christianity. . . . It was the conspiracy of the *Sophisters of Impiety*, or the ANTICHRISTIAN CONSPIRACY.
> 2dly.   This school of impiety soon formed the *Sophisters of Rebellion* . . . , combining their conspiracy against kings with that of the Sophisters of Impiety. . . .
> 3dly.   From the Sophisters of Impiety and Rebellion, arose the *Sophisters of Impiety and Anarchy*. These latter conspire not only against Christ and his altars, but against every religion natural or revealed: not only against kings, but against every government, against all civil society, even against all property whatsoever.[58]

As fellow plotters in the 'triple conspiracy against God, the King, and Society',[59] Barruel named Voltaire, d'Alembert, Diderot, Rousseau, and other leading Enlightenment figures.[60] In subsequent volumes he carried the thesis further still, laying the guilt for having set the revolution in motion at the door not only of the *Philosophes* but of the Freemasons and the German Illuminati as well.[61]

A ready ally of Barruel, with his anti-Masonic, conspiratorial theory of the revolution, was John Robison, ex-soldier of fortune, Scottish professor, and future *Anti-Jacobin* reviewer (q.v.). Himself a Mason, Robison wrote with the express purpose of lifting the shadow of suspicion from the British Masonic lodges and drawing a distinction between them and the 'perverted' form of Freemasonry in existence on the Continent.[62] In his *Proofs of a Conspiracy against All the Religions and Governments of Europe, Carried on in the Secret Meetings of Free Masons, Illuminati, and Reading Societies* Robison argued that the Masonic lodges of France and Germany had fallen under the influence of the French *Philosophes* and become nurseries of immorality, irreligion, and political radicalism. Of all the Masonic orders in German territory the most dangerous, in Robison's opinion, was the secret society of the Illuminati, an extremist offshoot of German Freemasonry, whose 'express aim . . . was to abolish Christianity, and overturn all civil government'.[63] Though suppressed in Brandenburg, the order had surfaced again in the German reading societies, which various Illuminati organised to spread their radical philosophy. In France as well, Robison claimed, the Illuminati were one of the leading forces behind the emergence of revolutionary ideas, subtly infiltrating Masonic lodges in Paris and the provinces and turning the entire order into a network for subversion. 'Thus were the Lodges of France converted in a very short time into a set of secret affiliated societies, corresponding with the mother Lodges of Paris, receiving from thence their principles and instructions, and ready to rise up at once when called upon, to carry on the great work of overturning the state.' Though many contemporaries felt that in damning Freemasons and Illuminati wholesale the *Proofs of a Conspiracy* went too far, Robison himself was entirely convinced by the mass of circumstantial evidence he had built up. 'After all these particulars, can any person have a doubt that the Order of Illuminati formally interfered in the French Revolution, and contributed greatly to its progress?' he asked.[64]

In Britain, though Barruel's and Robison's theories enjoyed an admittedly mixed reception, their writings did provide fuel for the fire of those who perceived a clear connection between irreligion and political rebellion. Not all English anti-Jacobins by any means would agree that the *Philosophes*, the Freemasons, and the Illuminati actually conspired to create the French Revolution. All recognised the overriding importance of political events and attitudes as moving forces in setting the stage for the Jacobin takeover in Paris. But all did assign a crucial role in the preparation of a revolutionary climate to Barruel's and Robison's army of religious sceptics, who had undermined the restraints Christianity placed upon conduct, sown dissatisfaction with the Church as an institution, and regarded themselves as above the law.

In the face of such widespread anti-Jacobin charges of secret conspiracies, threatened insurrection, and French revolutionary influence upon the British Radical movement, certain questions cannot go unanswered. To what extent *did* the French Revolution influence developments across the Channel? To what degree *was* Britain threatened with revolution? Were the anti-Jacobins justified in their fears, or not? In other words, to what extent was the danger really real?

On the matter of French influence upon British Radicalism, the centrepiece of British anti-Jacobin thought at the time, every indication is that such influence was minimal at best until the late 1790s. Decades of determined scholarship have failed to unearth any proof of the existence of an organised secret conspiracy directed by French Jacobins and aimed at undermining Church, State, and society in Britain, whether by Freemasons, reprints of Deist works, or any other means. Of course there is the unanswered question of the previously mentioned 'insurrection plot' of December 1792, in which French operatives, planted among the thousands of *émigrés* in London, were rumoured to have plotted with the English Radical societies to stage an uprising and seize the capital. Existing evidence, however, is far from sufficient to warrant any conclusion on the matter.[65] Of course, too, there were numerous examples of contact between the French revolutionaries and the British Jacobins. Radical societies in Britain exchanged fraternal addresses with the French Convention in the fall of 1792, and some British societies collected money, muskets, and shoes for the French army. Various British and Irish Radicals travelled in France during the revolutionary epoch, including Paine, Priestley, Wordsworth, Mary Wollstonecraft, Wolfe Tone of the United Irish, and Thomas Muir and Lord Daer of the Scottish Society of Friends of the People. There were as well deliberate attempts by British Radicals to imitate their French Jacobin counterparts, attempts which can generally be put down to hero worship. Some British Jacobins cropped their hair, for example, and some Radical ladies built miniature guillotines. Delegates to the British Convention meeting in Edinburgh in late 1793, in addition to dating their minutes 'first year of British liberty, one and indivisible, by the appointment of the rabble of sans culottes', ostentatiously called themselves 'citizen', borrowed procedural methods and terminology from the French revolutionary government, opened their reports with the words 'Vive la Convention!' and closed them with 'Ça ira', and voted to draft a declaration of the rights of man.[66] There were thus undoubtedly some cases of cross-pollination in the French and British Radical movements. It was not, however, until the late 1790s, with the overt, treasonous conspiracy of the United Irish and the LCS with the French government, that the French revolutionaries had any direct influence upon the course of Radicalism across the Channel. For most of the decade R. R. Palmer's assessment is clearly correct: Jacobinism in Britain was a *British* movement arising out of the *British* Radical aims of annual parliaments and universal manhood suffrage, albeit inspired and emboldened by the encouraging example of France. 'It was a plant with native roots', says Palmer, which burst into brilliant bloom in the warmth of the French Jacobin sun.[67]

As for the second issue, the question of whether or not Britain was in real danger of a full-scale insurrection during in 1790s, the answer by informed hindsight appears to be no. The Ministry's success in repressing seditious meetings and publications and breaking up the Radical societies; the marshalling of counter-revolutionary public opinion by the Crown and Anchor Association, loyalist writers and journalists, and religious groups (such as Evangelical and Methodist societies and Sunday Schools); the presence of the Volunteer Corps; native English Francophobia; and the sobering prospect of French invasion all seem to have combined in neutralising the threat of revolution in Britain. Yet even now, after extensive scholarly investigation, that conclusion is far from decisively proved. As for the *appearance* of danger, that is another matter altogether. By every indication the entire conservative camp in Britain genuinely, sincerely believed that the nation was in very real danger of insurrection, or at least severe public unrest, and with good reason. A glance at the 1790s displays all manner of danger signs: Radical societies spreading (at least in the early period) by leaps and bounds; the political consciousness of the working classes suddenly aroused by *The Rights of Man*, thus offering the prospect of wide support for insurrection if it did come; dangerous instances of rioting and popular disorder over the years; the absence of an effective police force trained in crowd control; Deistical propaganda undermining religious faith among certain elements of the population; French agents operating in the capital; economic hard times during part of the decade, coupled with discouraging news from the battlefronts; Ireland ripe for explosion; and the very real possibility of a French invasion, made more serious after 1797 by the fear of another naval mutiny. In addition there was the disturbing parallel with France itself, where revolution had been set in motion by moderate, middle-class reformers agitating for a restructuring of the States-General – the French equivalent of parliamentary reform; where those moderates had then begun losing ground to a well-organised, vocal radical minority; and where a few radical leaders with mobs behind them had then toppled the monarchy and established a dictatorship. In short, Britons in the 1790s were facing a highly volatile situation that looked very dangerous indeed to those persons living through it, unaided by historical hindsight and engaged in fighting a war.[68] One must not allow the strident tone of the anti-Jacobins' writings, their hyperbolic rhetorical style, and their willingness to let their imaginations run away with them concerning organised plots and conspiracies to belie the fact that they had an undoubted cause for alarm. The danger was real – very real – and the English anti-Jacobins' Great Fear[69] was eminently justified.

What then could an individual English conservative do to contribute his mite to the struggle against Jacobinism? If he could do nothing else, he could *write* for the counter-revolutionary cause. There were hundreds of ardent Church-and-King Tories, motivated by patriotism and fear, writing for the public in various capacities during the 1790s. Their single overriding characteristic was their profound sense of mission, a consciousness of service to be performed that inspired an army of volunteers – parsons and magistrates, civil servants and schoolmasters, professional journalists and bookish amateurs – 'to wield the pen, and shed the ink'[70] in the war of words against Jacobinism.

There were, of course, many avenues open to talented writers. There was the government kept press, paid out of Secret Service funds to disseminate the ministerial political line and represented in Pitt's day by an army of Treasury pamphleteers and assorted subsidised newspapers, in particular the *True Briton* and the *Sun*. While Burke's Act of 1782 had tightened restrictions on the use of Secret Service money, limiting to £10,000 per annum the amount that could be spent on pensions and propaganda writing combined, the available fund was still large enough for the government to exert a varying degree of influence upon a number of newspapers and pamphleteers.[71] There were as well a few pro-Ministry but independent newspapers, of which William Cobbett's two dailies, *Porcupine's Gazette* (1797–9) and the *Porcupine* (1800–1), were the leading examples. There was also the realm of sermons, tracts, homilies, and didactic novels, produced by hundreds of private citizens of varying degrees of literary ability and presided over by the eminently successful Hannah More, whose *Cheap Repository Tracts*, a 'Burke for Beginners',[72] sold 300,000 copies in the space of six weeks.[73] There were, finally, the independent, conservative literary reviews. In a struggle which crystallised more and more into a contest between two ideologies, it is difficult to conceive of a tool better suited (albeit for an audience limited to the middle and upper classes) to the tasks of disseminating information, bestowing encouragement upon like-minded authors, and combatting opposing views.

Foremost in the ranks of these 'literary police'[74] were three periodicals: the *Gentleman's Magazine* – already a longtime supporter of Church and Constitution and rededicated in the epoch of the French Revolution to countering the 'machinations' of French and British Jacobin conspirators;[75] the *British Critic* – founded in the summer of 1793, expressly to fight Jacobinism, by the High-Church Society for the Reformation of Principles by Appropriate Literature and published by the staunchly religious and unswervingly Tory firm of Rivingtons; and the *Anti-Jacobin Review* — which appeared upon the scene in July 1798 (in the immediate aftermath of the Irish rebellion) and threw itself headlong into the foray on the side of counter-revolution and the established order.

The *Anti-Jacobin Review* was unique among the leading periodicals of its day in that it was in part the offspring of a newspaper by the same name. The *Anti-Jacobin; or, Weekly Examiner* came into being in late 1797, 'a number of men of brilliant talents and high connection [in Pitt's circle] . . . having determined to establish a weekly paper, for the purpose of exposing to deserved ridicule and indignation the political agitators by whom the country was then inundated'.[76] The aim of the paper was twofold: to launch a counter-attack against the *Monthly Magazine* and certain other 'Jacobin' periodicals and to serve as a gadfly to the Opposition politicians in Parliament. The leader of the project was George Canning, assisted on the literary front by George Ellis and John Hookham Frere and supported politically by such Ministeralists as Charles Long (later Lord Farnborough); John Fitzgibbon, the Earl of Clare; Charles Jenkinson (afterwards the Earl of Liverpool); and Lord Mornington (later Marquis Wellesley and brother of the future Duke of Wellington).[77] William Gifford, noted for his able translations of Juvenal and for his cutting satirical attacks upon the Della Cruscan poets in his *Baviad* and *Maeviad*, was at the last minute chosen editor to replace the founders' first choice, the ailing Dr Grant (q.v.).

According to Edward Hawkins, an early authority on the *Anti-Jacobin* weekly, the newspaper entered the world amid an atmosphere of intrigue and high secrecy:

> [John] Wright, the publisher of the *Anti-Jacobin* [newspaper], lived at 169 Piccadilly, and his shop was the general morning resort of the friends of the ministry. . . . About the time when the *Anti-Jacobin* was contemplated, Owen, who had been the publisher of Burke's pamphlets, failed. The editors of the *Anti-Jacobin* took his house, paying the rent, taxes, &c., and gave it up to Wright, reserving to themselves the first floor, to which a communication was opened through Wright's house. Being thus enabled to pass to their own rooms through Wright's shop, where their frequent visits did not excite any remarks, they contrived to escape particular observation.[78]

To safeguard the conspirators' identity still further, Wright's assistant, William Upcott, was hired to make fair copies of all contributions to the paper in order to protect the authors' handwriting from detection by the printer.[79] The newspaper itself was printed on Sundays on the *Sun* press, for which service Wright, the *Sun*'s publisher, received a guinea a week.[80]

Number 169 Piccadilly quickly became the headquarters of Canning and his fellow writers, who spent most Sundays secreted in their hidden offices, giving themselves up to literary inspiration. According to Hawkins the contributions, especially those in verse, were highly extemporaneous:

> What was written was left open upon the table, and as others of the party dropped in, hints or suggestions were made; sometimes whole passages were contributed by some of the parties present, and afterwards altered by others, so that it is almost impossible to ascertain the names of the authors.[81]

Another indication of the spontaneous nature of the project may be found in William Gifford Cookesley's memoir of William Gifford, with its references to the 'festive' dinner parties attended by Pitt, Frere, Gifford, Jenkinson, Canning, and others, at which 'many of the most exquisite papers in the Anti-jacobin were concocted'.[82]

Certainly the main strength of the *Anti-Jacobin* newspaper lay in the brilliance of its staff. From the beginning the paper enjoyed a crew of exceptionally talented contributors. Canning, Ellis, and Frere were the leading spirits, three men who would later be associated with the like-minded *Quarterly Review*. Canning and Frere had earlier written satirical pieces for Eton's *Microcosm*, while Ellis, a diplomat, courtier, and conversationalist, had been a co-founder of the *Rolliad*. A former opponent of Pitt, Ellis had recently switched sides out of fear of the French Revolution, and now he brought his formidable gift for satire to the service of the Prime Minister.[83] Other contributors included Lord Grenville (William Wyndham Grenville, Pitt's Foreign Secretary), George Howard (Viscount Morpeth), Hiley Addington, George Hammond, Edward Nares, John MacDonald, and perhaps John Bowles (q.v.).[84] Pitt himself has generally been credited with three articles defending his financial policy,[85] but aside from them his direct involvement with the writing of the paper was slight. Canning clearly hoped for more from the Prime Minister and frequently saved space for him until the last minute, but Pitt was rarely forthcoming. His influence upon the project waned after the paper's establishment, and he met only once with the staff at Wright's.[86]

Though Canning, Ellis, and Frere supplied some of the brightest wit of the *Anti-Jacobin* newspaper, its actual day-to-day direction fell to William Gifford, the friend of Wright's who had so unexpectedly inherited the paper's management. The case of William Gifford, editor of the *Anti-Jacobin* weekly and, in later years, of the *Quarterly Review*, is surely one of the most unusual in the history of the English periodical press.[87] The elements of his early life resemble nothing so much as an eighteenth-century *Oliver Twist*: improvident, alcoholic, poverty-stricken parents; grotesque physical deformity (Gifford was a dwarf and a hunchback, with one eye turned outward and a permanent spinal injury); a cruel and tyrannical guardian, who made off with his ward's inheritance and bound him apprentice to a brutal cobbler; a tenacious struggle to acquire learning, secretly, single-handedly, by candlelight, and in perpetual fear of his master's wrath;[88] and finally rescue in the shape of a sympathetic country surgeon (William Cookesley), who bought out the eager apprentice's indenture for six guineas, adopted him into his family, sent him through Oxford, and died of pneumonia on the eve of his adopted son's academic triumph.

Gifford's youthful struggle must be taken into account, for in this case the child was clearly the father of the man. Indeed his early history is the key to every word he wrote for the cause of anti-Jacobinism. 'He was a firm believer in the social system that permitted him to rise as he did',[89] and with reason. A philanthropic English gentleman of the middling sort had rescued him from his miserable childhood; a lord had given him the copy of Juvenal that launched his career as a translator; Oxford had furnished him the scholarship that turned him into a gentleman; and Tory leaders Pitt and Canning had rewarded his diligent study with the appointment that was to win him a place in literary history and, ultimately, burial in Westminster Abbey. In Gifford's opinion, therefore, the English political and social systems were flawless, and his duty lay in an ardent defence of those systems and lifelong gratitude to his benefactors.

Accordingly William Gifford became one of the most virulent anti-Jacobins and anti-Gallicans in the entire conservative camp. Although William Cobbett (q.v.) attempted at the time to dismiss him as a sinecured propagandist and a hypocrite, there is no reason to doubt the sincerity of Gifford's expressed political views.[90] 'His political and religious attachments completely overshadowed his judgment and common sense at times', his biographer has noted.[91] John Taylor (q.v.), a fellow journalist and Gifford's contemporary, recorded much the same impression in his memoirs. 'Mr. Gifford', said Taylor, 'had no mercy on those who differed with him in political opinions. He was a stanch [sic] supporter of Mr. Pitt's administration, and was a firm and intimate friend of Mr. Canning.'[92] Even Gifford's editing of the old English dramatists bore the imprint of his political beliefs. When later engaged as editor of the *Quarterly Review* he became notorious for ransacking the contributions of his staff reviewers, deleting the faintest suggestions of political heresy and rewriting the pieces into Tory manifestos of pristine purity – a practice deeply resented by the mutilated contributors.[93] As for the French Revolution, his loathing was unbounded. '[A]s some people have a hatred of a cat, and others of a toad, so . . . [Gifford] felt uneasy when a Frenchman was named.'[94] It is no wonder that the reformist Leigh Hunt satirised Gifford in *The Feast of the Poets* or that Keats's Radical friend, Charles Brown, concocting a Faustian story of an old woman seduced by the devil and delivered of 'an infinite number of Eggs', assigned William Gifford a place as one of the newly hatched imps.[95]

In essence Gifford's technique was to strike at the Radical

propagandists with the latter's own weapons. Gifford devoted a sizeable portion of each weekly number of the *Anti-Jacobin* newspaper to a review of the current periodical press, broken down under the headings of 'Lies', 'Misrepresentations', and 'Mistakes'. Here he subjected hapless Jacobin journalists to a merciless scrutiny, trumpeting their errors of grammar and spelling, lifting statements out of context to distort their meanings, dismissing their assertions as 'lies' with no further comment, and ridiculing their puny snipings at the Jove-like Pitt.[96] Simply stated, as Roy Benjamin Clark has noted, Gifford's 'purpose was to break the influence of the Jacobins by fair means or foul . . . [and] to defend the King and government, the nobility, and the Church of England'.[97] If that purpose earned him the enmity of the entire Radical wing of the press, it was a price Gifford was more than willing to pay.

The *Anti-Jacobin* newspaper came to a close less than eight months after its inception. Various explanations have been offered for its end. Samuel Smiles believed that it folded when Canning became Under-Secretary of State for Foreign Affairs and no longer had leisure time to spend on the enterprise.[98] Others have suggested that it was considered too extreme by the Wilberforce wing of the party, perhaps because it became too intemperate and coarse for its readers to stomach, perhaps because Pitt felt that Canning and his companions were demeaning the Ministry by writing for such a scurrilous sheet, however brilliant.[99] Probably, though, it came to an end simply because its work was done. It had appeared, as promised, every Monday throughout the 1797–8 parliamentary session and had diligently attempted, as Canning put it, 'to set the mind of the people right upon every subject'.[100] When the parliamentary session ended, so did the *Anti-Jacobin; or, Weekly Examiner.*[101] Its final number appeared 9 July 1798, featuring Canning's poem 'The New Morality', as an audacious parting shot at the whole galaxy of Opposition politicians and Radical pressmen. The same month the *Anti-Jacobin Review and Magazine* rose to take its place, independent in staff and management, yet inspired by the same mission, namely, to defend Church and Constitution and to fight the spread of Jacobin revolution.

Between the *Anti-Jacobin* weekly newspaper and the *Anti-Jacobin Review* several important differences existed. In the first place, the *Anti-Jacobin Review* acquired a new editor, who also went by the name of Gifford – John Richards Green (1758–1818), an intensely patriotic, pro-Ministry writer who had changed his name to John

Gifford (q.v.) after a youthful fling with indebtedness. John Gifford had first earned the notice of the Pittite camp with his anti-Jacobinical *History of France* (published 1791–4) and had gone on to write Crown-and-Anchor pamphlets and (apparently) to edit the Treasury-funded *True Briton* newspaper. He would direct the affairs of the *Anti-Jacobin Review* from its establishment in 1798 until his death in 1818, steering it unswervingly along the path of Church-and-King conservatism. For his assorted efforts in favour of Pitt and counter-revolution Gifford was amply rewarded, receiving a Treasury pension and appointment to two consecutive police magistracies. It would be a mistake, however, to dismiss him as a mere propagandist for hire. There was nothing hypocritical in Gifford's hatred of the French Revolution or in his blind opposition to the English reform movement, and the vast quantities of reviews he wrote himself for the *Anti-Jacobin* during his twenty years as editor are among the most vicious and vindictive attacks upon Radicalism and revolution ever to appear in the contemporary periodical press.[102]

A second important difference between the *Anti-Jacobin Review* and its newspaper predecessor involved the make-up and tone of the staff. Gone was the *Anti-Jacobin* newspaper's circle of brilliant and daring young Canningite Tories, with their mordant wit and verve and slapdash London chatter. In their place the *Anti-Jacobin Review* relied on the services of a team of thoroughly sober and earnest contributors, competent writers, for the most part, with solid literary and journalistic experience, resolutely conservative (with a few notable exceptions which will be pointed out in due course), and sprinkled with a disproportionate number of clergymen. Thus no longer was it from the parliamentary antechambers and the London town houses that the *Anti-Jacobin* drew the greatest number of its recruits but from the parsonages and vicarages of rural England – from Warham All Saints in Norfolk, from Donhead St Andrew and Enford in Wiltshire, from Hackney and Hanwell, Teston and Epsom, from the West Country towns of Ruan Lanihorne and Exmouth and Manaccan. The consequence for the *Anti-Jacobin Review* was a production fully as rabid and vindictive in tone as its predecessor but solemn, humourless, ponderous in style, preoccupied with abstruse religious controversy, and even more fanatical on the subject of the dangers posed by the Jacobin movement.

There were other differences as well. Obviously, with the change from weekly newspaper to monthly literary review went a refocusing of staff attention away from day-to-day parliamentary politics and toward a comprehensive critical survey of current literature. Two special foes of the *Anti-Jacobin* newspaper – the Foxite Whigs in Parliament and the 'Lake School' poets, represented by Wordsworth, Coleridge, Southey, Charles Lamb, and Charles Lloyd – declined in relative importance as targets for the *Anti-Jacobin Review*, becoming just two groups among many for the contributors to censure. John Gifford and his staff spread their nets wide, and the *Review*, its numbers routinely divided into sections of 'Original Criticism', 'Reviewers Reviewed', miscellaneous material, and a valedictory 'Summary of Politics, Foreign and Domestic', scanned the horizon each month, searching for Jacobin opponents in every realm of politics or literature.

Throughout its career the *Anti-Jacobin Review* operated in accordance with several simple ground rules, rules it shared with the other conservative literary periodicals of the day. First, obviously, the *Anti-Jacobin* was a literary review with a mission, and that mission was to defend orthodoxy – political, religious, moral, and social – from those forces at home and abroad threatening to destroy it. Second, the *Anti-Jacobin*, though in name a literary review, by virtue of its *raison d'être* always allowed political and religious concerns to dominate literary ones. As a result, despite some reviewers' honest attempts at balance, critical decisions tended to reflect political and religious acceptability far more than literary merit. Third and last, although the *Anti-Jacobin*'s ranks did include a number of men who as individuals enjoyed government patronage (in the form of Treasury subsidies, crown livings, civil service places, and so on), its contributors were completely sincere in their counter-revolutionary opinions. The rewards and incentives some of them received from the hand of the Ministry should in no way obscure the fact that what they wrote, they wrote from conviction. As for the *Anti-Jacobin* itself, it apparently enjoyed no significant financial backing from the Ministry or any other group.[103]

It was on the ideological front that the *Anti-Jacobin* newspaper and the *Anti-Jacobin Review* were most in accord. Like their predecessors on the newspaper staff, most of John Gifford's reviewers were Burkean conservatives, though some of them would go farther than Burke in a wholehearted acceptance of the conspiratorial theory of Jacobinism, à la Barruel. Beginning with his prospectus John Gifford made it perfectly clear that his writers would hold unswervingly to the political course charted by the *Anti-Jacobin* newspaper. In addition Gifford reiterated the theme of the press's mission as a weapon of counter-attack that was so marked in conservative thought of the period. The *Anti-Jacobin Review* was established, said Gifford, in order to fight the lies of the Jacobin press, which was supporting and defending 'the Regicides of France and the Traitors of Ireland'. To protect the press from such Radical corruption, it had to be controlled, and the best way to exert that control, Gifford believed, was through the press itself. 'Falsehood is best opposed by the promulgation of truth. MAGNA EST VERITAS ET PRAEVALEBIT.'[104] The *Anti-Jacobin Review*, he said, would address its immediate efforts to blocking the flood of sedition pouring forth from the native Opposition *Monthly*, *Critical*, and *Analytical* reviews, but to be effective, the *Anti-Jacobin* must dam the stream of pollution at its source. He and his staff had learned 'that nearly all the presses on the continent of Europe are under the immediate influence either of FRENCH PRINCIPLES, or of FRENCH INTRIGUES. The same influence also prevails in *America*', he added. 'From these contaminated sources,' said Gifford, 'the poison of Jacobinism might be successfully diffused over our country, and, circulating through secret channels, disguised in various ways, might ultimately undermine that fabric which can never be destroyed by an *open* attack.'[105] The ultimate enemy, therefore, was the revolutionary philosophy of France, and the *Anti-Jacobin Review* took as its solemn mission the task of fighting that insidious foe with all its strength.

In terms of literary criticism the *Anti-Jacobin*, as noted earlier, judged all works chosen for review along strict politico-religious lines, a policy, of course, in keeping with the accepted practice of most of the rest of the periodical press of the day. A typical case in point is the *Anti-Jacobin*'s treatment of the Romantic movement in literature, which was in full swing throughout the *Review*'s years of existence. To the uninitiated the *Anti-Jacobin*'s reception of the Romantics would seem capricious indeed. Gifford and his staff totally ignored Blake and Keats, for example, not to mention Landor, Crabbe, Peacock, Clare, and De Quincey. In addition the *Review* virtually ignored Thomas Moore, Leigh Hunt, Hazlitt, Thomas Campbell, and Shelley, abandoning each after a single review article. The German and French Romantics fared no better. The *Anti-Jacobin*, despite its thousands of pages of critiques of foreign literature, never reviewed Friedrich and August Wilhelm von Schlegel's seminal lectures defining Romanticism as a literary school or their contributions to the *Athenaeum*, which became the mouthpiece of the movement in Germany. Nor did the *Anti-Jacobin* devote any review space to Madame de Staël's *De l'Allemagne*, which popularised the ideas of the Schlegel brothers and thus facilitated the spread of Romanticism from Germany to the rest of the Continent. Indeed the *Anti-Jacobin* never discussed German Romanticism as such, preferring to dismiss the productions of the German literati under a blanket condemnation on moral and religious grounds.[106]

As for those Romantic works that did win the notice of Gifford and his staff, the key to their treatment at the hands of the *Anti-Jacobin* was unquestionably their political and religious content, which far outweighed literary merit as a factor for assessing critical praise or blame. Thus the *Anti-Jacobin* censured Byron's monumental *Childe Harold's Pilgrimage* on grounds of irreligion and shaky morality[107] while commending Thomas Moore's little-remembered *Epistles, Odes, and other Poems* for its uncomplimentary picture of America, a nation the *Anti-Jacobin* detested.[108] Thus too the *Review* praised Madame de Staël's published memoirs for exposing Napoleonic tyranny[109] but warned readers against *Corinne* as being 'subversive of all chastity and rational virtue'.[110] Thomas Campbell's *Gertrude of Wyoming* drew condemnation for its approval of the American Revolution and for the common-law marriage of its hero and heroine.[111] Hazlitt's *Political Essays* received the same treatment for its political and religious Radicalism;[112] and Shelley's *St Irvyne* so disgusted one *Anti-Jacobin* staffer by its irreligion and immorality and overwrought literary style that the *Anti-Jacobin* never reviewed Shelley again.[113] Southey, like Madame de Staël, received mixed reviews from Gifford's team, with Richard Polwhele (q.v.) attacking the poet's youthful *Joan of Arc* as an unpatriotic, anti-English production shot through with Painite views on natural religion[114] while a later staffer praised Southey's edition of the *Chronicle of the Cid* for denouncing 'Popery'.[115] Then there was the case of the unfortunate Charles Lloyd, upon whose neck the *Anti-Jacobin* dropped its critical axe by mistake, having concluded from an erroneous reading of Lloyd's novel, *Edmund Oliver*, that Lloyd was a rabid anti-war Jacobin.[116] The only major exceptions among the Romantics to the politico-religious standard for criticism were Wordsworth, Coleridge, and Scott, whom the *Anti-Jacobin* chose to review primarily on literary content. Not that

that guaranteed an appreciative reception, of course. While William
Heath (q.v.) praised *Lyrical Ballads* for its 'genius, taste, elegance,
wit, and imagery of the most beautiful kind',[117] a later *Anti-Jacobin*
reviewer laughed Coleridge's separate edition of *Christabel* to scorn
as 'balderdash' and pronounced that 'a more senseless, absurd, and
stupid composition, has scarcely, of late years, issued from the
press'.[118] Scott for his part found that although the *Anti-Jacobin* gave
uniformly enthusiastic notices to the *Waverley* novels, it denigrated
his poetry for its plethora of antiquated and 'obsolete terms, of
far-fetched allusions, of distorted imagery, of jarring rhymes, and of
prosaic verses'[119] and for its insistence upon the use of Scottish
dialect 'disgusting' to English ears.[120] Of course, one reason for the
Anti-Jacobin's failure to formulate a comprehensive attitude toward
Romanticism as literature (as opposed to Romanticism as a vehicle
for political and religious statements) was its lack of regularity in
reviewing specific Romantic authors. The *Anti-Jacobin* reviewed
only Scott and Byron with any frequency and dropped the latter for
all practical purposes in 1814 after Byron's publication of *The Bride of
Abydos* and *The Corsair*, which the *Review* strongly condemned on
moral and religious grounds.[121]

A key variable in the *Anti-Jacobin*'s day-to-day performance was
provided by the contributors themselves. Though the *Anti-Jacobin
Review* quite obviously had a uniform political and philosophical
standard, that standard was to an extent the reflection of the
aggregate opinion of its contributors and was influenced by their
individual fears, concerns, and prejudices. An all-important
question thus becomes the make-up of the *Review*'s staff of writers.
Who were the contributors? What did they have in common of ideas
or experience? What were their professions? Their religious and
educational backgrounds? Their political views? Their personal
motivations for writing? How many were Dissenters, and how
many were *émigrés*? What was their geographical distribution? How
many rose from poverty? How many enjoyed government
patronage? How many knew each other? How well did their beliefs
fit into the anti-Jacobin mind-set of the age? Would it be possible, in
fact, through an analysis of common denominators, to arrive at a
'typical' *Anti-Jacobin* reviewer?

In terms of profession, by far the largest single group among the
seventy men known to have contributed to the *Anti-Jacobin Review*'s
first six volumes was that of the clergy. Thirty-seven – over half of
the known contributors – were or had been clerics of some sort when

they wrote for the *Anti-Jacobin*, and one more contributor, Arthur Cayley, took orders later, in 1813. Of this number several were Dissenters – Braidwood, Greatheed, Haldane, and Rivers (all of whom wrote letters to the *Review* protesting their political loyalty and their opposition to the French Revolution); one (William Atkinson) was a Methodist in his leanings (though he held Church of England appointments); another (Agutter) had inclinations toward Swedenborgianism; and another (Tabaraud) was an exiled Catholic abbot. The great majority of the thirty-seven, however, were beneficed clergymen in the Church of England. In addition, one more *Anti-Jacobin* contributor, Lawrence Hynes O'Halloran, posed illegally as a clergyman – so successfully in fact that he was able to make a career for life out of his fictitious orders.

The next largest professional groupings[122] among those contributors whose occupations are known were those of journalists and schoolmasters. Eleven men – Bisset, Boettiger, Cobbett, Giffard of Dublin, John Gifford, Grant, Montlosier, Rivers, Tabaraud, Taylor, and Willich – had worked as newspaper writers, as editors of newspapers, reviews, or magazines, or as pamphleteers by the time they wrote for the *Anti-Jacobin*, and three others, Blagdon, Greatheed, and Harral, would become editors of newspapers or reviews in later years. In addition, several others could be described as professional writers – Moser and Reid, the historians Volney and Andrews, and to an extent D'Israeli and Pye, the Poet Laureate. Surprisingly, fifty-seven of the seventy *Anti-Jacobin* contributors are known to have published works of their own (over and above newspaper and review articles) in the course of their lives. Meanwhile, fifteen of the *Anti-Jacobin*'s staff had had some connection with the teaching profession before starting work for the *Review*: Bisset, Boucher, Croft, Kelly, and O'Halloran (who had all been headmasters of schools in England or America); Barclay (an anatomy lecturer); Robison (a chemistry professor at the University of Edinburgh); Blagdon and Cobbett (who had given language lessons); Boettiger, Mounier, Tabaraud, and Volney (who had all been connected with *collèges* or *gymnasia* on the Continent); and Randolph and Walker (who had been private tutors). In other categories six *Anti-Jacobin* contributors were physicians or scientists (Barclay, John Heath, Kelly, Pears, Robison, and Willich), two were barristers or legal scholars (John Bowles and Reeves),[123] several were politicians (notably three Frenchmen – Montlosier, Mounier, and Volney),[124] Cooke was a bookseller, Stevens was a wealthy hosier, and Mavor had some connection with a London counting house.

The geographical distribution of the *Anti-Jacobin* contributors provides some hints about the drawing power of the *Review*. Of the contributors whose whereabouts at the time are known, the largest single group – twenty-two or twenty-three persons (including a large number of journalists), or about one-third of the total list of seventy known contributors – lived in London or its vicinity. Another one-third (including a large number of clergy) were scattered throughout England: two or three in the West Country, one in Bath, one in Oxford, one or two in Wiltshire, three in Surrey, three in Kent, three or four in the East Anglian counties of Norfolk and Suffolk, one in Bedford, three in the West Midlands, one in the Lincolnshire–Nottinghamshire vicinity, and one or two in Yorkshire. In addition, seven of the contributors are known to have come from Scotland, one was a Dubliner, and three were foreign writers living on the Continent.

In a number of cases recruitment of writers for the *Anti-Jacobin* can be explained at least in part by patterns of acquaintance. Taylor, Reeves, and John Bowles dined together from time to time, in company with George Chalmers of the Board of Trade and Plantations (himself a government propaganda writer); and Taylor for his part knew Fitzgerald, John Gifford, and Pye. Pye's literary protégé was D'Israeli, and John Gifford was a personal friend of Harral and an acquaintance of Cobbett. Agutter published a pamphlet in conjunction with John Bowles,[125] and Tabaraud issued a French translation of Bowles's *Reflections submitted to the Consideration of the Combined Powers*, while Cobbett was a good friend of Reeves and numbered John Bowles, Brand, and Boucher among his correspondents. Meanwhile among the Church-oriented contributors Stevens was a pivotal figure. He worked with Skinner in the cause of Scottish Episcopacy and was a friend of Prince, Randolph, Jones of Nayland, and Boucher. Moreover, Stevens introduced Boucher to Jones of Nayland and to Samuel Glasse, George Henry Glasse's father. J. J. Watson, a future leader of the High-Church party, was a friend of John Bowles and Stevens and was as well the former curate of Jonathan Boucher at Epsom. Several of the Scots were known to each other: Gleig, Robison, and Walker were acquaintances, and so were Gleig and Skinner (though not on the best of terms). Polwhele and Whitaker, two of the *Anti-Jacobin Review*'s most important contributors, were close friends and neighbours, and Blagdon was Willich's private secretary.

As the vast majority of the *Anti-Jacobin Review*'s writers were devotees of Burkean conservatism of the counter-revolutionary, Church-and-King stamp, the question naturally arises whether or not any of them knew Burke personally. Judging by the massive Copeland edition of Burke's correspondence, a few of the *Anti-Jacobin* writers did have a connection with Burke, but those relations seem to have been distant and negligible. John Reeves, who received support from Burke and William Windham when his *Thoughts on the English Government* was under parliamentary attack, seems to have had the only dealings with Burke of any significance.[126] Several *Anti-Jacobin* writers – Moser, Gifford, and John Bowles – obsequiously sent copies of their works to Burke, the great man, to read, and Burke wrote courteous but perfunctory letters of thanks in reply.[127] In addition, Brand, Glasse, Montlosier, Mounier, and Stewart each wrote at least one letter to Burke.[128]

A very important common denominator among a number of the *Anti-Jacobin*'s contributors was government patronage, taking the form of pensions, direct grants from the Secret Service funds, clerical appointments, civil service posts, and the like.[129] Several *Anti-Jacobin* writers were recipients of direct Treasury subsidies: Boucher received several small Treasury grants after returning to England from America, culminating in a regular pension starting at £100 per annum. Taylor had a regular salary from Secret Service funds for supporting the ministerial line in the press, as did the *Anti-Jacobin*'s editor, John Gifford, and (in later years) F. W. Blagdon. For his part Giffard of Dublin received £600 per annum for his efforts in defending ministerial policy and the Protestant cause in Ireland, in particular through his work as editor of the *Dublin Journal*. In addition, John Bowles and Donald Grant also enjoyed substantial pensions from Secret Service funds for their writings in support of government.

A number of *Anti-Jacobin* contributors held valuable posts in the civil service, some sinecures, some not. Reeves headed the list with his appointments as commissioner of bankrupts, law clerk to the Board of Trade, chief of the Standing Committee of the Mint, receiver to the police, Chief Justice of the Court of Judicature in Newfoundland, High Steward of the Manor and Liberty of the Savoy, joint patentee of the office of King's Printer, and joint superintendent of the Alien Office. In November 1792, before he had acquired the last three posts, the *Star* estimated that his various government offices brought him £1,000 per annum.[130] John Giffard, a member of the Dublin Corporation, was as well a place holder in the Irish customs for a number of years. Fitzgerald held various posts in the Navy Pay Office, John Bowles was appointed commissioner of bankrupts and commissioner for the sale of Dutch prizes, Mounier was a British secret agent in Switzerland for two years in the mid 1790s (and was offered the position of Chief Justice of Canada, which he refused). Gifford, John Bowles, Pye, Moser, Polwhele, W. L. Bowles, and Booker were magistrates, and Pye was appointed poet laureate. Then there were the Church appointments. Boucher was given the vicarage of Epsom as a reward for his Tory stand in America and was considered for the Episcopal see in Edinburgh, though he never received the latter appointment. Randolph was chaplain to the Duke of York and prebendary of Bristol, in the gift of the Lord Chancellor; Booker and W. L. Bowles both served as chaplain to the Prince Regent; Croft was presented to the rectory of Thwing in Yorkshire by his college friend, Lord Eldon, a conservative stalwart; and Brand was rewarded with the lucrative living of St George's, Southwark, by Lord Loughborough (then Lord Chancellor) in recognition of Brand's recent pamphlet supporting Pitt and the war with France. Of course in this connection the caveat mentioned earlier should be reiterated here, and that is that the fact that many of the *Anti-Jacobin*'s staff writers accepted patronage, either before or after their affiliation with the *Review*, in no way belies the sincerity of the views they expressed in their writings. There is indeed absolutely no evidence to indicate that any of the above men were anything but genuine in their support for Church and State.

As for other categories for comparison, the *Anti-Jacobin*'s ranks included a large number of university-educated men. Sixteen are known to have attended Oxford colleges, most taking degrees; nine were Cambridge men; and two included in those numbers – William Jones of Nayland and Charles Edward Stewart – held degrees from both universities. Three others had studied at the University of Edinburgh, one at the University of Glasgow, and one at King's College, Aberdeen, while W. T. Fitzgerald had been a student at the Royal College of Navarre in the University of Paris. Most of the contributors whose birth dates are known started writing for the *Anti-Jacobin* while in their thirties or forties, although three (Cayley, Cheetham, and Blagdon) were in their early twenties and William

Jones of Nayland was seventy-four. Five – Lachassagne, Montlosier, Mounier, Tabaraud, and Willich – were *émigrés* to England, the first four (at least) fleeing the French Revolution. As previously mentioned, four of the contributors – Braidwood, Greatheed, Haldane, and Rivers – were Dissenters and a fifth, William Hamilton Reid, was an ex-Dissenter who had undergone a change of heart and turned to orthodoxy.[131] Reid was also typical of another small minority among the *Anti-Jacobin* contributors – those individuals who had risen above poverty and disadvantages of birth and become, for a time at least, staunch conservatives, deeply appreciative of the social system that had allowed them to rise. Reid, Boucher, Brand, Croft, and Cobbett were all examples of such 'grateful Toryism'.

The pattern of staff assignments provides a few additional clues about the management of the *Anti-Jacobin* during its early years. In the first place, it is worth noting that the reviewers' careers or areas of competence by no means dictated the choice of assignments. The *Anti-Jacobin* during the course of its first six volumes reviewed a wide range of literature, drawn from both English and foreign authors. By far the largest single category of works reviewed (about two out of every five articles) was that of political publications – pamphlets and speeches; commentaries on current events, especially in France; polemical works on the Irish union; patriotic sermons for fast days; political poetry; arguments concerning Pitt's income tax; and the like. Next in numerical importance came works on divinity (including non-political sermons) and historical publications, constituting approximately one-sixth and one-eighth of the reviewers' agenda, respectively. Poetry (excluding political satire), novels and plays, travel (including the popular scenic tours of the School of the Picturesque), and medico-scientific works were likewise strong areas, accounting, when added together, for another one-fourth of the *Review*'s critical space. In addition, the *Anti-Jacobin* contained a handful of reviews in the categories of drama, law, philology, the Classics, geography, philosophy, education, and the like. Gifford to be sure sometimes did assign review articles according to the expertise of the staff. For example, Dr Heath reviewed medical publications; Kelly, the mathematician and astronomer, covered technical works in those fields; Harral, a novelist and playwright himself, did drama, novels, and tales; Blagdon, a professional translator, covered foreign literature; Agutter, Prince, Croft, and Skinner, all clerics, concentrated on theological publications. But assignments according to staff competence were by no means always the case, and a number of contributors blithely reviewed works outside their fields as a matter of routine.

Finally, although the *Anti-Jacobin* staff reviewed both friendly and unfriendly authors in large quantities, an interesting footnote is the frequency with which they reviewed works by each other.[132] In the first six volumes Gifford reviewed publications by Bisset, Polwhele, Cobbett, Samuel Henshall, Munkhouse, John Bowles, Stewart, O'Halloran, Hutton, Rivers, Reid, and Brand. Bisset reviewed D'Israeli, and W. L. Bowles covered Polwhele. Watson did Thomas, Prince, and Glasse; and Whitaker reviewed Samuel Henshall, Glasse, Croft, and Gifford. Boucher did Gleig, John Bowles did Boucher, Bisset did Gifford, and Samuel Henshall did Gifford, O'Halloran, and Munkhouse. Gleig reviewed Braidwood, Taylor did Pye, and Glasse covered Jones of Nayland. Such a system obviously produced a built-in bias, but it was a practice from which none of the reviewers shrank. One of their duties was to encourage authors who defended Church and King and Constitution, and if those authors happened to be their fellow contributors, it was of no matter to the *Anti-Jacobin* staffers.

What then can be said of the typical contributor to the *Anti-Jacobin Review*? Based on known information, the typical *Anti-Jacobin* reviewer was a clergyman in the Church of England, although journalism and teaching were strong contenders for alternate careers. If a clergyman, he lived in the provinces; if a journalist, he lived in London. Again, if a clergyman, he probably had attended a university at least temporarily, though less than half of the contributors as a whole were university-educated. He was in his thirties or forties when he first started writing for the *Anti-Jacobin*. He would publish at least one work of his own (exclusive of reviews) sometime in the course of his life, and his contributions for the *Anti-Jacobin* did not necessarily fall into his own area of expertise. He was a friend of at least one other contributor, and it would not be unusual if he had some personal connection with the government, either through a pension or subsidy, a Crown living, service as a magistrate, or some other government post or reward. He was a political conservative of the Church-and-King stamp, with marked counter-revolutionary opinions. Finally, he was completely sincere and serious in his journalistic endeavours, regarding it his clear duty to uphold the established order in Church and State and to support the *Review* in its campaign to fight 'the malignant genius of Jacobinism'.[133]

Fight the *Review* did for twenty-three years, though changes in publishers, amalgamation with other journals, and declining interest made its attacks increasingly less effective.[134] Although it has been the purpose of this account to concentrate on the *Anti-Jacobin Review* in its early, formative years, a few general trends in its later history might be sketched out to complete the picture of the *Review* as it grappled with the new political complexities of the nineteenth century. The *Anti-Jacobin* would continue under John Gifford's leadership until his death in 1818, and it would maintain until it ceased publication in 1821 its steadfast conservative philosophy and vehement support for Tory ministries.[135] Vindictiveness and stridency of language would continue to be its hallmarks, and the rise to power of Napoleon would give it a target of fit proportions upon which to vent its journalistic wrath. Church and King would remain the twin pillars of its allegiance, and partnership with the *Protestant Advocate* in particular would lead it to devote a tremendous amount of its space to a scurrilous anti-Catholic campaign. The parliamentary reform agitation of the post-1815 epoch would quite predictably find it warning its readers with great alarm 'that the very same arts which demoralized France, and produced in that unhappy country all . . . [manner of] horrors, are now in full activity in England',[136] and in Henry Hunt's parliamentary reform campaign it would perceive no less than Jacobinism alive again.[137] In December 1821, after twenty-three years and sixty-one volumes of ceaseless struggle for the conservative cause, the *Anti-Jacobin Review* would disappear from the literary scene.

In any study such as this involving the periodicals, the ultimate concern must be the matter of the effectiveness of the review in question in carrying out its self-appointed task. Did the *Anti-Jacobin Review*, in this case, really influence the attitudes of the reading public? Did it enjoy sufficient sway over readers to stimulate the sale of those works of which it approved and drive out those of which it did not? Did it successfully alert the British public to what it perceived to be the dangers of the Jacobin menace?

Most historians of the English periodicals would agree that the question of the reviewers' influence is unfortunately impossible to answer with any degree of exactitude. First, there is the highly debatable matter of the periodicals' ability to stimulate or retard sales. Obviously good reviews were bound to help a book, while bad reviews did not necessarily hurt its chances and sometimes actually stimulated sales out of curiosity or partisanship. Byron, for example, believed that the *Quarterly Review*'s attack upon Shelley in 1818 'sold an edition of the "Revolt of Islam" which otherwise nobody would have thought of reading',[138] while cheap pirated copies of Byron's own *Don Juan* enjoyed an enormous sale after his publisher, John Murray, prudishly attempted to keep the poem out of the hands of the lower orders.[139] Lady Morgan's *France* also seems to have enjoyed a *succès de scandale* after the *Quarterly Review* condemned it in 1817,[140] and even Keats once admitted that 'the attempt to crush me in the Quarterly has only brought me more into notice'.[141] John Clive put the problem in its true perspective in his study of the *Edinburgh Review*: if every reader of the periodicals had recorded in his diary the articles he read and his conclusions with regard to them, as William Windham did concerning the *Edinburgh*'s review of Southey's *Madoc*,[142] then and only then could historians estimate accurately the impact of the periodicals' reviews on readers' opinions.[143]

Aside from the difficulty of assessing the reviewers' influence over their readership, there is the related problem of determining what segment of the population actually read the reviews. Literacy statistics suggest a natural starting point for investigation, and recent figures by Lawrence Stone place literacy rates high in Britain, indicating that in 1800 well over two-thirds of all British males could sign their names.[144] On the other hand, of course, it must be remembered that signing one's name is the barest form of literacy and also that many persons who could read chose not to.[145] The relatively high price and limited sale[146] of eighteenth-century periodicals need not in themselves have prevented the working classes from reading them, as coffee-houses frequently took in communal copies that passed through many hands.[147] However, the very nature of their material precluded a truly wide readership among the less educated lower orders. This was especially true with literary periodicals of a conservative stripe, like the *Anti-Jacobin*, whose political bias would assure that they would have little appeal among the working classes. All things considered, it must be acknowledged that the conservative literary critics did not reach a wide spectrum of the population with their anti-Jacobinical message.

That being the case, a final question must be asked. If indeed the *Anti-Jacobin* was designed for the propertied middle and upper classes and geared to appeal to those elements, was its existence at all necessary? Did the *Anti-Jacobin*'s conservative contributors really need to tell their middle- and upper-class readers that Jacobinism was a threat to the established order? Were not their readers already in agreement with them on that issue?

The reviewers themselves were not blind to this question, and their own response would be a carefully reasoned yes and no. Yes, the British upper and middle classes would have recoiled at the idea of a revolution such as France had suffered taking place in their country. Yes, they feared the march of revolutionary Jacobinism and the political upheaval in Europe as much as any *Anti-Jacobin* reviewer. But loathing for Robespierre and for the political ramifications of Jacobinism was not all that concerned the Church-and-King literary reviewers. Since they believed in the existence of moral and religious Jacobinism as well as the more common political manifestation, they would say without hesitation that all social ranks should take warning, since immorality and irreligion did not follow class lines. Also, as the reviewers honestly believed that they could shame an erring writer into giving up the profession or convince him to recant his errors, they felt that they had a duty to speak their minds, hoping to win back the reprobate or at least sting him into silence. Moreover, since a certain number of clergymen and country gentlemen could be counted on to buy up and circulate among their parishioners and dependents inexpensive publications defending religion, morality, patriotism, and respect for the social hierarchy, the reviewers believed that they could encourage this salutary instruction of the lower orders, rewarding the Hannah Mores and Sarah Trimmers with their approval and assisting the clergy and gentry in choosing the best tracts for circulation.

Finally one must remember the motivation of the reviewers themselves. They were patriots who saw their country besieged by a movement which they believed could destroy it – revolutionary, conspiratorial Jacobinism. They were loyal churchmen who saw their religion subjected to daily attack. The danger was real, and they earnestly wanted to do their part in resisting these threats. Though their approbation or censure of a work might have little effect, though the audience they addressed was small, though the classes that presented the most danger to conservatism would never see their reviews, yet they felt they must persist in their duty to defend Church and King, morality and hierarchy, to the best of their ability. 'I am sure', Coleridge once wrote, 'it is time not only for all good men who love the constitution to unite; but to use all honorable means & vehicles of diffusing the right feelings and principles.'[148] The *Anti-Jacobin* contributors and their brother Tory reviewers could not have agreed more.

NOTES

1. [Robert Nares(?) or William Beloe(?)], *British Critic*, xvi (July–December 1800) i–iii.
2. 'Conservative' and 'anti-Jacobin' are used throughout in a wide sense to designate those persons who supported the established order in Church and State – that is, monarchy, hierarchy, privilege, property, religious orthodoxy, and an unreformed Parliament. Identified as they were with the parties of William Pitt and later of Lord Liverpool, they were thus Ministerialists until 1830, when the coming of Lord Grey to power made them the Opposition. Though nominally Whigs at the beginning of the period, they came increasingly to reserve that designation for the followers of Charles James Fox and Lord Holland, preferring to call themselves 'Pittites' and, by the 1820s, 'Tories'. The adjectives 'conservative' and 'anti-Jacobin' are therefore used interchangeably with 'Pittite', 'Ministerialist', 'Tory', and 'Church-and-King'.
3. [Robert Nares(?) or William Beloe(?)], *British Critic*, xviii (July–December 1801) i.
4. The *Analytical Review*, established by Joseph Johnson in 1788, was the mouthpiece of a notable group of Radicals and Dissenters, including Mary Wollstonecraft, William Cowper, Blake, Godwin, Priestley, Paine, and Henry Fuseli. A number of them contributed review articles to the *Analytical Review*.
5. British Library Reading Room catalogue entry P.P.3596.
6. It should be noted that for the purposes of this study the word 'contributor' has been defined broadly to include any person whose work is known to have been printed in the first six volumes of the *Anti-Jacobin* or reprinted therein from another current source. Such matters as frequency and regularity of contributions, while undoubtedly significant, have not been used as determinants for deciding whether or not to include a given name on the list. Researchers familiar with the British Library's annotated copy of the *Anti-Jacobin* may note that three persons listed in its pages have in fact been excluded from consideration – Bertrand de Moleville (credited with material appearing in the *AJ*, v [January 1800] 48–56; v [February 1800] 162–72; v

[March 1800] 277–89), R. Farrell (*AJ*, III [May 1799] 49), and Stebbing Shaw (*AJ*, I [August 1798] 237–9). In the first two cases the handwritten attribution of authorship in the British Library copy was obviously a careless error, since Bertrand de Moleville and Farrell were actually the authors, not the reviewers, of the material in question. In the third case Stebbing Shaw's 'article' was simply a reprint of a poem by Anna Seward, which was published in Shaw's *History and Antiquities of Staffordshire* a number of years before the *Anti-Jacobin* came into existence. Accordingly it has not been considered a legitimate contribution to the *Review* in any sense of the word. Conversely, reprinted items by three other contributors have been included – material by William Cobbett (*AJ*, I [October 1798] 479; I [November 1798] 591–3; I [December 1798] 725–8; VI [August 1800] 466–8), K. A. Boettiger (*AJ*, VI [Appendix to May–August 1800] 576–8), and the Count de Volney (*AJ*, II [March 1799] 331–4; II [April 1799] 443–6). In all three cases, though the articles are reprints from other periodicals, they are contemporary material, unlike Anna Seward's poem, which was simply extracted from an old and unrelated work.

7. With regard to the identification of clergymen a meticulous effort has been made to enumerate each individual's church appointments. This has been done for the convenience of researchers in the field, who often find to their exasperation that eighteenth-century memoirs frequently differentiate reverend authors only by their ecclesiastical preferments. Thus, for example, contemporary memoirs refer to John Brand the mathematician as the Rev. Mr Brand, rector of St George's, Southwark, while John Brand the secretary of the Society of Antiquaries appears as the Rev. Mr Brand, rector of St Mary-at-Hill. For extra accuracy in identification, university degrees have been listed where available as well.

8. *AJ*, I (July 1798) 29.

9. [Richard Gough(?) or William Beloe(?)], *GM*, LXIII–1 (January–June 1793) iii. (John Nichols, 'Preface', *General Index to the 'Gentleman's Magazine'*, *GM*, index vol. III [1787–1818] Pt 1, lxxiii, lists Gough and Beloe among the possible authors of this preface.)

10. This attitude coincided with, and fuelled the fires of, an already existent trend toward moral reform and improvement of manners in the late eighteenth century, a trend manifested in William Wilberforce's revival of the Society for the Reformation of Manners in 1787, the growth of the Sunday School movement, campaigns in favour of Sabbatarianism and the purification of literature and the theatre, and efforts to curb drinking and to outlaw blood sports and public executions. See Ford K. Brown, *Fathers of the Victorians: The Age of Wilberforce* (Cambridge: Cambridge University Press, 1961); Maurice J. Quinlan, *Victorian Prelude: A History of English Manners, 1700–1830* (rev. edn; Hamden, CT: Archon Books, 1965); and Richard A. Soloway, 'Reform or Ruin: English Moral Thought During the First French Republic', *Review of Politics*, xxv (January 1963) 110–28.

11. [Robert Grant(?)], *Quarterly Review*, IV (August 1810) 230. (The article is attributed to Grant in Hill Shine and Helen Chadwick Shine, *'Quarterly*

Review' Under Gifford: Identification of Contributors, 1809–1824 [Chapel Hill: University of North Carolina Press, 1949]. Other possible authors are, in order, George Canning, John Davison, and J. H. Frere.)

12. *British Critic*, xii (October 1798) 427.
13. *AJ*, i (July 1798) 25, 28.
14. An estimated 200,000 copies of the *Rights of Man* found their way to the working classes within two years of publication (see Richard D. Altick, *The English Common Reader: A Social History of the Mass Reading Public, 1800–1900* [Chicago: University of Chicago Press, 1957] p. 70).
15. W. T. Laprade's charge (in *England and the French Revolution, 1789–1797* [New York: AMS Press, 1970; reprint of 1909 edn]) that Pitt manufactured a national emergency out of thin air in late 1792 in an effort to divide the parliamentary opposition and enhance his own strength has been completely discredited. See Clive Emsley's careful study of the rumoured plot in 'The London "Insurrection" of December 1792: Fact, Fiction, or Fantasy?', *Journal of British Studies*, xvii (Spring 1978) 66–86. Albert Goodwin also dismisses the charge, though he adds that Pitt, a practical politician, probably had 'the ulterior motive of wishing to play on the conservative fears of the Portland Whigs in order to draw them into a coalition Ministry and thus split the Whig Opposition' (Albert Goodwin, *The Friends of Liberty: The English Democratic Movement in the Age of the French Revolution* [Cambridge, MA: Harvard University Press, 1979] p. 207). For his part, John Ehrman in his magisterial biography of Pitt convincingly argues that Pitt's actions in late 1792 sprang out of genuine alarm over the rapidly worsening domestic situation and the growing probability of war with France (John Ehrman, *The Younger Pitt: The Reluctant Transition* [Stanford, CA: Stanford University Press, 1983] pp. 214–25). Moreover, Clive Emsley has convincingly demonstrated that Pitt's actions overall were a measured response to Radicalism and fully within the traditional legal framework and that in no way did they constitute a 'White Terror' (see Clive Emsley, 'An Aspect of Pitt's "Terror": Prosecutions for Sedition during the 1790s', *Social History*, vi [May 1981] 155–84; and his 'Repression, "Terror" and the Rule of Law in England during the Decade of the French Revolution', *English Historical Review*, c [October 1985] 801–25).
16. Eugene Charlton Black has questioned whether a bona fide organisational meeting was actually held, suggesting that Reeves's pre-prepared resolutions may have been designed merely to give the appearance of coming from a large group of earnest and loyal gentlemen (see Eugene Charlton Black, *The Association: British Extraparliamentary Political Organization, 1769–1793*, no. liv of Harvard Historical Monographs [Cambridge, MA: Harvard University Press, 1963] p. 237).
17. *GM*, xcix–2 (November 1829) 468–9. See Gayle Trusdel Pendleton, 'Three Score Identifications of Anonymous British Pamphlets of the 1790s', *Notes and Queries*, n.s. xxvi [June 1979] 209–10, for the identification of Reeves as the author of the Association's resolution.
18. Black, *The Association*, p. 237.

19. In 1794, when Reeves petitioned William Windham, the new Secretary at War, for an appointment as King's Printer, Reeves noted the Ministry's signal disregard for his anti-revolutionary efforts. 'You will understand', he assured Windham, 'that I do not mean to reproach anyone, as if the government had a connection with the . . . [Crown and Anchor Association], which gave me any claim upon them. In my opinion they had none such. It began without any communication with any of them. Mr. Pitt had the curiosity to make enquiries after it – I saw him twice, or thrice upon it – and he gave me the use of the post office to send our packets. That is the only thing we ever had of the government, and we were thankful for it' (see Windham Papers, Add. MS. 37874, fols 32 and 42, cited in Maurice J. Quinlan, 'Anti-Jacobin Propaganda in England, 1792–1794', *Journalism Quarterly*, xvi [March 1939] 14–15).
20. The memoir of Reeves in the *Annual Biography and Obituary*, drawing upon John Gifford's account in his 1809 *History of the Political Life of the Rt Hon. William Pitt*, supports Reeves's claim that, contrary to popular speculation, the Ministry played no role in organising the Crown and Anchor meeting and only learned of Reeves's intention to form the Association from newspaper advertisements. 'Mr. Pitt,' noted Reeves's biographer, 'far from giving his countenance to . . . [the meeting], in the first instance had great doubts of its policy and expediency.' Pitt, in fact, had originally favoured a bill to outlaw all political meetings whatsoever except those for the drafting of petitions. It was only later, after Pitt learned that Reeves's group was determined to proceed despite government objections, that the Prime Minister 'altered his mind . . . [and] expressed his approbation of the [Crown and Anchor] committee, when their names were read to him' (*Annual Biography and Obituary*, xiv [1830] 288). Reeves's memorialist further stated that Pitt 'never afforded the associations the smallest pecuniary or other assistance' (ibid.). Later historians have failed to resolve the issue. Lucyle Werkmeister (*The London Daily Press, 1772–1792* [Lincoln: University of Nebraska Press, 1963] p. 359) contends that the Crown and Anchor Association was indeed subsidised by the Treasury. Albert Goodwin notes that the Association was 'launched' by the government but does not investigate the point further (Goodwin, *Friends of Liberty*, p. 264). Ehrman considers it highly likely that the Ministry had some prior knowledge of Reeves's plans to form the Association (Ehrman, *Younger Pitt: The Reluctant Transition*, pp. 230–2). Robert R. Dozier takes a middle view, suggesting that Reeves inaugurated the Crown and Anchor Association without government knowledge but received some aid from the Ministry after the fact (Robert R. Dozier, *For King, Constitution, and Country: The English Loyalists and the French Revolution* [Lexington: The University Press of Kentucky, 1983] pp. 57–9).
21. Dozier, *For King, Constitution, and Country*, p. 62. Reeves's group set the figure higher, claiming 2000 Associations (*Association Papers*, preface, p. v, cited in Austin Mitchell, 'The Association Movement of 1792–3', *Historical Journal*, iv [1961] 62).
22. Black, *The Association*, pp. 256–7. Occasionally Dissenters took part in the Association movement, but for the most part they preferred to

meet separately and draft their own declarations of loyalty (ibid., p. 241).

23. The local Associations' war on Radicalism took many forms. In addition to supplying officials with evidence concerning seditious activities and pressuring magistrates to take more vigorous action locally, the Associations frequently threatened booksellers with the prospect of prosecution if they did not remove seditious literature from their shelves and threatened publicans with the loss of their licenses if they did not close their meeting rooms to Radicals (Mitchell, 'Association Movement', pp. 67–71; Black, *The Association*, pp. 261–6).

24. Crown and Anchor Association pamphlets fill twenty volumes, each containing several tracts.

25. The Victualling Office was officially instructed to hand out Crown and Anchor pamphlets to the seamen and dockworkers of Portsmouth (Black, *The Association*, p. 240).

26. In Black's, Mitchell's, and Dozier's view the Crown and Anchor Association, by moulding public opinion solidly against the Radicals, assisting in government prosecutions, generating local repression of seditious activity, and demonstrating a show of support for conservative political ideology, constituted one of the most important elements in the crushing of Radicalism in the 1790s. Donald Ginter disagrees, pointing out that the reformers, especially the Friends of the People, often used the Association movement to stage meeting that professed loyalty but urged reforms. Thus, says Ginter, descriptions of the Crown and Anchor Association fusing the nation into a solid Church-and-King bloc must not be overdrawn (see Donald E. Ginter, 'The Loyalist Association Movement of 1792–93 and British Public Opinion', *Historical Journal*, IX [1966] 179–90).

27. *Proceedings on the Trial of William Skirving, on an Indictment charging him with Sedition*, in Thomas B. Howell and Thomas Jones Howell (eds), *Cobbett's Complete Collection of State Trials and Proceedings for High Treason and Other Crimes and Misdemeanors from the Earliest Period to the Present Time . . . from the Ninth Year of the Reign of King Henry, the Second, A.D. 1163, to . . . George IV, A.D. 1820*, XXIII (London: R. Bagshaw, 1817) 446.

28. *Proceedings on the Trial of Joseph Gerrald, on an Indictment charging him with Sedition*, ibid., col. 933.

29. The leaders of the British Convention of 1793 – Maurice Margarot, Joseph Gerrald, and William Skirving – were convicted of sedition and sentenced to fourteen years in the penal colony in Botany Bay. Although Thomas Hardy, J. H. Tooke, John Thelwall, and the other leaders of the LCS and SCI were acquitted of treason charges, lawyers' fees and other expenses (combined with the rank-and-file moderates' fears of prosecution) sufficed to destroy the SCI and cripple the LCS.

30. The first Volunteer corps were established in 1793, the numbers of units increasing in 1794 and growing tremendously in 1797–8. Though intended for home defence against French invaders, the Volunteers also constituted a potential reserve for use in time of insurrection (J. R.

Western, 'The Volunteer Movement as an Anti-Revolutionary Force, 1793–1801', *English Historical Review*, LXXI [October 1956] 605, 611–13).

31. The mutiny of the Channel fleet at Spithead (April 1797) was a well-organised sit-down strike against brutality and poor conditions. LCS incitement has been suggested by some historians but never proved, though some of the mutinous sailors had read Paine and were political Radicals. The Spithead mutiny ended peacefully with the mutineers reaffirming their loyalty and willingness to fight the French, and the authorities making concessions on pay and shipboard conditions and granting full pardon. The mutiny of the North Sea fleet at the Nore (May 1797) was far more ominous in its overtones. There the mutineers tarred and feathered officers, hanged and shot Pitt and Dundas in effigy, and blockaded the Thames. More importantly for the government, the rebels even considered joining forces with the French. The Admiralty offered a pardon but no concessions, the mutineeers became divided over demands, and the mutiny collapsed in June, the government executing or transporting a number of the mutineers (Goodwin, *Friends of Liberty*, pp. 407–8). For convincing evidence of United Irish involvement in both mutinies see Marianne Elliott, *Partners in Revolution: The United Irishmen and France* (New Haven, CT: Yale University Press, 1982) pp. 142–4.

32. The French did land a contingent of some 1200 troops in Pembrokeshire in early 1797, but the French soldiers soon surrendered, and the danger passed. ([Excerpt from the *London Gazette* of 25 February 1797], quoted in the Historical Appendix, *A Collection of State Papers relative to the War with France*, v [London: Debrett, 1798] p. 18; Clive Emsley, *British Society and the French Wars, 1793–1815* [Totowa, NJ: Rowman and Littlefield, 1979] p. 56.)

33. *British Critic*, x (August 1797) 157.

34. Edmund Burke, *Reflections on the Revolution in France* (New York: Penguin Books, 1968) p. 119.

35. Ibid., p. 121.

36. Though agreeing with many of John Locke's ideas, most 1790s conservatives rejected Locke's view that government originated with a mutual contract, since that idea had been pre-empted by the Radicals. Instead, they believed in a prescriptive Constitution – that is, a Constitution built up over many centuries through custom and trial-and-error experience (see H. T. Dickinson, *Liberty and Property: Political Ideology in Eighteenth-Century Britain* [New York: Holmes and Meier, 1977] pp. 294–300).

37. A few exceptions come to mind: John Reeves, whose *Thoughts on the English Government* compared the Constitution to a tree in which the monarchy was the trunk and the two houses of Parliament were branches; and William Jones of Nayland and the *British Critic*'s publisher, John Rivington, who both kept 30 January as a day of humiliation in memory of the martyred Charles I.

38. Carl B. Cone, *Burke and the Nature of Politics*, vol. II: *The Age of the French Revolution* (n.p.: University of Kentucky Press, 1964) p. 285.

39. *AJ*, XXIII (February 1806) 217.

40. *British Critic*, x (December 1797) 681.
41. Ibid., xiii (April 1799) 420.
42. *GM*, lxix–1 (February 1799) 139.
43. *AJ*, xv (May 1803) 41.
44. [Robert Bisset], *AJ*, i (July 1798) 98.
45. *AJ*, xiv (April 1803) 402.
46. *British Critic*, viii (August 1796) 181.
47. Ibid., xlvii (March 1816) 258.
48. [William Beloe], *GM*, lxvii–1 (January–June 1797) iii.
49. Burke, *Reflections*, p. 164.
50. Quoted in [William Hamilton Reid], *AJ*, vi (August 1800) 471.
51. *GM*, lxix–1 (April 1799) 306.
52. Robert Boucher Nickolls, *The political as well as moral Consequences resulting respectively from religious Education, and its Reverse, deduced from History and Example* (London: F. and C. Rivington, 1798) p. 28, quoted in *GM*, lxx–2 (July 1800) 644.
53. This was not the first time that a Radical society had sponsored Paine's works. The SCI and assorted local Radical groups throughout the country had already facilitated the publication and mass distribution of cheap editions of *The Rights of Man* (Altick, *English Common Reader*, pp. 70–1). As for *The Age of Reason* it is noteworthy that the LCS's sponsorship of a cheap edition of that work alienated considerable numbers in the Society's pro-Christian wing (see E. P. Thompson, *The Making of the English Working Class* [New York: Random House, 1963] pp. 148–9).
54. *British Critic*, iv (November 1794) 551.
55. *GM*, lxviii–1 (February 1798) 148.
56. Barruel, a Jesuit, had edited the anti-revolutionary *Journal Ecclésiastique* in France until just before his escape to England in September 1792 (see Bernard N. Schilling, *Conservative England and the Case against Voltaire* [New York: Columbia University Press, 1950] p. 249).
57. Augustin de Barruel, *Memoirs, Illustrating the History of Jacobinism*, trans. Robert Clifford (4 vols; 2nd edn; London: printed by T. Burton, 1798) i, xiii.
58. Ibid., i, xiv.
59. Ibid., i, xv.
60. Although Barruel's work constitutes the most extended and best-known indictment of the *Philosophes* as plotters of the French Revolution, England had even before the Jacobin epoch begun to view Voltaire as the author of a concerted plot against Christianity (Schilling, *Conservative England*, pp. 215–17). See, for example, Burke's opinion, voiced in the *Reflections*, that the *Philosophes'* 'literary cabal had some years ago formed something like a regular plan for the destruction of the Christian religion' (Burke, *Reflections*, p. 211).
61. As far as Freemasonry is concerned, it should be noted that Barruel was indicting the Continental and not the British form of the Masonic order. Rooted in the Newtonian Enlightenment and in mid seventeenth-century Puritan and radical thought, Freemasonry had officially arisen in 1717 with the formation of the Grand Lodge in London (Margaret

C. Jacob, *The Radical Enlightenment: Pantheists, Freemasons and Republicans*, in J. H. Shennan (ed.), Early Modern Europe Today [London: George Allen and Unwin, 1981] *passim*). Freemasonry was imported into the Continent from Britain in the 1720s and spread rapidly over Western Europe in the first half of the century and into Poland and Russia in the second half. The lodges were open to all classes and included on their rolls priests, nobles, and the brothers of Louis XVI as well as members of the bourgeoisie. Meetings formed a natural forum for debate of current philosophical ideas, and the society itself placed special emphasis upon trusting in reason instead of dogma, the encouragement of a sense of brotherhood that cut across class and national lines, and the promotion of natural religion. Condemned twice by Rome (1738 and 1751), Freemasonry would often be accused of fostering sedition and participating in a conspiracy to set the French Revolution in motion. No solid evidence has ever been advanced to substantiate the charges, though the lodges did contain a number of French revolutionary leaders.

A potent offshoot of German Freemasonry was the Illuminati movement, a secret society of rationalists with mystical leanings and Freemason ties established in Bavaria by Adam Weishaupt in the late 1770s. Founded to fight continued Jesuit influence in Bavaria and to promote a transformation of society along rational and egalitarian lines, the Illuminati movement spread rapidly through southern Germany, Italy, the Habsburg lands, and parts of eastern France, often by infiltrating and then taking over Masonic lodges. The Illuminati society was officially dissolved in 1785 by order of the alarmed Bavarian government, amid a spate of arrests, seizures of incriminating secret correspondence, and charges of conspiring against Church and State.

62. J. M. Roberts, *The Mythology of the Secret Societies* (New York: Charles Scribner's Sons, 1972) p. 208.
63. John Robison, *Proofs of a Conspiracy against All the Religions and Governments of Europe, Carried on in the Secret Meetings of Free Masons, Illuminati, and Reading Societies* (2nd edn; London: T. Cadell Jr and W. Davies, 1797; Edinburgh: W. Creech, 1797) p. 105.
64. Ibid., pp. 405, 411.
65. See Emsley, 'The London "Insurrection" of December 1792', pp. 66–86, for a full treatment of the subject. Albert Goodwin for his part does not believe that such a plot existed (Goodwin, *Friends of Liberty*, p. 266).
66. See the records of the trials of Alexander Scott, William Skirving, and Joseph Gerrald in Howell and Howell (eds), *State Trials*, xxiii, cols 383–602, 803–1011.
67. R. R. Palmer, *The Age of the Democratic Revolution: A Political History of Europe and America, 1760–1800*, vol. ii: *The Struggle* (Princeton, NJ: Princeton University Press, 1964) p. 465.
68. Albert Goodwin (*Friends of Liberty*) and Carl B. Cone (*The English Jacobins: Reformers in Late 18th Century England* [New York: Charles Scribner's Sons, 1968]) are in agreement on this point.
69. For a comparison of Britain's Great Fear with the French *grande peur* of the late summer of 1789 see Emily Lorraine de Montluzin, 'Jacobinism

and the Reviewers: The English Literary Periodicals as Organs of Anti-Jacobin Propaganda, 1792–1832' (Ph.D. dissertation, Duke University, NC, 1974) pp. 2–3. Clive Emsley makes the same comparison in 'The London "Insurrection" of December 1792', p. 86.

70. [Robert Nares(?) or William Beloe(?)], *British Critic*, xviii (July–December 1801) i.

71. A[rthur] Aspinall, *Politics and the Press, c. 1780–1850* (London: Home and Van Thal, 1949) pp. 66–7. Of course there were other less direct means of government influence upon the newspaper press as well: indirect subsidies via advertisements or the printing of official government proclamations; government purchase of copies of newspapers and pamphlets to circulate to various officials or to send to provincial newspapers, with directions to reprint certain passages; the furnishing of information or news items ahead of time to favoured newspapers; the supplying of official memoranda by cabinet members and under-secretaries to friendly newspapers to be used verbatim or rewritten as 'exclusives', and so on (ibid., *passim*).

72. M. G. Jones, *Hannah More* (Cambridge: Cambridge University Press, 1952) p. 134.

73. 3 March–18 April 1795 (Altick, *English Common Reader*, p. 75).

74. [Henry John Stephen and William Gifford(?)], *Quarterly Review*, ii (August 1809) 146. Other possible authors are John Wilson Croker, William Gifford (alone), and John William Ward, Lord Dudley. See Shine and Shine, *'Quarterly Review' Under Gifford*.

75. See, for example, *GM*, lxi–1 (January–June 1791) iii; lxiii–1 (January–June 1793) iii; and lxvii–1 (January–June 1797) iii.

76. [William Gifford Cookesley ('Eponymos')], ['Memoir of William Gifford'], in John Nichols, *Illustrations of the Literary History of the Eighteenth Century* (8 vols; London: printed for the author, 1817–58) vi, 5.

77. Roy Benjamin Clark, *William Gifford: Tory Satirist, Critic, and Editor* (New York: Columbia University Press, 1930) p. 83.

78. Edward Hawkins, 'Authors of the Poetry of the Anti-Jacobin', *Notes and Queries*, 1st ser., iii (3 May 1851) 349. Edward Hawkins was a researcher in the then British Museum. Using four early copies of *The Poetry of the Anti-Jacobin* (including Canning's and Wright's), he put together the list of *Anti-Jacobin* poetry contributors contained in his article.

79. Ibid.

80. Wendy Hinde, *George Canning* (New York: St Martin's Press, 1973) p. 58.

81. Hawkins, 'Authors of the Poetry of the Anti-Jacobin', p. 349.

82. [Cookesley ('Eponymos')], ['Memoir of William Gifford'], in Nichols, *Illustrations*, vi, 6.

83. Owen E. Holloway, 'George Ellis, the *Anti-Jacobin* and the *Quarterly Review*', *Review of English Studies*, x (January 1934) 56.

84. Cobbett may or may not have been correct that Bowles, a later contributor to the *Anti-Jacobin Review*, collaborated in the early days of the *Anti-Jacobin* newspaper as well, withdrawing after the leaders decided that his personality was too domineering and his material too ponderous (*Cobbett's Political Register*, xv [22 April 1809] 603–4). For

Grenville's contributions to the *Anti-Jacobin* newspaper see Emsley, *British Society and the French Wars*, p. 66.
85. Hinde, *George Canning*, p. 63. Clark suggests that Pitt occasionally contributed satirical poetry as well (Clark, *William Gifford*, p. 83; see also Ehrman, *Younger Pitt: The Reluctant Transition*, pp. 39–40).
86. Hawkins, 'Authors of the Poetry of the Anti-Jacobin', p. 349.
87. The chief source material pertaining to Gifford's life is his own brief autobiography contained in the introduction of the 1802 edition of his translation of the *Satires* of Juvenal. The account is reprinted, in whole or in part, in several early memoirs of Gifford, including those in Nichols's *Illustrations*, the *Gentleman's Magazine*, the *Annual Biography and Obituary*, and *Public Characters*.
88. Gifford's early studies consisted almost entirely of mathematics, since the only books he owned were treatises on algebra. When his master detected a waning interest in shoemaking on Gifford's part and confiscated his books, pens, and paper, Gifford discovered that he could beat out thin pieces of leather and scratch his equations on them with an awl. In this manner he continued his studies in secret for several years.
89. Clark, *William Gifford*, p. 34.
90. Ibid., pp. 30–1. For Gifford's services to the *Anti-Jacobin* newspaper Pitt appointed him Paymaster of the Band of Gentlemen Pensioners at an annual salary of £1000 – a sum soon augmented by £100 from a double commissionership of the Lottery (ibid., p. 18).
91. Ibid., pp. 164–5.
92. John Taylor, *Records of My Life* (New York: J. and J. Harper, 1833) p. 441.
93. Robert Southey in particular was outraged at the emasculation of his articles. See, for example, Southey's letter to Thomas Southey, 14 March 1809, in Kenneth Curry (ed.), *New Letters of Robert Southey* (2 vols; New York: Columbia University Press, 1965) I, 503.
94. R. W. Hay, letter to John Murray III, 7 July 1856, in Samuel Smiles, *A Publisher and His Friends: Memoir and Correspondence of the Late John Murray, with an Account of the Origin and Progress of the House, 1768–1843* (2 vols; London: John Murray, 1891) II, 179.
95. John Keats, letter to George and Georgiana Keats, 14 February–3 May 1819, in Hyder Edward Rollins (ed.), *The Letters of John Keats, 1814–1821* (2 vols; Cambridge, MA: Harvard University Press, 1958) II, 61.
96. Clark, *William Gifford*, pp. 86–7.
97. Ibid., p. 87.
98. Smiles, *Publisher and His Friends*, I, 91.
99. J. D. C., 'The "Anti-Jacobin"', *Athenaeum*, 3268 (14 June 1890) 769.
100. George Canning, letter to George Ellis, 19 October 1797, quoted in Hinde, *George Canning*, p. 58.
101. Hinde, *George Canning*, p. 64.
102. For a more complete account of John Gifford's career see his biographical sketch below.
103. Donald H. Reiman (ed.), *The Romantics Reviewed: Contemporary Reviews of British Romantic Writers* (9 vols; New York: Garland, 1972) part A, I, 22.
104. *AJ*, I (July 1798) 2.

105. Ibid., pp. 4–5.
106. See, for example, James Walker's contributions to the *AJ*, v (Appendix to January–April 1800) 568–80; vi (July 1800), 343–9; vi (Appendix to May–August 1800) 494–8, 562–76[?], 578–80. For a lengthy discussion of the reception of German literature in the British press during the period under study see Bayard Quincy Morgan and A. R. Hohlfeld (eds), *German Literature in British Magazines, 1750–1860* (Madison: University of Wisconsin Press, 1949) pp. 37–75.
107. *AJ*, xlii (August 1812) 349, 356.
108. Ibid., xxiv (July 1806) 263–71.
109. Ibid., lxi (December 1821) 303–15.
110. Ibid., xxxii (Appendix to January–April 1809) 454.
111. Ibid., xxxiv (September 1809) 4–5.
112. Ibid., lvii (December 1819) 312–24.
113. Ibid., xli (January 1812) 69–71.
114. Ibid., iii (June 1799) 120–28.
115. Ibid., xxxi (October 1808) 151–65; and xxxi (November 1808) 234–45.
116. [Robert Bisset], ibid., i (August 1798) 176–80; ibid., ii (April 1799) 428–9; [Robert Bisset], ibid., iii (June 1799) 188–92. Also see below, p. 59, n. 9. As for Charles Lamb, Lloyd's partner in their youthful volume of *Blank Verse*, the former was warned by the *Anti-Jacobin* that his *Tales from Shakespeare* was indecent and improper for children to read (ibid., xxvi [March 1807] 298).
117. Ibid., v (April 1800) 434.
118. Ibid., l (July 1816) 635.
119. Ibid., xlix (November 1815) 471.
120. Ibid., xxxviii (March 1811) 231.
121. Ibid., xlvi (March 1814) 209–37.
122. Note that all of the categories used for grouping the *Anti-Jacobin* reviewers overlap. A clergyman like Boucher who also had a career as a schoolmaster, for example, appears in two lists: those of clergymen and teachers.
123. Samuel Egerton Brydges was called to the Bar but did not practise.
124. In addition, Pye, S. E. Brydges, and (after 1832) Cobbett were Members of Parliament.
125. Agutter's *Pamphlet relative to the late Duke of Bedford, in conjunction with Mr. John Bowles* (Upcott, *Biog. Dict.*, p. 3).
126. See Edmund Burke, letter to William Windham, 25 November 1795, in Thomas W. Copeland *et al.* (eds), *The Correspondence of Edmund Burke* (10 vols; Cambridge: Cambridge University Press, 1958–78; Chicago: University of Chicago Press, 1958–78) viii, 346–7; Burke, letter to Henry Dundas, 6 December 1795, ibid., p. 353; John Reeves, letter to Burke, 8 [December] 1795, ibid., pp. 355–7.
127. Burke, letter to Joseph Moser, 5 April 1796, ibid., pp. 456–8; John Gifford, letter to Burke, 25 February [1796], ibid., p. 391; Burke, letter to Gifford, 7 March 1796, ibid., pp. 407–8; Burke, letter to Gifford, 1 May 1797, ibid., ix, 320–1; Burke, letter to John Bowles, *c.* 12 March 1796, ibid., viii, 414–15.
128. Ibid., x, 102, 133, 156, 182.

129. For all citations of evidence on this topic see the notes following the contributors' individual biographical sketches.
130. Mitchell, 'Association Movement', p. 59, n.18.
131. Another 'contributor', Volney, was a Deist. He only technically qualifies as an *Anti-Jacobin* contributor, since the *Review* merely reprinted an excerpt from one of his works uncomplimentary to Joseph Priestley.
132. Derek Roper (*Reviewing before the 'Edinburgh', 1788–1802* (London: Methuen, 1978) p. 182) accepts without question the handful of annotations in the British Library copy that list the author of a work as the reviewer of his own publication. In fact, the very rarity of such instances militates against taking them at face value. It is more likely that the attributions in question were careless errors in which the author's name was mistakenly transposed for the reviewer's name in the office copy of the *Review*.
133. [John Gifford], *AJ*, I (July 1798) iii.
134. The *Anti-Jacobin Review* appeared under the following names as it amalgamated with other periodicals:
    Vols I–xxxv (July 1798–April 1810): *Anti-Jacobin Review and Magazine; or, Monthly Political and Literary Censor.*
    Vols xxxvi–l (May 1810–August 1816): *The Antijacobin Review, and True Churchman's Magazine; or, Monthly, Political, and Literary Censor.*
    Vols li–lv, no. 2 (September 1816–October 1818): *The Antijacobin Review; True Churchman's Magazine; and Protestant Advocate: or, Monthly, Political, and Literary Censor.*
    Vols lv, no. 3–lxi (November 1818–December 1821): *The Antijacobin Review; and Protestant Advocate: or, Monthly, Political, and Literary Censor.*
135. Interestingly, two contributors during these later years were a Radical (John Horne Tooke) and a Benthamite (James Mill), who 'handled works of a non-literary nature' (Walter James Graham, *English Literary Periodicals* (New York: Thomas Nelson and Sons, 1930) p. 223).
136. *AJ*, lvii (February 1820) 556.
137. See, for example, ibid., li (January 1817) 481–502; li (February 1817) 642–3, 665–7; lvii (September 1819) 59–69; and lvii (December 1819) 312–24.
138. George Gordon, Lord Byron, letter to John Murray, 24 November 1818, in Smiles, *Publisher and His Friends*, I, 399.
139. Hugh J. Luke, Jr, 'The Publishing of Byron's Don Juan', *PMLA*, lxxx (June 1965) 199–209.
140. A. S. Collins, *The Profession of Letters: A Study of the Relation of Author to Patron, Publisher, and Public, 1780–1832* (London: George Routledge and Sons, 1928) p. 223.
141. Keats, letter to George and Georgiana Keats, 14–31 October 1818, in Rollins (ed.), *Letters of John Keats*, I, 394. Adverse reviews were not alone in sometimes stimulating sales. Legal prosecution of a work also at times had the perverse effect of driving up sales through notoriety, as happened when charges were brought against the new 1818 edition of Paine's *Age of Reason* (Altick, *English Common Reader*, p. 327).

142. William Windham, entry for 20 November 1805, in Mrs Henry Baring (ed.), *The Diary of the Right Hon. William Windham, 1784 to 1810* (London: Longmans Green, 1866) p. 454.
143. John Clive, *Scotch Reviewers: The Edinburgh Review, 1802–1815* (London: Faber and Faber, 1957) p. 12.
144. Stone's figures are 65 per cent of all English and Welsh males and 88 per cent of all Scottish males in 1800 (Lawrence Stone, 'Literacy and Education in England 1640–1900', *Past & Present*, XLII [February 1969] 120). See also R. K. Webb's earlier estimate that two-thirds to three-quarters of the *working* classes could read by the 1840s (Robert K. Webb, 'Working Class Readers in Early Victorian England', *English Historical Review*, LXV [July 1950] 349).
145. Webb, 'Working Class Readers', p. 349.
146. A few figures exist for the sale of periodicals in the late eighteenth century:
    Gentleman's Magazine: 4550
    British Critic: 3500
    European Magazine: 3250
    Universal Magazine of Knowledge and Pleasure: 1750
    Analytical Review: 1500
    New Annual Register: 7000–8000 (per year)
    (C. H. Timperley, *Encyclopaedia of Literary and Typographical Anecdote* [2nd edn; London: Henry G. Bohn, 1842] p. 795).
147. The coffee-houses and public houses also subscribed to newspapers for the use of their patrons, and the *Westminster Review* estimated in 1829 that every copy of a London newspaper averaged thirty readers (*Westminster Review*, X [April 1829] 478, cited in Aspinall, *Politics and the Press*, pp. 24–5).
148. Samuel Taylor Coleridge, letter to William Mudford, 19 March 1819, in Earl Leslie Griggs (ed.), *Collected Letters of Samuel Taylor Coleridge* (6 vols; Oxford: Clarendon Press, 1956–71) IV, 928.

The Contributors

AGUTTER, Rev. William (1758–1835)

AJ contributions: III, 76–7; V, 46–8, 84, 90–1, 318–20, 338–9.

William Agutter was a popular preacher and, after 1797, chaplain and secretary to the Asylum for Female Orphans in London. He seems to have held no Church preferment, perhaps because of his unorthodox leanings towards Swedenborgian doctrine.[1]

Agutter published a number of patriotic sermons, among them *Christian Politics, or, the Origin of power, and the grounds of subordination*; *Deliverance from Enemies*; and *The Faithful Soldier and True Christian, and the Miseries of Rebellion considered*. His best-known work was a sermon *On the Difference between the Deaths of the Righteous and the Wicked*, contrasting the last hours of Samuel Johnson and David Hume. For the *Anti-Jacobin* Agutter wrote several reviews and letters to the editor, criticising the Evangelicals as crypto-Calvinists and denouncing the *Monthly Magazine* as a 'vile compendium of Jacobinism'.[2]

Notes

1. William Prideaux Courtney, 'Agutter, William', *DNB*, I, 180. Agutter was an Oxford graduate (BA, 1781; MA, 1784, Magdalen College [*Alumni Oxon.*, I, 11]). For other sources of the scanty information available concerning Agutter's life see the *GM*, n.s. IV (July 1835) 98; and John Nichols, *Literary Anecdotes of the Eighteenth Century* (9 vols; London: printed for the author, 1812–15) IX, 39n–40n.
2. *AJ*, V (March 1800) 338.

ANDREWS, John (*c.* 1736–1809)

AJ contributions: IV, 489–503[?]; VI, 481–94.

John Andrews, LL D, was an historian and political writer 'well known in the literary world'[1] of his time. Little information about him survives today except for the list of his numerous publications, which included works on European political history, essays on manners and mores, and writings on political theory.[2] The

Gentleman's Magazine called Andrews 'an able historian, a profound scholar and politician, and a man ever ready to take up his pen in his Country's cause'.[3] Certainly his 1783 *Essay on Republican Principles* (written in reply to John Adams) was very much the sort of work that would find favour with Andrews's fellow *Anti-Jacobin* reviewers, as it was 'replete with judicious remarks and acute observations on the inconvenience of republican government'.[4] Andrews supplied only one known piece for the *Anti-Jacobin*, a review of Arnould's *Système Maritime et Politique des Européens*.[5]

Notes

1. *GM*, LXXIX (February 1809) 186.
2. Lists of Andrews's known publications may be found in the *BLGC*, in Watt's *Biblio. Brit.*, I, 31, and in Arthur Henry Bullen's sketch of Andrews in the *DNB*, I, 408. His principal publications included his *History of the War with America, France, Spain, and Holland* (1785), *The History of the Revolutions of Denmark* (1774), *A Defence of the Stadtholdership* (1787), *The Present Relations of War and Politics between Great Britain and France* (1806), *An Account of the Character and Manners of the French* (1770), *Historical Review of the moral, religious, literary, and political character of the English nation, from the earliest periods* (1806), *An Inquiry into the manners, taste, and amusements of the two last centuries, in England* (1782), *Letters to a Young Gentleman, on his setting out for France* (1784), *Remarks on the French and English Ladies* (1783), *An Inquiry into the Principles, Dispositions, and Habits of the People of England . . . since the Reign of Queen Elizabeth* (1807), *Characteristical Views of the past and of the present state of the people of Spain and Italy* (1808), *An Analysis of the Principal Duties of Social Life: written in imitation of Rochefoucault* (1783), *Free Disquisitions on the Sentiments and Conduct requisite in a British Prince* (1805), and *An Essay on Republican Principles* (1783).
3. *GM*, LXXIX (February 1809) 186.
4. David Rivers, *Literary Memoirs of Living Authors of Great Britain* (2 vols; London: R. Faulder, 1798) I, 14.
5. *AJ*, IV (Appendix to September–December 1799) 489–503(?), and VI (Appendix to May–August 1800) 481–94. (Andrews's name is signed to the second instalment of the review. Presumably he did the first half, which is missing from the British Library copy, as well.)

ATKINSON, Rev. C. W.

AJ contribution: V, 99–100.

Identification of the Rev. C. W. Atkinson has proven impossible. He, like William Atkinson (q.v.), may have been a member of the large Atkinson family settled in Yorkshire and the Lake District, but this is mere conjecture. C. W. Atkinson submitted only one contribution to the *Anti-Jacobin*, a letter to the editor attacking Priestley and the Socinians, Mary Wollstonecraft, the *New Annual Register* (a 'superannuated vehicle of democracy'),[1] and the religious and political Radicalism of the *Analytical Review*.

Note

1. *AJ*, v (January 1800) 99.

ATKINSON, Rev. William (1757–1846)

AJ contribution: III, 82–84.

William Atkinson of Thorp Arch, Yorkshire, MA and fellow of Jesus College, Cambridge,[1] was lecturer at the parish church of Bradford, Yorkshire, and from 1792 to 1845 rector of Warham All Saints, Norfolk.[2] He was a member of the Methodist wing of the Church, and his father (Christopher Atkinson of Queen's, Oxford, b. 1713) and two of his brothers (Christopher Atkinson of Trinity Hall, Cambridge, d. 1795; and Miles Atkinson of Leeds) were leaders in the Methodist–Evangelical revival.[3] Known as 'Parson Atkinson' and considered rather eccentric in his day, William Atkinson 'kept a printing press in his home, and issued pamphlets and broadsheets on ecclesiastical and political topics',[4] his chief target being the Dissenters. His publications include, in addition to his *Poetical Essays* of 1786, *A Candid Inquiry into the Democratic Schemes of the Dissenters during these troublesome times* (1801), *A Letter in answer to one suspected to have been written by a stranger, assisted by the Jacobin Priests of the West-Riding* (1801), and *The Guilt of Democratic Scheming fully proved against the Dissenters* (1802).[5]

Notes

1. Admitted sizar, 1775; BA, 1780; MA, 1783; fellow, 1782–91 (*Alumni Cantab.*, pt 2, I, 96).
2. He also held the perpetual curacy of Thornton, near Bradford, 1799–1801 (ibid.).
3. *Alumni Oxon.*, I, 38; *Alumni Cantab.*, pt 2, I, 92, 94; J. S. Reynolds, *The Evangelicals at Oxford, 1735–1871* (Oxford: Basil Blackwell, 1953) pp. 9–10; *A New Catalogue of Living English Authors* (London: C. Clarke, 1799) I, 113.
4. *Alumni Cantab.*, pt 2, I, 96.

5. *BLGC*; Thompson Cooper, 'Atkinson, William', *DNB*, ɪ, 698. His letter to the *Anti-Jacobin* (ɪɪɪ [May 1799] 82–4) in answer to Greatheed's defence of the Dissenters is written in the same vein.

BARCLAY, Dr John (1758?–1826)[1]

AJ contributions: v, 194–200; vɪ, 177–84, 416–28.

One of the *Anti-Jacobin*'s occasional reviewers of scientific works was John Barclay, Edinburgh physician and professor of anatomy. Barclay, the nephew of the Rev. John Barclay (the founder of the schismatic Barclayan or Berean Churches in Scotland),[2] had originally intended on a career in the Scottish Church. After a course of study at the College of St Andrew's, he was licensed as a preacher by the Presbytery of Dunkeld, whereupon he embarked upon a brief career as a private tutor to the families of Charles Campbell of Loch Dochart and Sir James Campbell of Aberuchill. It was while he was thus employed that Barclay began the study of natural history and anatomy that would occupy the rest of his life. He continued to preach occasionally and was for many years a member of the General Assembly of the Church of Scotland, but from the commencement of his study of anatomy the focus of his ambition became medicine.

Barclay's medical career may be briefly summarised. He obtained his degree as a physician from the University of Edinburgh in 1796 and in 1797 began teaching anatomy to private pupils in Edinburgh. In 1804 the Royal College of Surgeons certified his programme of lectures as equivalent to the regular anatomy courses offered by the Royal Colleges of Surgeons of London, Edinburgh, or Dublin. Two years later Barclay, now well known as an anatomist, was admitted a fellow of the Royal College of Physicians of Edinburgh. He continued to lecture until 1825 while in the meantime assembling an impressive private anatomical museum which he willed to the Royal College of Surgeons at his death in 1826.[3] His published works include his *Introductory Lectures to a Course of Anatomy* (1827), *A New Anatomical Nomenclature* (1803), studies on the structure and operations of the muscles and the arteries, and the article on physiology for the third edition of the *Encyclopaedia Britannica* (1797).[4]

Notes

1. The *DNB* lists the year of Barclay's birth as 1758 (George Thomas Bettany, 'Barclay, John', *DNB*, I, 1086–7). Barclay's assistant and early biographer, George Ballingall, gave the date as 1759 or 1760 (see George Ballingall, [Introductory Memoir] in John Barclay, *Introducing Lectures to a Course of Anatomy, Delivered by the Late John Barclay* [Edinburgh: Maclachlan and Stewart, 1827] p. i).
2. John Struthers, *Historical Sketch of the Edinburgh Anatomical School* (Edinburgh: Maclachlan and Stewart, 1867) pp. 56–7; Bettany, 'Barclay', p. 1086.
3. Barclay delighted in dissecting rare or unusual animals. His celebrated collection included such anatomical curiosities as 'skeletons of . . . the elephant, boar, camel, ox, deer, horse (including the Arabian, the great cart horse, the pony, and the ass), bear, walrus, seal, dolphin, narwhal, and the ostrich' (Struthers, *Historical Sketch*, p. 67).
4. Barclay may possibly have written in addition the review of Dr Monro's work on hernia in the *Edinburgh Review*, III (October 1803) 136–46 (see *Wellesley Index*, I, 433).

BISSET, Robert (1759–1805)

AJ contributions: I, 51–4, 91–102, 109–111, 160–4, 176–90, 191–7, 223–7, 247–9, 253–63, 331–6, 359–62, 387–98, 415–23, 515–23[?], 588–91, 634–6[?], 685–90[?], 712–18[?]; II, 57–63, 71–5, 113–22, 133–46, 155–6, 252–7, 262–7, 275–80, 353–61[?], 372–80[?], 388–93[?], 428–33[?]; III, 33–7, 39–42, 91–8, 113–20, 138–43, 146–50, 188–92, 194–8, 225–30, 246–59, 267–76, 369–76[?], 413–21[?]; IV, 12–18, 39–58, 67–76, 103–5, 150–70, 174–84.

With the sole exception of John Gifford no contributor furnished more reviews for the *Anti-Jacobin*'s early volumes than Robert Bisset. Information concerning Bisset's career is regrettably scanty. He is known to have edited the *Historical Magazine*, a short-lived periodical established in 1799.[1] In addition he published during his lifetime two novels and several works on politics and history – principally his 1796 *Sketch of Democracy*, two tracts defending the slave trade, a *Life of Edmund Burke* (1798), and a six-volume *History of the Reign of George III. to the termination of the late war* (1803). Finally, his obituary in the *Gentleman's Magazine* reports that he held the degree of Doctor of Laws, that he maintained himself as 'master of an academy in Sloane-street, Chelsea', and that he died at forty-six, 'chagrin, under embarrassed circumstances . . . [having] broken his heart'.[2]

Judging by his writings, Bisset was one of the most fanatical Jacobin-haters in John Gifford's pay. To Bisset the English Jacobin societies represented no less than 'a faction inimical to religion, morals, government, property, and order'.[3] 'Whoever is the enemy of Christianity and natural religion, of monarchy, of order, subordination, property and justice, I call a Jacobin', he wrote.[4] Like many of his fellow contributors, Bisset believed without question in the existence of an actual Jacobin conspiracy to overthrow the Constitution in Church and State, by force of arms and in collaboration with a French army of invasion.[5] Accordingly, in dozens of review articles and in his series of essays entitled 'The Rise, Progress, and Effects of Jacobinism', which appeared at intervals in the *Anti-Jacobin Review*, Bisset sought to alert his readers against the foes he saw on all sides: the political Jacobins of the party of Paine, Thomas Hardy, the Edinburgh Friends of the People, and the United Irish; the social Jacobins such as the playwright Thomas Holcroft, who (Bisset believed) used the theatre to inculcate social levelling;[6] the religious Jacobins such as Joseph Priestley, at war with the Church Establishment and Christianity itself; the moral Jacobins of the Wollstonecraft–Godwin school, with their attacks upon marriage, their advocacy of adultery, and the unedifying spectacle of their daily practice of 'JACOBIN MORALITY'.[7] Of all of Bisset's *bêtes noires*, however, the greatest was democracy, a principle which he realised must prove destructive to the monarchical–aristocratic Constitution of the eighteenth century and a principle he fought relentlessly in his *Anti-Jacobin* reviews[8] and in his polemical *Sketch of Democracy*.

A hallmark of Robert Bisset's literary style was the extreme intensity and personal hatred with which he approached his opponents in the press. In an age when vitriolic reviewing was the norm, Bisset's critiques were in a class by themselves.[9] In more ways than one, therefore, he was a pacesetter for Gifford's staff. In tone as well as principles the *Review* clearly owed much to the man who referred to himself proudly as 'that zealous Anti-Jacobin, Dr. Bisset'.[10]

Notes

1. The periodical's full name was the *Historical, Biographical, Literary and Scientific Magazine* (*BLGC*).

2. *GM*, lxxv-1 (May 1805) 494.
3. *AJ*, I (July 1798) 109.
4. Ibid. (August 1798) 223.
5. Ibid. (July 1798) 111.
6. See, in particular, ibid. (July 1798) 51–4; (August 1798) 160–4, 193–5.
7. Ibid. (July 1798) 98.
8. See, for example, ibid. (October 1798) 387–98, and (November 1798) 515–23.
9. Typical was his review of the hapless Charles Lloyd, a minor poet whom Bisset assumed (erroneously, it proved) to be a Jacobin. See *AJ*, I (August 1798) 177 and 178n; II (April 1799) 428–33; III (June 1799) 188–92. For a lengthy consideration of Charles Lloyd's political philosophy in the late 1790s see also Burton R. Pollin, 'Charles Lamb and Charles Lloyd as Jacobins and Anti-Jacobins', *Studies in Romanticism*, XII (Summer 1973) 633–47.
10. *AJ*, II (February 1799) 140.

BLAGDON, Francis William (1778–1819)

AJ contributions: v, 557–64, 566–8; vi, 517–25.

Francis William Blagdon was a self-styled professor of the French, Italian, Spanish, and German languages, a translator of foreign publications, and a paid Treasury journalist for the Perceval Ministry of 1809–12. During 1800 he supplied several reviews of foreign works for the *Anti-Jacobin Review*. His obituary in the *Gentleman's Magazine* describes Blagdon as

> an active and laborious writer for the press, and some time co-editor of the Morning Post newspaper. He began his career as a horn-boy to vend the Sun newspaper, whenever it contained extraordinary news; then became amanuensis to the late Dr. Willich, under whom he studied the German and French languages; and afterwards set up for himself as editor of a monthly volume of translated Travels . . . [and] an annual volume, called the Flowers of Literature.[1]

Though successful as a translator, Blagdon was largely unfortunate in his journalistic endeavours. His first newspaper venture, the *Phoenix*, failed. A second paper, *Blagdon's Weekly Political Register* (founded in 1809 in express opposition to Cobbett's *Political Register* and subsidised by the Treasury), collapsed in less

60 *The Anti-Jacobins*

than a year, ruining Blagdon financially.[2] A third newspaper, the name of which is unknown and which was likewise subsidised by the Perceval Ministry, disappeared sometime before mid-1812.[3] Thereafter Blagdon subsisted on his salary as co-editor of the *Morning Post*, until 'incessant care undermined his constitution, and he sunk under a general decline'.[4]

In 1805 Blagdon spent six months in King's Bench prison for publishing (under the signature Aristides) a pamphlet critical of the naval administration of Lord St Vincent.[5] Despite that experience, 'his connections and immediate interests led him to support the administration and measures of the day'.[6] His reviews for the *Anti-Jacobin* reflect in particular his disgust at the 'evil tendency' of so-called immoral novels and his condemnation of the irreligion of those writers who followed 'the new philosophical principles' of revolutionary France.[7]

Notes

1. *GM*, LXXXIX-2 (July 1819) 88.
2. Ibid.; Watt, *Biblio. Brit.*, I, 119; Alexander Andrews, *The History of British Journalism from the Foundation of the Newspaper Press in England, to the Repeal of the Stamp Act in 1855, with Sketches of Press Celebrities* (2 vols; London: Richard Bentley, 1859) II, 39; A[rthur] Aspinall, *Politics and the Press, c. 1780–1850* (London: Home and Van Thal, 1949) p. 86.
3. Aspinall, *Politics and the Press*, p. 86. After these reverses Blagdon wrote to Lord Kenyon, begging him to persuade the government to arrange further subsidies as a reward for Blagdon's past loyalty and as a means for him to continue his support of ministerial policies. Though Blagdon's letter was forwarded to the Home Office, the outcome of his request is not known (see F. W. Blagdon, letter to Lord Kenyon, 4 July 1812, quoted in ibid., pp. 87–8).
4. *GM*, LXXXIX-2 (July 1819) 88.
5. Upcott, *Biog. Dict.*, pp. 28–9.
6. *GM*, LXXXIX-2 (July 1819) 88.
7. *AJ*, V (Appendix to January–April 1800) 564, 567.

BOETTIGER, Karl Augustus (1760?–1835)[1]

AJ contribution: VI, 576–8.

Boettiger was a German archaeologist, journalist, and little-known intimate of Goethe's circle in Weimar. After an early career in the Church, he became acquainted with Herder, who secured for him the position of director of the *gymnasium* of Weimar, which he occupied from 1791 until 1804. There he became the friend of Wieland, Schiller, Goethe, and others at the court of Duke Charles Augustus, indulged his early interest in archaeology, and embarked at the same time upon a career in journalism. For a number of years (under the name of Bertuch) he published his *Journal des Luxus und der Moden* and from 1796 until 1810 edited Wieland's *Der neue Deutsche Merkur.* He was also involved in the publication of a Weimar-based journal entitled *London und Paris*, while supplying various articles for the *Allgemeine Zeitung* and for foreign periodicals, including William Jerdan's *Literary Gazette.*[2] In addition, he published numerous works in the field of archaeology, which was becoming more and more his central interest. He capped his career in 1804, when he was appointed a councillor at court, director of the academy for pages at Dresden, and director of the Museum of Antiquity.[3]

Boettiger is of only peripheral importance to the *Anti-Jacobin.* When John Robison (q.v.) and the Abbé Barruel published their controversial claims that the German literati and Illuminati were implicated in the so-called Jacobin conspiracy, Boettiger took umbrage at what he considered to be a blanket condemnation of German intellectual circles. He accordingly submitted a 'Postscript' to *Der neue Deutsche Merkur*, denouncing Robison's and Barruel's alarmist charges and suggesting that the two men were hired propagandists for the English Ministry. It was this charge that involved Boettiger in an exchange of angry letters with Robison's friend James Walker (q.v.) in the pages of the *Anti-Jacobin Review.* For his part Boettiger sought only to clear the majority of the German intelligentsia of the stigma of complicity with (as he put it) 'the most wicked profligates, those Jacobins of terror and regicide fanatics'. As for himself, he vigorously affirmed his personal opposition to anarchy and his support for the restoration of the French monarchy.[4]

Notes

1. Boettiger's date of birth is listed alternately as 1760 and 1762.
2. William Jerdan, *The Autobiography of William Jerdan* (4 vols; London: Arthur Hall, Virtue, 1852–3) II, 178.
3. Concise summaries of Boettiger's life and publications are to be found in 'Bottiger ou Boettiger (Charles-Auguste)', *Biographie des Hommes Vivants* (5 vols; Paris: L. G. Michaud, Imprimeur-Libraire, 1816–19) I, 423–4;

'Boettiger (Charles-Auguste)', *Nouvelle Biographie Générale* (46 vols; Paris: Firmin Didot Frères, Éditeurs, 1853–66) VI, 372–3; the *Catalogue Général des Livres Imprimés de la Bibliothèque Nationale* (216 vols; Paris: Paul Catin, Éditeur, 1924–73); and the *BLGC*.
4. *AJ*, VI (Appendix to May–August 1800) 576–7.

BOOKER, Rev. Luke (1762–1835)

AJ contribution: V, 332–5.

Luke Booker, vicar of Dudley, Staffs.,[1] Justice of the Peace for the counties of Worcester, Hereford, and Stafford, and chaplain in ordinary to the future George IV, was a poet and charity preacher of considerable fame during his lifetime. His published works consist mainly of sermons and poems (*The Hop-Garden*; *The Highlanders*; *Malvern*; *Poems on Subjects Sacred, Moral and Entertaining*; and so on), plus scores of original epitaphs.[2] He is chiefly known for his career as a preacher of charity sermons, in the course of which he is said to have delivered 173 sermons and raised nearly £9000 for assorted causes.[3] His son described him in the *Gentleman's Magazine* as 'a loyal and exemplary subject', who was 'a fearless and un-compromising antagonist with the emissaries of atheism and infidelity, in the early stage of his career; and at a later period [with] the Roman Catholic and Unitarian opponents of our Protestant faith'.[4] He contributed one signed letter to the *Anti-Jacobin Review*.

Notes

1. Booker, who took orders in 1785 without a living and, apparently, without a university degree, served in turn as lecturer of the Collegiate church of Wolverhampton; curate of Old Swinford; minister of St Edmund's chapel of ease in Dudley; rector of Tedstone Delamere in Herefordshire; and finally, from 1812 until his death, vicar of Dudley ([Rev. Mr Booker (son of Luke Booker)], *GM*, n.s. V [January 1836] 93–4; Alexander Gordon, 'Booker, Luke, LL.D.', *DNB*, II, 830; *Index Eccles.*, p. 19).
2. Booker's most famous epitaph was composed 'as a warning to female virtue, and a humble monument of female chastity' for the grave of one Mary Ashford, 'who, in the 20th year of her age, having incautiously repaired to a scene of public amusement without proper protection, was brutally violated and murdered on the 27th May, 1817' (quoted in William Bates, ' "The Mysterious Murder" ', *Notes and Queries*, 2nd ser., XI [1 June 1861] 432). Booker had been erroneously credited with the authorship of a melodrama based on the case – *The Mysterious Murder, or*

What's o'clock – written, in fact, by George Ludlam. He did, however, publish a controversial pamphlet pertaining to the murder, *A Moral Review of the Character and Conduct of Mary Ashford* (Bates, ibid.; Gordon, 'Booker', p. 831).
3. [Booker], *GM*, n.s. v (January 1836) 94.
4. Ibid.

BOUCHER, Rev. Jonathan (1738–1804)

AJ contributions: I, 62–72, 303–8, 613–20[?]; II, 3–10, 157–60, 287–9, 297–8, 299–300; III, 42–3, 168–71, 179–80; IV, 27–39, 90–7, 190–9, 249–60; V, 326–32, 405–10, 439–41; VI, 27–33, 81–4.

Jonathan Boucher, American Loyalist and lexicographer, brought to the services of the *Anti-Jacobin Review* an already considerable reputation as a defender of conservative political principles. Born in Blencogo, Cumberland, into an impoverished family and largely self-educated,[1] Boucher emigrated to America in 1759 as tutor to the sons of a well-to-do merchant in Port Royal, Virginia. After taking orders he embarked on the dual career of clergyman[2] and headmaster of a boarding school for boys, one of his pupils being John Parke Custis, the stepson of George Washington.[3] Boucher prospered in America, accumulating land and slaves as well as the valuable patronage of Robert Eden, the Royal Governor of Maryland, who presented him to two valuable livings[4] – a favour Boucher repaid by serving as Eden's political manager in the Maryland Assembly. As his own circumstances improved, as his ties with Eden and the wealthy planter society deepened, and as hostility between Britain and the Colonies mounted, Boucher drifted more and more into the Tory, or Court, party, a development that infuriated Whig elements in his congregation.[5] Locked out of his church, twice denounced before local pro-American vigilante organisations, subjected to threatening letters, hostile demonstrations in the midst of his sermons, and (if Boucher himself is to be believed) an abortive conspiracy to assassinate him in his own pulpit,[6] Boucher, who had preached for six months with a brace of loaded pistols on his velvet cushion, decided to abandon the Colonies. After assuring his angry congregation that '*As long as I live*, . . . yea, whilst *I have my being*, will I, with Zadok the priest, and Nathan the prophet, proclaim, *God save the King!*'[7] Boucher sailed for

England, proscribed as a traitor by the Americans and forced to abandon his library and about £5000 in slaves and land to be confiscated by the revolutionary authorities.[8]

After his return to England Boucher spent years in obscurity, living in hopes of ultimately being rewarded for his loyalty to the Crown and supporting himself by writing for the newspapers, especially the *Public Advertiser*.[9] In 1776 he received the curacy of Paddington and shortly thereafter met William Stevens (q.v.), who introduced him to William Jones of Nayland (q.v.), Samuel Glasse (the father of George Henry Glasse [q.v.]), and the Dean of Canterbury. Through Stevens's aid Boucher became Assistant Secretary to the Society for the Propagation of the Gospel in Foreign Parts; and in 1785 when Samuel Glasse left the vicarage of Epsom, Boucher received the living in reward for his loyalty in America.[10] He spent the rest of his life preaching, writing, corresponding with learned societies,[11] and pursuing philological studies. His writings on English dialects, the product of years of research, were left unfinished at his death and were published posthumously as *Boucher's Glossary of Archaic and Provincial Words; A supplement to the dictionaries of the English language, particularly those of Dr. Johnson and Dr. Webster*.

Boucher, like his conservative friends, regarded with horror the collapse of Louis XVI's monarchy and the establishment of the French revolutionary government.[12] When John Gifford established the *Anti-Jacobin Review* in 1798, Boucher became one of his most prolific contributors, pouring out articles in praise of patriotic sermons and denunciations of 'the hideous monster, *Jacobinism*'.[13] It was a fitting end for his career. As far as Boucher was concerned, he had been fighting republicanism, levelling, and assaults upon the established order all his life.

Notes

1. According to Boucher's *Reminiscences of an American Loyalist* the Boucher (or, as it was originally spelled, Bourchier) family was reputedly of Norman origin. In the Civil Wars one Sir John Bourchier signed Charles I's death warrant and as a result was later stripped of his estate, accounting in part for the family's decline in prosperity. In Boucher's own day the family was in very reduced circumstances, and Boucher himself was forced to acquire a sketchy education in the intervals of ploughing fields and hauling coal, peat, and turf to supplement the paternal income. As a result he never had any university training, and his only degree was an honorary MA from King's College in New York

(now Columbia University), given, Boucher said, 'expressly because of the services I had rendered to Church and State' (Jonathan Boucher, *Reminiscences of an American Loyalist, 1738–1789*, ed. Jonathan Bouchier [Boston: Houghton Mifflin, 1925] p. 100).

2. Boucher was appointed, in order, rector of Hanover in King George's County, Virginia (1761, though he did not actually begin his duties until 1762); of St Mary's in Caroline County, Virginia (1764); of St Anne's, Annapolis (1770); and of Queen Anne's parish in Prince George's County, Maryland (1771).

3. As far as Washington was concerned, this circumstance, Boucher later wrote, 'laid the foundation of a very particular intimacy and friendship, which lasted till we later separated, never to unite again, on our taking different sides in the late troubles' (Boucher, *Reminiscences*, p. 48). When in 1797 Boucher published *A View of the Causes and Consequences of the American Revolution*, he dedicated the work to Washington as a 'tender of renewed amity' (Jonathan Boucher, [Dedication], *A View of the Causes and Consequences of the American Revolution* [London: printed for G. G. and J. Robinson, 1797]).

4. St Anne's, Annapolis, and Queen Anne's parish, Prince George's County, Maryland (see above).

5. There has been considerable debate among American colonial historians as to the reasons for Boucher's adoption of the principles of the Court party. Michael D. Clark, for example, has placed paramount importance upon Boucher's loyalty to the Church, arguing that Boucher saw colonial attacks upon the British government as a danger to the Church he so conscientiously served (see Michael D. Clark, 'Jonathan Boucher's *Causes and Consequences*', in Lawrence Leder (ed.), *The Colonial Legacy*, vol. I: *Loyalist Historians* [New York: Harper and Row, 1971] p. 97; see also by the same author 'Jonathan Boucher: The Mirror of Reaction', *Huntington Library Quarterly*, xxxiii [November 1969] 19–20). Anne Young Zimmer and Alfred H. Kelly on the other hand have found the causes of Boucher's espousal of the royalist position in a set of social and political circumstances: his lucrative appointment to St Anne's parish, his connections with the Dulany family and with Governor Eden, his championing of the cause of an American episcopate (of which American Whigs disapproved in principle), and his heated controversy with two Whig politicians, Samuel Chase and William Paca, over the legality of the tobacco tax levied in Maryland for Church support. These circumstances, Zimmer and Kelly argue, tended to draw Boucher more and more into line with the Court party (see Anne Young Zimmer and Alfred H. Kelly, 'Jonathan Boucher: Constitutional Conservative', *Journal of American History*, lviii [March 1972] 905–7; Anne Y. Zimmer, 'The "Paper War" in Maryland, 1772–73: The Paca-Chase Political Philosophy Tested', *Maryland Historical Magazine*, lxxi [Summer 1976] 177–93; Anne Y. Zimmer, *Jonathan Boucher: Loyalist in Exile* [Detroit: Wayne State University Press, 1978] pp. 94, 263).

It is worth noting also that, though he was unquestionably a conservative with regard to such issues as the monarchy, the Anglican Establishment, and the primacy of the law and Constitution, Boucher held a very liberal view for his day on a number of other issues (Zimmer and Kelly, 'Jonathan Boucher: Constitutional Conservative', pp. 898–9). In addition to entertaining an attitude toward the rights of Indians and Roman Catholics that was decidedly more liberal than the prevailing pattern of thought in the Colonies, Boucher was noted for his humanitarian treatment of the slaves with whom he came in contact as planter and priest and for his advocacy of the gradual abolition of slavery as an institution. Certainly he was not 'Jonathan Boucher, Toryissimus', in the words of Richard Gummere, or the 'extremest expression of American Toryism', as Vernon Louis Parrington called him (Richard M. Gummere, 'Jonathan Boucher, Toryissimus', *Maryland Historical Magazine*, LV [June 1960] 138–45; Vernon Louis Parrington, *Main Currents in American Thought*, vol. I: *1620–1800: The Colonial Mind* [New York: Harcourt Brace, 1927] p. 214).

6. For Boucher's own spirited account of the incident see Boucher, *Reminiscences*, pp. 121–3.

7. Boucher, *Causes and Consequences*, p. 588.

8. Clark, 'Jonathan Boucher's *Causes and Consequences*', p. 100.

9. He received several small grants from the Treasury and finally a regular pension starting at £100 per annum (Boucher, *Reminiscences*, p. 144).

10. Margaret Evans (ed.), *Letters of Richard Radcliffe and John James of Queen's College, Oxford, 1755–83* (Oxford: Clarendon Press, 1888) p. xvii. Once mentioned as a possible candidate for the bishopric of Nova Scotia, he was tentatively considered for the Episcopal see in Edinburgh in 1793; but when the plan drew criticism for creating political power for Episcopal bishops in Scotland, Boucher withdrew his name (John Parker Lawson, *History of the Scottish Episcopal Church from the Revolution to the Present Time* [Edinburgh: Gallie and Bayley, 1843] pp. 346–7).

11. Boucher was a member of the Society of Antiquaries of London, the Society of Antiquaries of Scotland, and the Royal Society of Edinburgh (*List of the Society of Antiquaries of London* [London: n.p., 1800] p. 5; Samuel Hibbert-Ware and David Laing, 'Account of the Institution and Progress of the Society of the Antiquaries of Scotland', [Appendix to] *Archaeologica Scotica: or Transactions of the Society of Antiquaries of Scotland*, III [Edinburgh: printed for the Society, 1831] 19; *Transactions of the Royal Society of Edinburgh*, V [Edinburgh: T. Cadell Jun. and W. Davies, 1805] 121).

12. Predictably, Boucher could at first see no difference between the revolutions in America and in France, as he regarded both as rebellions against authority (Clark, 'Jonathan Boucher: The Mirror of Reaction', pp. 22, 30). By the late 1790s, however, he had begun to feel that it was the French and not the Americans who were 'the enemies of this country, and of the human race' (*AJ*, III [June 1799] 180). Encouraged by John Adams's stand against American military aid to France, Boucher urged the formation of an Anglo-American alliance against Jacobinism, with joint citizenship, a defence partnership, and the hope of a future 'foederal [*sic*] union' of the two nations (Boucher, *Causes and Consequences*, p. lxxvi).

13. *AJ*, V (April 1800) 407.

BOWLES, John (1751–1819)

AJ contributions: I, 25–33, 112, 133–40, 263–8, 674–8[?]; II, 83–90, 222–4.

John Bowles, barrister, magistrate, place-holder,[1] and paid Treasury writer,[2] was one of the Crown and Anchor Association's leading pamphleteers and a mainstay of the *Anti-Jacobin Review*. Contemporary accounts offer a number of enlightening glimpses into his pro-Church-and-King opinions. David Rivers noted that John Bowles 'was one of the first writers, and one of those most successful, in exposing Paine's Rights of Man: his pamphlet, entitled A Protest against that publication, was received with uncommon applause'.[3] John Taylor (q.v.), who dined from time to time in company with Bowles, John Reeves (q.v.), and George Chalmers,[4] always found his pamphleteering friend to be 'firmly loyal and honourable', adding that 'Mr. Bowles was warmly attached to Mr. Pitt'.[5]

It is Bowles's own writings, many of which were circulated among the lower orders under the auspices of the Crown and Anchor Association,[6] that provide the best evidence of his political views. Bowles was a firm believer in the existence of the so-called Jacobin plot to undermine Britain politically, spiritually, morally, and socially, as described by Barruel and Robison. In Bowles's opinion France without question had produced a 'sect of Infidels' that was endeavouring to wipe out religion and substitute atheism.[7] 'The founder of this infernal sect, or rather the framer of this Infidel Conspiracy, [was] Voltaire', who, together with his anti-Christian supporters, Bowles declared, had worked for years in secret 'not only to make proselytes to their system, and to establish secret societies of infidels, but to destroy . . . all sense of Religion in mankind'.[8] From religion the corrupting influence of Jacobinism had spread to morality. A new 'modern philosophy' had arisen, fed by the German literati, whose 'licentious' plays and novels were sapping the moral fibre of British womankind, capitalising on that 'obvious and indissoluble connection, which [exists] . . . between female chastity and the welfare and safety of civil society'.[9] It was on the question of the political ramifications of Jacobinism, however, that Bowles most often concentrated, as he sought again and again to warn his readers against the myriad horrors of the 'Revolutionary system', a witches' brew of 'tumult, sedition, treason, rebellion and regicide', of 'oppression, tyranny, confiscation, judicial murder, war and universal excitement to revolt'.[10] Without doubt, in John Bowles the Church-and-King party possessed one of its most valuable allies in the struggle to combat 'the malignant genius of JACOBINISM',[11] in all of its assorted forms.

Notes

1. Bowles, in addition to serving as a magistrate for Surrey, was appointed a Commissioner of Bankrupts and a Commissioner for the sale of Dutch prizes (*GM*, LXXXIX-2 [December 1819] 565).
2. The Secret Service accounts contain records of several subsidies paid to Bowles: £15 on 9 July 1792; £100 on 10 November 1792; £15 on 10 July 1793; and £100 on 6 November 1793 (Chatham Papers [P.R.O. 30/8], vol. 229, pt 2, fols 291a and 292a).
3. David Rivers, *Literary Memoirs of Living Authors of Great Britain* (2 vols; London: R. Faulder, 1798) I, 62.
4. George Chalmers, a clerk on the Privy Council's committee for trade and foreign plantations, was the author of an unflattering biography of Thomas Paine, published under the pseudonym of Francis Oldys.
5. John Taylor, *Records of My Life* (New York: J. and J. Harper, 1833) pp. 357, 358.
6. Typical of Bowles's propaganda pamphlets were such works as *Dialogues on the Rights of Britons, between a Farmer, a Sailor, and a Manufacturer* (1792), *The Real Grounds of the present War with France* (1793), *A short Answer to the Declaration of the Persons calling themselves Friends of the Liberty of the Press* (1793), and *The Dangers of Premature Peace* (1795). (*GM*, LXXXIX-2 [December 1819] 565; *BLGC*.)
7. John Bowles, *A View of the Moral State of Society, at the Close of the Eighteenth Century. Much Enlarged, and Continued to the Commencement of the Year 1804* (London: F. and C. Rivington, 1804) pp. 8–9.
8. Ibid., pp. 9n., 10.
9. Ibid., pp. 10, 26–7, 37.
10. John Bowles, *Reflections on the Political and Moral State of Society, at the Close of the Eighteenth Century* (London: F. and C. Rivington, 1800) p. 43.
11. [John Gifford], *AJ*, I (July 1798) iii.

BOWLES, Rev. William Lisle (1762–1850) [*AJ*: 'Rev. W. Bowles'[1]]

AJ contribution: III, 171–4.

William Lisle Bowles is one of those marginal figures of literature who are remembered almost exclusively through their connections with greater men. In Bowles's case it is his strong influence upon the young Coleridge and Wordsworth, together with his literary *querelle* with Byron over the merits of the poetry of Pope, upon which his fame now rests.[2] Indeed in most modern readers' minds Bowles is known chiefly through the dubious distinction of being immortalised, like Southey and Pye, in a stinging couplet in Byron's *English Bards and Scotch Reviewers*:

> Bowles! in thy memory let this precept dwell,
> Stick to thy Sonnets, Man! – at least they sell.[3]

Byron's antagonism notwithstanding, Bowles was in his own day a highly regarded poet and pamphleteer and an eminently successful clergyman. A prize-winning student at Winchester and at Trinity College, Oxford,[4] Bowles moved quickly up the ecclesiastical ladder, becoming in time vicar of the lucrative living of Bremhill, Wilts.,[5] prebendary and later canon-residentiary of Salisbury cathedral, and chaplain to the Prince Regent.[6] The duties of his various appointments were not overly demanding, and the income and prestige he derived from them gave Bowles ample opportunity to live the life of a gentleman-poet he so much enjoyed.

That leisurely existence was centred upon the Wiltshire vicarage of Bremhill, pleasantly located within convenient distance of Salisbury, Bath, and the Marquis of Lansdowne's house parties at Bowood.[7] Bowles spent the happiest part of his life at Bremhill, entertaining visitors, composing verse, superintending his parish, and 'improving' his grounds with neo-gothic abandon. 'His parsonage-house at Bremhill is beautifully situated,' wrote Bowles's friend Thomas Moore, 'but he has a good deal frittered away its beauty with grottos, hermitages, and Shenstonian inscriptions: when company is coming he cries, "Here, John, run with the crucifix and missal to the hermitage, and set the fountain going." . . . [B]ut he is an excellent fellow notwithstanding.'[8]

Bowles's personality was an unusual mixture of the tranquil and the fearful, the benevolent and the argumentative. '[H]e was remarkably simple, naïve, credulous', an 'astonishingly absent-minded' man, wrote Garland Greever, the editor of his correspondence.[9] He was as well 'an active but lenient magistrate'[10] who by William Jerdan's report 'educated and clothed nearly all the poorer class of children in the parish of Bremhill'.[11] He was passionately fond of music, playing the flute, violin, and cello with competence and taking delight in superintending the parish choir at Bremhill and the cathedral music at Salisbury. On the other hand he was, according to Southey, 'literally afraid of every thing'[12] and was 'said to have measured the distance between his prebendal house and Salisbury Cathedral to ascertain whether he would be in danger if the spire were to fall, and at one time to have "lived in such fear of mad dogs as to wear stout overalls to prevent being bitten" '.[13] In matters of religion and politics he was a foe alike of liberal and Radical ideas, noted for 'his stubbornness, his combativeness, his extreme conservatism in social, economic, and political affairs, [and] his religious intolerance'.[14] On the philosophical score, at least, he was thus the very sort of man who was drawn to the support of the anti-Jacobin party. Surprisingly, he is known to have contributed only two short articles to the first six volumes of the *Anti-Jacobin Review*, both of them apolitical critiques of his fellow poet, Polwhele.

Notes

1. William Lisle Bowles habitually signed his name as 'W. L. Bowles' or 'Lisle Bowles', not 'W. Bowles', as the name appears in the British Library staff copy. That the *Anti-Jacobin's* 'Rev. W. Bowles' was indeed William Lisle Bowles is confirmed by the fact that the *Anti-Jacobin* referred to the Vicar of Bremhill by the same inappropriate title of the 'Rev. W. Bowles' in the index to vol. II, p. 581.
2. The Byron–Bowles–Pope controversy, fought over the question of 'whether poetry be more immediately indebted to what is sublime or beautiful in the works of nature or the works of art' (as one pamphlet title expressed it), began with Bowles's publication of a highly derogatory ten-volume edition of Pope's works, together with an unfavourable memoir of the latter, in 1806. It continued intermittently for years as Byron, Campbell, and others challenged Bowles's contention that Pope's poetry was marred by artificiality (see J. J. van Rennes, *Bowles, Byron and the Pope-Controversy* [Amsterdam: H. J. Paris, 1927]).
3. Byron, *English Bards and Scotch Reviewers*, lines 361–2.
4. BA, 1786; MA, 1792 (*Alumni Oxon.*, I, 144; *GM*, n.s. xxxiii [June 1850] 672).
5. Bowles was collated to the vicarage of Bremhill by a grateful Archbishop Moore, whose own advancement in the Church had been furthered by the recommendation of Bowles's maternal grandfather, Dr Grey (*GM*, n.s. xxxiii [June 1850] 673).
6. Bowles served in order as deacon to the curacy of Knoyle, Wilts. (1788); curate of Donhead St Andrew, Wilts., a family living which had been occupied by his grandfather and uncle (1792); absentee vicar of Chicklade, Wilts. (1792); absentee rector of Dumbleton, Glos. (1797); vicar of Bremhill, Wilts. (1804); prebendary of Stratford in the cathedral church of Salisbury (1804), which he exchanged in 1805 for the prebend of Major Pars Altaris; chaplain to the Prince Regent (1818); and canon-residentiary of Salisbury (1828) (see *GM*, n.s. xxxiii [June 1850]

673; *Index Eccles.*, p. 21; William Barclay Squire, 'Bowles, William Lisle', *DNB*, ii, 977; Garland Greever (ed.), *A Wiltshire Parson and His Friends: The Correspondence of William Lisle Bowles* [Boston, MA: Houghton Mifflin, 1926] pp. 6–9).

7. Greever, *Wiltshire Parson and His Friends*, p. 8.
8. Thomas Moore, *Diary of Thomas Moore*, entry for 1 September 1818, in Lord John Russell (ed.), *Memoirs, Journal, and Correspondence of Thomas Moore* (8 vols; London: Longman, Brown, Green, and Longmans, 1853–6) ii, 153.
9. Greever, *Wiltshire Parson and His Friends*, p. 9.
10. Squire, 'Bowles', p. 978.
11. William Jerdan, *The Autobiography of William Jerdan* (4 vols; London: Arthur Hall, Virtue, 1852–3) i, 151n.
12. Robert Southey, letter to Katherine Southey, 16 November 1836, in Charles Cuthbert Southey (ed.), *The Life & Correspondence of the late Robert Southey* (6 vols; London: Longman, Brown, Green and Longmans, 1849–50) vi, 315.
13. Greever, *Wiltshire Parson and His Friends*, p. 10. For more on Bowles's eccentricities and irrational fears see Caroline A. Bowles, letter to Robert Southey, 12 July 1832, in *The Correspondence of Robert Southey with Caroline Bowles*, ed. Edward Dowden, Dublin University Press Series (Dublin: Hodges, Figgis, 1881; London: Longmans Green, 1881) pp. 253–4; and A. G. Bradley, *Round about Wiltshire* (8th edn; London: Methuen, 1948) p. 174.
14. Greever, *Wiltshire Parson and His Friends*, p. 10. Though it is true that Bowles campaigned against the Dissenters in his parish, as the *New Monthly Magazine* reported (xiv [1 November 1820] 483), it should be noted that Bowles was tolerant enough to accompany his friend Thomas Moore to Mass (*Diary of Thomas Moore*, entry of 22 August 1824, in Moore, *Memoirs, Journal, and Correspondence*, ii, 235).

BRAIDWOOD, Rev. William

AJ contribution: v, 463–4.

Nothing is known of Braidwood except that he was a Dissenting minister residing in Edinburgh. He may or may not have been related to Thomas Braidwood (*c.* 1745–1806) and John Braidwood (1756–98) of Edinburgh who together established a highly respected academy in Hackney for the instruction of the deaf and dumb.[1]

The British Library's *General Catalogue* lists William Braidwood as the author of several sermons and collections of discourses published during the period from 1796 to 1816. Judging by one of those works, his *Loyalty enforced by Arguments which are founded upon just Views of Civil Government, as an Ordinance of God* – a sermon preached in the Baptist Meeting-house, Richmond Court, Edinburgh, on 4 August 1799 – he was a man of at least moderately conservative principles. In that work (reviewed in the *Anti-Jacobin*) Braidwood declared his support of the duty of loyalty to the civil authorities, the divine origin of government, and the justness and necessity of defensive war.[2] A subjoined essay, *A Vindication of some Dissenting Congregations, who have been charged with disloyalty, by the late General Assembly of the Church of Scotland*, as well as a signed letter to the *Anti-Jacobin* on the same subject, offers further evidence of his political conservatism.

Notes

1. *GM*, lxviii–2 (October 1798) 908; ibid., lxxvi-2 (November 1806) 1082; Weeden Butler, Jr., ibid., lxxvii-1 (January 1807) 36–8; ibid., lxxxix-2 (October 1819) 377. The Braidwood academy is praised in a number of Scottish histories and travel books including Samuel Johnson's *Journey to the Hebrides*.
2. [George Gleig], *AJ*, v (March 1800) 297–300.

BRAND, Rev. John [Fitz-John] (1743–1808)

AJ contributions: i, 56–62, 165–71, 314–24[?], 434–44; iii, 198–207; vi, 525–9.

The Rev. John Brand, rector of St George's, Southwark,[1] was a mathematician, pamphleteer, and acknowledged expert on political economy. A loyal Tory and prolific writer, he proved to be one of the *Anti-Jacobin*'s staunchest allies, pouring out denunciations of Radicalism and revolution in the pages of the department entitled the 'Reviewers Reviewed'.

According to William Beloe, whose *Sexagenarian* is the best source for the early period of Brand's singular career,[2] Brand was the son of a Norwich saddler of slender means. After travelling for several years on the Continent, during which time he perfected his knowledge of foreign manners and customs to such an extent that his friends later referred to him in jest as 'the Abbé', Brand returned to England and entered Caius College, Cambridge. After taking his degrees Brand was presented in 1775 to the impoverished vicarage of Wickham Skeith in Suffolk,[3] where he settled into his meager establishment and, for the sake of propriety, married his housekeeper, 'a servant of all work, plain, ignorant, and of the meanest extraction. . . . The consequence was a numerous family and the most deplorable poverty'.[4] In order to eke out his salary and to provide for his increasing family, Brand plunged into literature, turning out assorted pamphlets on politics and political economy and a series of articles on mathematics for the *British Critic* and other periodicals. It was through his contributions to the *British Critic* that Brand came to the attention of Lord Loughborough, then Lord Chancellor,[5] who in 1797 presented him to the valuable rectory of St George's, Southwark – a lucrative reward for his pamphleteering skill in support of Pitt and the war effort.[6]

Brand was a man of decided opinions and mercurial temperament. At an early point in his career he became involved in a literary feud with the followers of Richard Price, the Dissenting minister. When Price's nephew published a scathing attack upon Brand in the *Monthly Review*, the latter demanded satisfaction in a manner most unusual for a clergyman:

> Mr. Brand called as usual on . . . [the younger Price], and requested his company to take a walk. . . . When they had proceeded to some distance, and come to a retired spot, the critic was not a little astonished at seeing his companion strip to his shirt, and, with many and bitter reproaches, insist upon satisfaction for the baseness and treachery with which he had been treated. . . . The result was, . . . that [Price] . . . , who was the more athletic of the two, proved the conqueror, and the mortified and discomfited Abbè [sic] retired from the contest with one of his ribs broken.[7]

Brand was equally aggressive in his political beliefs. As one biographer noted, he 'was a staunch tory, and his toryism coloured all his disquisitions'.[8] In his pamphlet in defence of John Reeves's *Thoughts on the English Government* in particular he energetically supported Reeves in his ultra-monarchical interpretation of the Constitution and proudly aligned himself with Reeves's Crown and Anchor Association – 'a set of men who have already preserved legal Government in the extremity of danger, and will, I trust, preserve it from future danger'.[9] As for his contributions to the *Anti-Jacobin*, they uniformly consisted of a litany of warnings against revolutionary tendencies (especially literary subversion), complete

with fervent calls for the nation to stand ever-vigilant in its support
of Church and King.[10]

Notes

1. The *Anti-Jacobin*'s Rev. John Brand, rector of St George's, Southwark,
   should not be confused with the Rev. John Brand (*c.* 1743–1806) of
   Lincoln College, Oxford, rector of St Mary-at-Hill and secretary of the
   Society of Antiquaries.
2. Beloe devoted two chapters of his memoirs to Brand and Brand's
   two sisters, though never mentioning their names (William Beloe, *The
   Sexagenarian; or, the Recollections of a Literary Life* [2 vols; 2nd edn;
   London: F. C. and J. Rivington, 1818] I, 141–53). John Nichols reprinted
   this material, largely verbatim, in his memoir of Brand (see John
   Nichols, *Illustrations of the Literary History of the Eighteenth Century* [8
   vols; London: printed for the author, 1817–58] VI, 528–37).
3. Brand's appointment to the vicarage of Wickham Skeith was but one in
   a long list of ecclesiastical positions which he filled. Brand served as
   curate of Brandon Parva and Welborne, Norfolk (1766); rector of
   Wickham Skeith (1775–1808); rector of Hainford, Norfolk (1776–81);
   vicar of Egmere (1780–98); rector of Worlingworth, Suffolk (1780); rector
   of Wortham Everard (1780); and rector of St George's, Southwark
   (1797–1808) (*Alumni Cantab.*, pt 2, I, 362).
4. Nichols, *Illustrations*, VI, 531.
5. Francis Espinasse, 'Brand, John', *DNB*, II, 1122.
6. A[rthur] Aspinall, *Politics and the Press, c. 1780–1850* (London: Home
   and Van Thal, 1949) p. 176, n. 2.
7. Nichols, *Illustrations*, VI, 530.
8. Espinasse, 'Brand', p. 1122.
9. J[ohn] Brand, *A Defence of the Pamphlet Ascribed to John Reeves, Esq. and
   Entitled, 'Thoughts on the English Government'* (London: T. N. Longman,
   1796) p. xiv.
10. Any account of the life of John Brand would be incomplete without
    mention of his eccentric and politically antipodal sister, Hannah Brand,
    who (in conjunction with a second sister, Mary) ran 'a very respectable
    seminary for French education' in Norwich (Nichols, *Illustrations*, VI,
    534). After a promising beginning the enterprise was wrecked by the
    capriciousness and the political Radicalism of Hannah Brand. As a
    disgusted William Beloe put it, 'She was of the Wolstoncraft [*sic*] school,
    a great stickler for the dignity of the sex, and the rights of women' (see
    Beloe, *Sexagenarian*, I, 147–8). After failing as a teacher, as an author,
    and as an actress, she became a governess in the home of a former
    pupil, where she busied herself in preaching feminist doctrines and
    turning her pupil (now the mistress of the house) against her husband.
    The latter, 'a well-meaning, good sort of man', was understandably
    indignant and 'very naturally insisted that the governess should be
    dismissed. The foolish wife, however, resisted. . . . The husband was
    firm, and the result was that the indiscreet wife sacrificed three young
    children and the society of her husband, with whom she had hitherto

lived happily, to share with her female friend the disgrace, contempt, and privations which accompanied their departure' (Nichols, *Illustrations*, VI, 535). Pursued by the wrath of the husband and a series of injunctions from Doctors' Commons, Hannah Brand and her admiring ex-pupil fled England and lived out their days together in retirement in a distant colony. This bizarre circumstance provides an interesting insight into the successful diffusion of Radical principles in England in the 1790s, despite the best efforts of John Gifford, John Reeves, and their literary allies. It offers as well a useful frame of reference in which to view the arch-conservative principles of Hannah Brand's professional anti-Jacobin brother John.

BRIDGES, W[illiam?]

AJ contribution: II, 213–14.

W. Bridges's identity remains unknown. He was the author of one contribution to the *Anti-Jacobin*, a brief description of the medal struck in honour of Nelson's victory in the Battle of the Nile.[1]

Note

1. Although the name 'Wm. Brydges' is signed in the British Library staff copy to the second part of a review of Stebbing Shaw's *History and Antiquities of Staffordshire* (*AJ*, IV [October 1799] 171–4), the actual author of the article was obviously Samuel Egerton Brydges, who wrote the first part of the review (*AJ*, IV [September 1799] 1–11).

BRYDGES, Sir Samuel Egerton (1762–1837)

AJ contributions: IV, 1–11, 171–4.

Samuel Egerton Brydges, would-be poet, antiquarian, and thoroughgoing eccentric, was born at Wootton Court, Kent, the second son of Edward Brydges. Educated at the King's School in Canterbury and at Queens' College, Cambridge (which he left in 1782 without a degree),[1] Brydges embarked upon a lacklustre career at the Middle Temple, whence he was called to the Bar in 1787. Finding the law 'utterly abhorrent to his taste',[2] he never practiced, settling down instead to a life devoted to literature, antiquarian and genealogical researches,[3] and (after 1792) the improvement of his expensive country house.

In 1790 Brydges initiated the fruitless genealogical controversy which was to occupy his lifelong attention and was to prove a source of comic relief to court and literary circles for decades. The last duke of Chandos having died, Brydges persuaded his (Brydges's) elder brother, the Reverend Edward Tymewell Brydges, to lay claim to the barony of Chandos, basing his contention on his supposed descent from a sixteenth-century Brydges who had been a son of the first baron.[4] After years of investigation of the subject the House of Lords finally ruled in 1803 that the Reverend Mr Brydges had not proved his case, to the great discomfiture of his younger brother, who had been the driving force behind the suit from the start. Undaunted by this setback, Egerton Brydges poured out poems, novels, pamphlets, and genealogical studies passionately laying claim to what he had by now convinced himself was his family's rightful peerage.[5] After his brother's death in 1807 Brydges took the coveted title upon himself, insisting that the common law would vindicate his rights despite the ruling of the House of Lords. His letters from this time on bear the signature 'S. E. Brydges, per legem terrae, B.C. of S.' – Baron Chandos of Sudeley – an impropriety in which he indulged for the rest of his life.

In February 1808 Brydges accepted with profound delight a knighthood in the Equestrian, Secular, and Chapteral Order of St Joachim, a bogus order based in Stockholm which (the *Gentleman's Magazine* sarcastically noted) 'had been established by some junior members of the sovereign houses in Germany, but was managed by an English adventurer, who called himself *Sir* Levett Hanson, and who regularly returned the election of any applicant that had *moyenné* a certain sum at a banking-house in Pall Mall'.[6] The 'honour', if such it could be called, led Brydges to re-style his name fore and aft, his signature now appearing 'Sir Samuel Egerton Brydges, K.J.'. With that he had to be content until 1814, when he at last acquired a legitimate English baronetcy.

In 1818 Brydges betook himself and his title to the Continent, where he lived for the rest of his life, having tired of public service after six uninspired years as Member of Parliament for Maidstone (1812–18) and having run up substantial debts printing limited editions of old English poetry on a private press set up in a vacant room in his son's home of Lee Priory. Henceforth he devoted his life to literature, for which he had always imagined himself to have had great talent, adding to his scores of verses, novels, essays, reprints of forgotten poets, and genealogical pamphlets[7] and finally capping his literary career with the publication of his rambling and fanciful *Autobiography*. Though he wrote extensively for the *Gentleman's Magazine*[8] and other periodicals during the course of his remarkable life, Brydges contributed only one article to the *Anti-Jacobin*, a two-part non-political review of his old friend Stebbing Shaw's *History and Antiquities of Staffordshire*.

Notes

1. *Alumni Cantab.*, pt 2, I, 377. While at Cambridge Brydges met Thomas Fyshe Palmer, who in 1793 would be sentenced to be transported for sedition. According to Brydges's *Autobiography*, Palmer 'was very anxious to make a radical and a dissenter of me, and crowded my table with all sorts of mischievous pamphlets, as these propagandists are in the habit of doing. . . . In London he carried me to political meetings, where I heard Horne Tooke, and the Duke of Richmond, and John Cartwright, speak.' The Whiggish Brydges insisted, however, that Palmer's concentrated doses of Radicalism 'never could make the least impression on me' ([Samuel] Egerton Brydges, *The Autobiography, Times, Opinions, and Contemporaries of Sir Egerton Brydges* [2 vols; London: Cochrane and M'Crone, 1834] I, 62).
2. Samuel Egerton Brydges[?], 'Mr. Egerton Brydges', *Public Characters*, VII (1805) 252. The *Gentleman's Magazine* attributed this memoir to Brydges himself (*GM*, n.s. VIII [November 1837] 534).
3. Brydges, who was already beginning to be famous – or notorious – as a genealogical researcher, was elected to the Society of Antiquaries in 1795 (John Nichols, 'A List of the Members of the Society of Antiquaries of London, from Their Revival in 1717, to June 19, 1796' [Supplement to] *Bibliotheca Topographica Britannica*, x [London: John Nichols, 1798] 58).
4. For a summary of the claim see Warwick William Wroth, 'Brydges, Sir Samuel Egerton', *DNB*, III, 165.
5. According to G. F. Beltz, the Lancaster herald, who in his *Review of the Chandos Peerage Case* (1834) undertook an exhaustive study of the controversy, Brydges was not above the use of foul play in his pursuit of the title. As the *Gentleman's Magazine* summarised it, it appeared that he 'tampered, and that in several instances, with the documentary evidence that existed of his actual ancestors; though such was the devotion with which he ever adhered to his favorite illusion, that one would fain have concluded that he had created in his own mind a sincere conviction of the justice of his claims' (*GM*, n.s. VIII [November 1837] 535).
6. *GM*, n.s. VIII [November 1837] 536.
7. His most popular novels date from his early career – *Mary de Clifford* (1792) and the loosely autobiographical *Arthur Fitz-Albini* (1798). For lengthy lists of Brydges's publications see the *BLGC* and Watt, *Biblio. Brit.*, I, 164.
8. Upcott, *Biog. Dict.*, p. 43.

CAYLEY, Rev. Arthur (*c.* 1776–1848)

AJ contribution: III, 87–90.

Arthur Cayley was a Yorkshire clergyman and the author of a *Life of Sir Walter Ralegh* (1805) and *Memoirs of Sir Thomas More, with a new translation of his Utopia, his History of King Richard III, and his Latin poems* (1808). He is said in addition to have published some satirical epistles modelled on the *New Bath Guide*.[1]

Very little is known of the earlier period of Cayley's life when, as a young man just out of Cambridge, he submitted his single documented contribution to the *Anti-Jacobin*. The nature of his political principles at that time is particularly unclear. On the one hand he 'is reported to have been refused a fellowship [at Trinity] on account of the detestation of the jacobinical principles of the day, which he had expressed in two elegant English orations, composed by him as college exercises'.[2] However, in his letter to the *Anti-Jacobin*, written in examination of charges of Jacobinism which had been levelled at St John's College, Cambridge, Cayley avowed himself to be an opponent of Jacobinism and 'a lover of my King, my country, and its constitution'.[3] Whatever Cayley's earlier principles, it seems evident that he sooner or later committed himself to the cause of the established authorities, as he took holy orders in 1813 and served quietly as rector of the country parish of Normanby, Yorks., for thirty-four years until his death in 1848.[4]

Notes

1. *BLGC*; Upcott, *Biog. Dict.*, p. 59; Gordon Goodwin, 'Cayley, Arthur', *DNB*, III, 1299.
2. Upcott, *Biog. Dict.*, p. 59.
3. *AJ*, III (May 1799) 87.
4. *Alumni Cantab.*, pt 2, I, 545; *Index Eccles.*, p. 32; *GM*, n.s. xxx (July 1848) 101.

CHEETHAM, Robert Farren (1778–1801)

AJ contribution: II, 326–7.

Robert Farren Cheetham contributed one signed letter to the *Anti-Jacobin*. Little is known of him except that he was a native of

Stockport in Cheshire, was an Oxford graduate (BA, Brasenose College, 1800),[1] and published two collections of poetry, his *Odes and Miscellanies* of 1796 and his *Poems* of 1798.[2] The latter work – devoted to 'British valour, and the achievements of our national heroes'[3] – drew special praise from the *Anti-Jacobin* for its denunciations of French 'Philosophism' and Thomas Paine.[4]

Notes

1. *Alumni Oxon.*, I, 243.
2. *BLGC*.
3. *AJ*, I (November 1798) 537.
4. Ibid., pp. 538–9.

COBBETT, William (1762–1835)

AJ contributions: I, 479, 591–3, 725–8; VI, 466–8.

William Cobbett, whose career offers one of the best examples of political 'apostasy' in his day, hardly qualifies as a writer for the *Anti-Jacobin*. His 'contributions', strictly speaking, were only reprints, inserted in the *Review* by his friend John Gifford.[1] However, since Gifford and company in effect *made* Cobbett one of themselves by adopting him into their ranks, he has been included in the list of contributors.

Cobbett's early career[2] was undoubtedly of the sort guaranteed to lift anti-Jacobin hearts. Born a peasant in Surrey in 1762, self-educated, and ambitious for a wider life,[3] Cobbett enlisted in the Army and, after eight years' service, emigrated to America. Arriving in Philadelphia in October 1792 he found himself in a hotbed of partisan politics, most of it pro-French and anti-British. It was largely a matter of course for Cobbett, who was deeply patriotic, to throw himself into the foray on the side of his King and Country,[4] and by 1796 he had become the most formidable and hated Tory pamphleteer in America – the celebrated 'Peter Porcupine', bitter foe of republicans and proud owner of a brazenly Tory book-shop in Philadelphia. After several years of stormy partisan politics and defeat in a devastating libel suit[5] brought against him by Dr Benjamin Rush, whose method of copious bleedings and heroic purges he had ridiculed during the 1797 yellow fever epidemic, Cobbett returned to England in 1800, financially ruined but trailing a reputation for Toryism that had already made him the hero of the Church-and-King camp.[6]

Once more in London, Cobbett pursued a strictly independent course as a journalist. Refusing all offers of ministerial patronage,[7] he nevertheless sturdily supported government policy in his two newspapers, the *Porcupine*[8] and the *Political Register*, exulting in his journalistic integrity as a Tory upon principle with no strings attached. In 1804, however, Cobbett began undergoing a political metamorphosis, turning more and more against the so-called 'Pitt System' of paper money, high taxation, debt funding, placemen, and the elevation to power of parvenu bankers and financiers. When Pitt died in 1806 and the Grenville coalition ministry succeeded him, Cobbett came to the pessimistic conclusion that the 'Pitt System' (or 'the Thing', as he dubbed it) was in fact not Pitt's alone but the *modus operandi* of the entire political establishment. Thenceforth Cobbett broke with all the parliamentary factions and, to the chagrin of his old admirers, embraced the cause of popular Radicalism.[9]

Cobbett's was an old-fashioned, strangely mutated form of Radicalism – almost a 'conservative' Radicalism, in the Cromwellian tradition. He has been called an archetypal British yeoman, a patriotic 'one-man country party',[10] committed to duty, hard work, and practical progress. At heart he was a reformer, supporting Francis Burdett's and Henry Hunt's campaigns for parliamentary reform, exposing Army corruption,[11] attacking the Corn Laws, and denouncing military flogging – a stand that won him a two-year sentence in Newgate prison for seditious libel.[12] After a brief self-exile in America,[13] he took up the unlikely cause of championing Queen Caroline in her 1820 trial for adultery, using the occasion as a stick with which to beat George IV. Finally, after campaigning vigorously in favour of Lord Grey's Reform Bill (and narrowly escaping another prison sentence for sedition in the process), Cobbett closed his career as Member of Parliament for Oldham in the reformed Parliament. The old Radical had rejoined the established order at last.

Notes

1. For an interesting glimpse of Cobbett's personal dealings with John Gifford, William Gifford, and John Wright see Pierce W. Gaines, 'Two Letters Written by William Cobbett from America', *Yale University Library Gazette*, XLVIII (July 1973) 44–55. Also, for a self-revealing

Cobbett letter to another *Anti-Jacobin* associate – Jonathan Boucher – see Thomas M. Debevoise, III, 'Another Cobbett Letter from America', *Yale University Library Gazette*, LIII (July 1978) 33–7.

2. Cobbett's life has been the subject of numerous studies, the best of which are G. D. H. Cole's *Life of William Cobbett* (New York: Harcourt Brace 1924), John W. Osborne's *William Cobbett: His Thought and His Times* (New Brunswick, NJ: Rutgers University Press, 1966), Daniel Green's *Great Cobbett: The Noblest Agitator* (London: Hodder and Stoughton, 1983), James Sambrook's *William Cobbett*, Routledge Author Guides, ed. B. C. Southam (London: Routledge and Kegan Paul, 1973), Asa Briggs's brief *William Cobbett*, Clarendon Biographies, ed. C. L. Mowat and M. R. Price (London: Oxford University Press, 1967), and George Spater's *William Cobbett: The Poor Man's Friend* (2 vols; Cambridge: Cambridge University Press, 1982), Spater's work being especially notable for its incorporation of a great deal of relatively new manuscript materials. W. Baring Pemberton's *William Cobbett* (Harmondsworth, Middlesex: Penguin Books, 1949) and Marjorie Bowen's gushing and Whiggish *Peter Porcupine: A Study of William Cobbett, 1762–1835* (London: Longmans Green, 1936) are less reliable. Cobbett's scattered autobiographical writings, including his *Life and Adventures of Peter Porcupine* (published in *Porcupine's Works* [12 vols; London: printed for Cobbett and Morgan, 1801] IV, 23–70), have been admirably spliced and edited by William Reitzel as *The Autobiography of William Cobbett: The Progress of a Plough-boy to a Seat in Parliament* (London: Faber and Faber, 1967 [first published in 1933 by Faber and Faber under the title *The Progress of a Ploughboy*]).

3. According to Cobbett's own account, the horizons of his narrow world first opened to him in 1774 when, aged eleven and clad in his peasant 'blue smock-frock and . . . red garters tied under . . . [the] knees', he journeyed to Kew to see the royal gardens and there bought his first book, Swift's *Tale of a Tub*. Swift's tale, which he devoured immediately, sitting in the shade of a Kew Gardens haystack, opened his eyes to the world of thought. '[I]t delighted me beyond description', he wrote, 'and it produced what I have always considered a sort of birth of intellect' (Reitzel, *Autobiography of William Cobbett*, pp. 18–19).

4. Cobbett was at that time engaged in teaching English to refugees from France and from the recent slave rebellion in the French West Indies. Asa Briggs and Sambrook are probably correct that Cobbett imbibed much of his anti-revolutionary sentiments from them (Briggs, *William Cobbett*, p. 17; Sambrook, *William Cobbett*, p. 45).

5. Cobbett claimed in his memoirs that the $5000 the vindictive Philadelphia court sentenced him to pay was 'a sum surpassing the aggregate amount of all the damages assessed for all the torts of this kind, ever sued for in [the United States] from their first settlement to the time of the trial' (Reitzel, *Autobiography of William Cobbett*, p. 74).

6. Cobbett's works were already enjoying a substantial sale in England, where his literary agent was John Wright, the bookseller who had published the *Anti-Jacobin* newspaper.

7. That Cobbett did not spend the next few years of his life comfortably

ensconced as a Treasury propagandist was solely the result of his own choice. Though regaled at the table of William Windham (Pitt's Secretary at War) in company with Canning, Pitt, and the *Anti-Jacobin* newspaper's George Ellis and John Hookham Frere, and though summoned to the Foreign Office and offered the editorship of the *True Briton* (a pro-government newspaper), Cobbett refused all ministerial patronage. Instead he remained a strictly independent agent, responsible to no one, not even to Windham, who had become his personal friend and who had advanced £600 for the establishment of the *Political Register* (Bowen, *Peter Porcupine*, pp. 81, 84–5; Briggs, *William Cobbett*, p. 24; Sambrook, *William Cobbett*, p. 53; Spater, *William Cobbett*, p. 115).

8. The *Porcupine*, established in October 1800, failed in November 1801. It was purchased by John Gifford, who merged it with the *True Briton* (Bowen, *Peter Porcupine*, p. 86).

9. *Cobbett's Political Register*, xi (23 May 1807) 935. There were other motives as well behind Cobbett's change of heart toward Pitt. When Pitt had suggested a place in his new cabinet for Charles James Fox, George III had refused to countenance the idea. Windham and Grenville in turn refused to serve without Fox, and Cobbett (Windham's personal friend) joined them in opposition as a matter of course (Pemberton, *William Cobbett*, pp. 44–5).

10. See Sambrook's chapter title, *William Cobbett*, p. 52. In Sambrook's view William Cobbett was the very epitome of the traditional 'country party' philosophy – industrious, deeply patriotic, devoted to the land, suspicious of vested interests and easy money. Thus much of what his contemporaries perceived as Radical behaviour – his attacks upon Army corruption, his calls for parliamentary reform, his defence of a Queen 'wronged' by a pleasure-loving, spendthrift husband, his hatred of German mercenaries who flogged English militiamen – was really conservatism in another guise. 'I am', Cobbett wrote, 'no republican in principle. . . . I hold, that this, which we have [in England] , is the best sort of government in the world. I hold that a government of king, lords, and commons, the last of which chosen by all men, . . . is the best of governments' (Reitzel, *Autobiography of William Cobbett*, p. 76). By urging Radical reforms, Sambrook argues, Cobbett merely strove to ensure that the old England he loved would endure. Thus the Radical was a conservative by another name.

On the purely personal level Cobbett's was a highly opinionated disposition, and the intrusion of his prejudices produced a decidedly unusual set of likes and dislikes. He approved of 'manly' sports (especially blood sports), Rousseauistic education for children, and honest, character-building agricultural labour. He despised poetry (unprofitable), Shakespeare (bawdy and ungrammatical), music (it clouded the brain and encouraged laziness), female coquetry (one step removed from harlotry), foreign luxury goods (morally debilitating), Italian opera singers (effeminate), Quakers, Methodists, Evangelicals, Unitarians, Jews, and Wilberforce's efforts to abolish the slave trade.

11. He aided Colonel Wardle in revealing the involvement of the Duke of

York's mistress, Mary Anne Clarke, in the sale of Army commissions and Church preferments – an exposé that cost the Duke of York his position as Commander-in-Chief.

12. The case concerned five English militiamen at Ely who mutinied over a pay stoppage and were ordered flogged by the German mercenary troops to whom their unit was attached. Ex-sergeant-major Cobbett took up the case, was charged with seditious libel, and was convicted in 1810 after mismanaging his own defence. Cobbett was sentenced to two years' imprisonment in Newgate prison plus a fine of £1000, bail of £3000 upon release, and two sureties of £1000 each for seven years' probation.

13. Cobbett in late 1816 began reprinting essays and other items from the *Political Register* and issuing them under separate cover. Since the publications contained no news as such, Cobbett was able to avoid the newspaper stamp duty and so sell copies of *Cobbett's Weekly Political Pamphlet* at the low price of 2d. each. The *Pamphlet* (dubbed by Castlereagh 'Twopenny Trash') rapidly outsold all other newspapers, rising to an estimated circulation of 40,000–50,000 copies sold a week and a readership of perhaps ten times that figure (Sambrook, *William Cobbett*, p. 87). The Ministry fought back after the 1817 Spa Fields Riot by securing passage of the Gagging Acts, which gave magistrates the power to judge whether or not reading-room materials were seditious, thus placing Cobbett in grave danger with regard to the contents of his *Pamphlet*. Consequently he chose to avoid the risk of prosecution by means of a two-year self-exile in America. It was, incidentally, upon his return from America in 1819 that he brought with him in his trunk the bones of Thomas Paine, personally exhumed from their resting place in New Rochelle, New York, and intended for exhibit to Paine's admirers, followed by ceremonious interment in a proper Radical memorial. Cobbett never did realize his ghoulish intent, and the bones lie buried in an unknown grave somewhere on Cobbett's estates.

COOKE, Joshua (c. 1753–1820) [*AJ*: 'Mr. Cooke']

AJ contributions: ɪ, 612[?]; v, 457–9.

A letter dated from Oxford, the printed signature 'Oxoniensis', and a handwritten attribution to one 'Mr. Cooke' in the British Library staff copy are the only clues to the identity of a contributor to the *Anti-Jacobin* whose letter to the editor (' "Nil Admirari," and "Peter not infallible!" ') appeared in the *Review*'s fifth volume.[1] It is virtually certain that the 'Mr. Cooke' in question was Joshua Cooke, a leading Oxford bookseller and raconteur.[2]

Cooke, the former partner and then successor of bookseller

Daniel Prince, operated a highly successful and prestigious shop near the Clarendon Press,[3] attracting a wide trade from the academic community and winning for himself the status of 'privilegiatus' of the University.[4] According to an anonymous acquaintance:

> Mr. Cooke's very amiable temper, and friendly disposition soon procured him an enviable distinction with the gentlemen of the University, by whom he was frequently invited to the honours of the *Common Room*, and received with the respect due to a man of engaging manners, and well-informed mind. His memory in literary anecdote was uncommonly retentive, and a long acquaintance with the eminent scholars of Oxford, their early history, and progress in public life, rendered his conversation highly interesting.[5]

Though noted among his friends for his conviviality and bonhommie, Cooke could apparently become as politically exercised as the next man when it came to the subject of Jacobinism. He was a self-professed political conservative and friend to the 'national establishments', as his only known contribution to the *Anti-Jacobin* shows. That contribution – the above-mentioned letter to John Gifford, congratulates the editor on his exposé of the *Monthly Review* ('this now tottering vehicle of Jacobinism, heterodoxy, slander, and abuse') and praises Hannah More's campaign against 'the amazonian cabal of Godwin and the new Philosophy'.[6]

Notes

1. *AJ*, v (April 1800) 457–9. Cooke may have contributed a second letter to the *AJ*, I (November 1798) 612. (See note concerning the attribution of the article on p. 170.)
2. A second possibility exists: the Rev. Edward Cooke, MA and LL B (Exeter College, Oxford), rector of Haversham, and contributor to the periodicals (see his lengthy obituary in the *Annual Biography and Obituary*, IX (1825) 401–2). However, the tone of the letter to the editor of the *Anti-Jacobin*, with its proud but vague reference to an affiliation with the University ('I am not a stranger to academic quiet' [*AJ*, v (April 1800) 457]), strongly suggests Joshua Cooke, 'privilegiatus' of the University, as the author.
3. *GM*, xc-1 (February 1820) 170; *BLGC*.
4. *Alumni Oxon.*, I, 289.

5. *GM*, xc-1 (February 1820) 178. The *Gentleman's Magazine*'s panegyric to Cooke's virtue and amiability is drawn in part from *Jackson's Oxford Journal*.
6. *AJ*, v (April 1800) 457–8.

CROFT, Rev. George (1747–1809)

AJ contributions: iii, 1–8, 211–12, 349–51; iv, 129–33; v, 1–9.

George Croft, headmaster, linguist, and divine, is an interesting example of the phenomenon which might well be termed 'grateful Toryism'. A child of humble family and slim financial resources, Croft, like William Gifford a generation later, owed his education and his career to the patronage of the religious and civil establishments. Again as in the case of William Gifford, Croft's gratitude to his benefactors – and his sense of indebtedness to the system that had allowed him to rise – led him to become an ardent Tory and a deeply committed supporter of the established order.

Croft's debt to ruling-class benevolence began early in his life. A brilliant student educated free of charge in the Bolton Grammar School, he matriculated at University College, Oxford, as a Bible clerk, his schoolmaster, the Rev. Thomas Carr, having raised a subscription to help with his expenses. Croft's rapid rise in the educational community fully justified his patron's trust. After taking his BA and being elected a scholar of University College, he proceeded MA, fellow, BD, and DD in rapid order,[1] capping his university attainments by preaching the Bampton Lectures of 1786. At the same time Croft was winning ecclesiastical preferments[2] and pursuing a career as a headmaster, first at Beverley Grammar School (1768–80) and then at the Grammar School of Brewood, Staffordshire (1780–91). His personal friends included Lord Eldon, who later presented him to the rectory of Thwing in the East Riding of Yorkshire, and Sir William Jones, the oriental scholar.

Like so many other products of his age who had risen from humble parentage to positions of status through upward social mobility, Croft was a convinced Tory and a wholehearted supporter of the system within which he had found his niche. He was ever 'firm and decided in his public character, hostile to the specious innovations of modern times'.[3] His contemporary and memorialist Rann Kennedy left a vivid portrait of Croft fighting the forces of

Jacobinism and Dissent in Birmingham with more zeal than science:
'[H]e entered into all the public business of the town, and during a
most eventful period, he was distinguished as a strenuous defender
of the constitution in church and state, and an active opposer of
every thing which he considered as tending to injure or endanger
them.'[4] One evidence of the drift of his sympathies was his
friendship for the French *émigrés*. *The Times* of 8 November 1793 lists
the 'Rev. G. Croft' among the contributors to the United Committee
of Subscribers for the Relief of the Suffering Clergy of France.[5] His
own works attest to his Tory principles, his list of publications
including *The Test Laws defended* (written in answer to Richard Price's
Old Jewry sermon) and his 1793 *Plans of Parliamentary Reform, proved
to be visionary* (arguing that a further extension of the suffrage would
place the nation in danger of riots and violence).[6] For the *Anti-Jacobin*
he wrote reviews of Biblical criticism (attacking Deist claims that the
Bible was largely fabulous) and biting letters to the editor, signed
'MISOFANATICUS' and filled with trenchant denunciations of
Evangelical 'enthusiasm'.[7]

Notes

1. *Alumni Oxon.*, I, 318.
2. Croft received the vicarage of Arncliffe in Craven in 1779 from University
   College. He held it as an absentee, leaving the post to a curate. Shortly
   afterwards he became chaplain to the Earl of Elgin and in 1791 was
   named lecturer at St Martin's, Birmingham, and chaplain of St
   Bartholomew's, Birmingham. In 1802 Lord Eldon presented him to the
   rectory of Thwing in the East Riding of Yorkshire.
3. *GM*, LXXIX-1 (May 1809) 485.
4. [Rann Kennedy], 'A Brief Sketch of the Author's Life', in George Croft,
   *Sermons, including A Series of Discourses on the Minor Prophets, Preached
   before the University of Oxford* (2 vols; Birmingham: printed by R. Jabet,
   1811) I, xxx.
5. Croft's subscription of £36 17s. 8d. was more than the annual income of
   many a clergyman.
6. William Arthur Shuffrey, *Some Craven Worthies* (London: F. E. Robinson,
   1903) p. 175.
7. See especially *AJ*, III (May 1799) 1–8; III (June 1799) 211–12; and III (July
   1799) 349–51.

D'ISRAELI, Isaac (1766–1848)

AJ contribution: III, 356–7.

Isaac D'Israeli, author of the *Curiosities of Literature* and father of Benjamin Disraeli, was a literary celebrity of considerable repute in the 1790's. Descended from Levantine Jews who had settled in Italy in the sixteenth century, D'Israeli was the London-born son of a merchant and stockbroker who had emigrated to England in 1748. Sent to school at Enfield and then Amsterdam, D'Israeli returned to England in 1782, determined, against his family's wishes, to follow a career in literature. Although he had broken into print in 1786 with a vindication of Dr Johnson in the *Gentleman's Magazine*,[1] it was his 1789 attack upon Peter Pindar in the *Gentleman's*[2] that first won him fame and the personal patronage of Henry James Pye (q.v.), who was soon to become Poet Laureate. It was Pye, in fact, who induced D'Israeli's father to accept his son's choice of a literary career.

That career does not appear to have been materially hampered by racial prejudice, perhaps in part because D'Israeli was not a practising Jew. Though proud of the heritage and history of his race, D'Israeli disagreed with the social separation practised by many in the Jewish community and considered most elements of Jewish religious ritual mere superstition.[3] Elected in 1813 against his will as warden of the London synagogue of Spanish and Portuguese Jews (of which he was a contributing member), D'Israeli refused to serve, declaring that the office was 'repulsive to his feelings' and that he could 'never unite in . . . [the synagogue's] public worship because, as now conducted, it disturbs instead of exciting religious emotions'.[4] For this outburst, as well as for refusing office, the elders of the synagogue fined D'Israeli £2, which precipitated a running battle between the author and the elders until 1817, when D'Israeli resigned from the congregation and had all of his children baptized at St Andrew's, Holborn.

Though D'Israeli experimented with poetry and romances,[5] his fame rests chiefly on two works – the aforementioned *Curiosities of Literature, consisting of Anecdotes, Characters, Sketches, and Observations, Literary, Critical, and Historical* (which was begun in 1791 and which eventually ran through six volumes and numerous revisions), and the five-volume *Commentaries on the Life and Reign of Charles I.* The latter work, which appeared from 1828 to 1830, aroused a literary controversy because of its royalist overtones and won D'Israeli a DCL at Oxford in 1832.[6] D'Israeli always enjoyed the friendship and respect of a wide literary acquaintance which included Walter Scott, Byron, Southey, Thomas Moore, Bulwer-Lytton, John Nichols, and (for a number of years) John Murray II, publisher of Byron and of the *Quarterly Review*.[7] D'Israeli wrote one contribution for the *Anti-Jacobin*, a letter to the editor concerning the *Review*'s comments on his *Curiosities of Literature*.

Notes

1. *GM*, LVI-2 (supplement for the year 1786) 1123–7.
2. *GM*, LIX-1 (July 1789) 648–9.
3. D'Israeli elaborated at length upon these views in his *Genius of Judaism* (1833).
4. Quoted in Sidney Lee, 'D'Israeli', *DNB*, V, 1023.
5. One of D'Israeli's novels, *Vaurien*, pleased the *Anti-Jacobin* by its critical attitude toward Godwin's philosophy and John Thelwall's political Radicalism (*AJ*, I [December 1798] 685–90).
6. For a full list of D'Israeli's publications, see the *BLGC*.
7. His circle of friends does not, however, appear to have included David Rivers, who in his 1798 *Literary Memoirs of Living Authors of Great Britain* wrote a sneering account of D'Israeli, criticising the supposed arrogance of the *Curiosities of Literature* and in general pointing out 'the petulance and conceit of this mighty Authorling'.

FITZGERALD, William Thomas (1759?–1829)

AJ contributions: I, 235; VI, 475.

William Thomas Fitzgerald, occasional contributor of poetry to the *Anti-Jacobin*,[1] was a leading spirit of the Literary Fund and a well-known writer of patriotic verse addresses. Born in England, the child of an Irish father connected with the family of the Duke of Leinster, Fitzgerald was educated at Greenwich and then in France, at the Royal College of Navarre in the University of Paris. While in France he was presented to Louis XVI and Marie Antoinette and, according to the *Gentleman's Magazine*, 'was invited to the balls and private parties of that Court; . . . even to the choice circle at the Petite Trianon'.[2] After returning to England, Fitzgerald entered the Inner Temple as the pupil of Sir Vicary Gibbs.[3] His interest in the law eventually waned, and in 1782 he became a clerk in the Navy Pay Office, where he served in various capacities for about twenty-five years.

Fitzgerald's chief enthusiasm was literature. He became a vice-president and firm supporter of the Literary Fund, which had been established by David Williams for the relief of indigent authors and their widows and orphans. He threw himself into poetry, turning out a profusion of verses and theatrical prologues, the latter written both for public performances and his own and others' private theatricals. As John Taylor (q.v.), his fellow member of the Keep the Line Club noted, 'Mr. Fitzgerald was a great lover of the drama, [and] he had frequently dramatic scenes represented at his house in the evening to parties of his friends, some of whom used to take part in the scenic amusements'.[4] Fitzgerald's private performances were well known among his acquaintances, who acclaimed him a highly accomplished actor.[5] His chief fame, though, lay with his loyal poems and addresses, recited with gusto by their author over a period of thirty-two years at the annual dinners of the Literary Fund. Very clearly they were the works of an intensely patriotic would-be Poet Laureate, their number including such self-revealing compositions as 'The Tribute of an humble Muse to an unfortunate captive Queen [Marie Antoinette]' (1793), 'Lines on the murder of the Queen of France', 'Britons, to arms! of apathy beware' (1803), and '"Britons never will be slaves!!" an Address to every loyal Briton on the threatened invasion' (1803); tributes and memorials to William Pitt, Nelson, Wellington, and the Spanish patriots; celebrations of the victories of Salamanca, Vittoria, and Waterloo; and an 1814 collected edition of poems castigating Napoleon, in the preface to which Fitzgerald plumed himself on his 'devoted love to his country, unbiased by party considerations, and . . . [his] undeviating detestation of the greatest and basest Tyrant that was ever permitted to desolate the earth'.[6]

Fitzgerald was by no means universally appreciated in his lifetime. James and Horace Smith parodied him in the 'Loyal Effusion' of their *Rejected Addresses*[7] and Byron enshrined him in his gallery of poetic mediocrity in *English Bards and Scotch Reviewers*:

> Still must I hear? – shall hoarse Fitzgerald bawl
> His creaking couplets in a tavern hall?

However, his John Bull chauvinism naturally made Fitzgerald a favourite among the anti-Jacobin and Francophobe wing of the periodical press. 'If ever muse deserved the much abused, but highly honourable epithet, *patriotic*', the *Anti-Jacobin* declared, 'Mr.

Fitzgerald's muse has an undoubted claim to it. She is ever vigilant, ever ready, to celebrate, in strains equal to the subject, her country's honour, her country's glory, and her country's triumphs.'[8]

Notes

1. W. T. Fitzgerald's 'A Jacobin Council' (signed 'Alfred') was printed in the *AJ*, I (August 1798) 235. His 'To the Author of the Epistle to Peter Pindar' (signed 'F.'), otherwise entitled 'To W. Gifford, Esq.', appeared in the *AJ*, VI (August 1800) 475. The latter poem was attributed in the British Library staff copy to 'G. W. Fitzgerald', as the *Anti-Jacobin* mistakenly referred to William Thomas Fitzgerald. See also a reference to the poet as 'G. W. T. Fitzgerald' in the *AJ*, III (July 1799) 303. Both poems are to be found in W. T. Fitzgerald's *Miscellaneous Poems* (London: printed by W. Bulmer, 1801) pp. 170–1, 189.
2. *GM*, XCIX-2 (November 1829) 471.
3. See his entry in *A Calendar of the Inner Temple Records*, ed. F. A. Inderwick and R. A. Roberts (5 vols; London: published by order of the Masters of the Bench, 1896–1936) V, 360.
4. John Taylor, *Records of My Life* (New York: J. and J. Harper, 1833) p. 453.
5. *European Magazine*, XLV (March 1804) 163; *GM*, XCIX-2 (November 1829) 471–2.
6. Quoted in *GM*, XCIX-2 (November 1829) 472.
7. Frank Thomas Marzials, 'Fitzgerald, William Thomas', *DNB*, VII, 152.
8. *AJ*, XII (June 1802) 205.

GIFFARD, John, of Dublin (1746–1819) [*AJ*: 'Alderman Gifford of Dublin']

AJ contribution: v, 91–9.

Surely one of the most fanatical of the *Anti-Jacobin*'s band of contributors was John Giffard, member of the Dublin Corporation, place-holder in the Irish customs, paid Treasury journalist,[1] and relentless crusader against Catholics and revolutionaries. Richard Polwhele (q.v.) called him a 'firm friend to the Constitution, in Church and State'.[2] In the more trenchant phrase of William Jerdan he was a 'red-hot Tory'.[3]

Giffard was born in Dublin, the son of a Devonshireman remotely connected with the great families of Windham, Granville, and Fane. Having originally intended to pursue a career in medicine, Giffard went into politics instead and 'was from his entry into public life the leading member of the Corporation of Dublin', making himself an arch-enemy of Home Rule and Irish separatist movements for nearly twenty-five years.[4] The key to his political behaviour was his intense loyalty to Protestantism, which he was convinced would be undermined by any tampering with the civil or religious establishment. Consequently he was an opponent of any change whatsoever in the governmental structure of Ireland or of any loosening of the control exerted over her by Britain. He had the fearlessness of a zealot, and his extreme views on the subject, openly displayed in impassioned harangues in public meetings and in the press, rapidly made him 'the idol of one party, while he rendered himself very obnoxious to the great body of the Irish nation'.[5]

The beginning of the war with France in 1793 saw Giffard, an ex-Volunteer,[6] return to military service as a captain in the Dublin Militia. He saw active service during the Irish insurrection of 1798, a crisis which cost him three members of his family. His nephew, Captain Ryan, was stabbed to death by the rebel Lord Edward Fitzgerald, whom Ryan had arrested for high treason. His brother-in-law died of privation while a prisoner of the revolutionists in Wexford gaol.[7] However, it was concerning his son William that 'the fury of rebellion fell most calamitously upon Mr. Giffard; his third son . . . was seized as he was travelling in a mail-coach, by a band of traitors, and required by them to lead them against a neighbouring post occupied by the King's troops; on his refusal, and that refusal being aggravated by his being known as the son of Mr. Giffard, he was savagely murdered on the spot'.[8] It was, as the *Gentleman's Magazine* noted, an event that could only exacerbate Giffard's hatred of 'every tendency to sedition and disturbance'.[9]

Giffard's last years of political life saw no diminution in his zeal for Church and State or in his penchant for the controversial. He was the only member of the Corporation of Dublin to support the Union in 1800, believing the measure to be Ireland's best chance for civil tranquillity and a strengthened Established Church. His 1805 petition in opposition to Catholic Emancipation offended the pro-Catholic Lord Lieutenant, Lord Hardwicke, and cost him his place in the Irish customs, which he had held since 1780. The Castle's decision to reappoint him in 1807 (this time as Accountant-General of the Customs) provoked a storm of protest from Henry Grattan and the Catholic Whigs and led to a counter display on Giffard's behalf on the floor of the House of Commons by his personal friend and compatriot, John Wilson Croker.[10] In addition

Giffard continued his longtime management of the *Dublin Journal*, a subsidised Treasury newspaper, which he made 'the oracle of the Loyal Protestants of Ireland'.[11] He died in 1819 at the age of 73 after a lifelong career as self-appointed guardian of the Constitution against the 'menace' of Catholics and reformers.[12]

Notes

1. Sometime between 1784 and 1787 Giffard was rewarded for his services to the Irish government with a secret pension of £300 per annum, which continued for the next thirty years and more. He acquired an additional £300 per annum for his efforts as conductor of the pro-Protestant *Faulkner's Journal* (later the *Dublin Journal*). For a full account of these and later secret service pensions paid to Giffard out of Treasury funds, see A[rthur] Aspinall, *Politics and the Press, c. 1780–1850* (London: Home and Van Thal, 1949) p. 115. It should be pointed out that the rewards in money and employment accorded to Giffard by the government in no way call in question the sincerity of his political convictions. All evidence indicates that he acted totally from principle and not as a mere Treasury hack.
2. R[ichard] Polwhele, *Reminiscences, in Prose and Verse* (3 vols in 1; London: J. B. Nichols and Son, 1836) I, 159n.
3. William Jerdan, *The Autobiography of William Jerdan* (4 vols; London: Arthur Hall, Virtue, 1852–3) II, 79–80.
4. *GM*, LXXXIX-1 (May 1819) 482.
5. 'John Giffard, Esq.', *Annual Biography and Obituary*, V (1821) 367.
6. An incident in Giffard's early military career provides ample evidence of the depth of his religious intolerance. An early and enthusiastic member of the Irish Volunteers (which had been organised to stem the threat of a French invasion in 1778), Giffard had become instantly alarmed when Catholics were permitted to join the Volunteer companies. 'Such . . . was his hatred to the catholics', one contemporary noted, 'that he resigned his commission the moment the gentlemen of that persuasion were admitted into their ranks' (ibid.).
7. Most of the Irish rebels of 1798 were Protestants. In Wexford, however, it was the Catholic influence that was paramount, as the insurrection in that area was spearheaded by Catholic priests. As a result, Wexford and its vicinity constitute a special case in the history of the rebellion, for the rising there took on all the overtones of a holy war against Protestants, notable for its killings of innocent civilians and general savagery (J. C. Beckett, *The Making of Modern Ireland, 1603–1923* [London: Faber and Faber, 1966] pp. 263–5).
8. *GM*, LXXXIX-1 (May 1819) 483. See also an earlier account of the murder, ibid., LXVIII (June 1798) 535–6.
9. Ibid., LXXXIX-1 (May 1819) 483.
10. Croker, M.P. (1807–32) and Secretary of the Admiralty (1810–30), was for many years a leading contributor to the Tory *Quarterly Review*.
11. *GM*, LXXXIX-1 (May 1819) 483.

12. Giffard left two prominent sons – one, the Hon. Hardinge Giffard, Chief Justice of the Island of Ceylon; the other, Lees Stanley Giffard, LL D, a barrister and the editor of the *Standard* (ibid., p. 484; Alexander Andrews, *The History of British Journalism* [2 vols; London: Richard Bentley, 1859] II, 168).

GIFFORD, John (1758–1818)

AJ contributions: I, i–viii, 1–25, 34–7, 42–51, 72–91, 107–8, 114–16, 119–31, 140–60, 171–6, 190–1, 197–201, 203–9, 211–12, 240–6, 280–303, 308–9, 324–31, 336–41, 350–1, 355, 362–3, 368–76, 403–9, 424–6, 483–95[?], 496–9[?], 501–15[?], 569–74[?], 605–11[?], 691–2[?], 734–9[?]; II, 10–17, 22–32, 42–9, 54–7, 75–9, 90–1, 97, 104–12[?], 128–33, 146–55, 160–90, 190[?], 191–209, 227–31, 233–41, 272–5, 280–7, 289–97, 302–4[?], 344–52[?], 457–64[?], 519–35[?]; III, 45–7, 50–2, 53, 73–4, 100–3, 105–11, 150–5, 176–7, 180–1, 192–4, 231–9, 286–97, 303–7, 309–18, 446–9[?], 451–7[?], 461–7[?], 489–96[?]; IV, vi–xvi, 79–90, 97–102, 106–15, 119–28, 138–50, 200–13, 225–6, 236–40, 241–8, 269–82, 420–7[?], 473–88[?], 570–80[?]; V, 37–46, 64–71, 111–19, 153–62[with Tabaraud], 172–9, 183–4[?], 184–94, 200–19, 233–40, 263–77, 289–95, 301–4, 304–8[with Taylor], 308–18, 348–60, 365–82, 391–404, 410–24, 428–30, 437–9, 441–3, 444–7, 476, 477–80, 484–91, 513–51, 556–7, 564–6; VI, 47–52, 59–80, 84₁–8, 105–8, 120, 146–56, 166–73, 189–91, 193–5, 197–214, 216–18, 228–9, 234–40, 287–301, 306–15, 321–9, 357–60, 398–406, 409–16, 432–5, 438–44, 446–9, 452–5, 460–4, 476–80[?], 480, 498–516, 530–61.

John Gifford, the *Anti-Jacobin Review*'s arch-Tory editor and chief writer, was born John Richards Green, the son of a barrister, grandson of a civil servant in the Post Office, and heir to an estate in Shropshire, held in copyhold by his family since the reign of Charles II. Despite the obvious advantages of his birth, Green's early years were anything but promising. Following a short stay at Oxford, which he left without a degree, he took chambers in Lincoln's Inn and embarked upon a career of 'amazing expenditure'[1] which ended only with bankruptcy. Green, his inheritance exhausted, his estate sold, and his creditors in hot pursuit, decamped for the Continent, where for six or seven years he underwent a sort of purgatory, first at Lille and then at Rouen.[2] By 1788 he was back in England, chastened by his experiences and 'metamorphos'd', as his contemporaries would say, into John *Gifford*, the name that he would use for the rest of his life.

Upon his return to England Gifford took up a career as a writer, putting his knowledge of the French language and political scene to good use in his multi-volume *History of France* (published in 1791–4). It was this work, with its marked anti-revolutionary bias, that first brought Gifford to the attention of Pitt's government. 'The zeal and writings of Mr. Gifford on this occasion, at length recommended him to the notice of ministers', a contemporary reported. 'His pen was found to be keen and serviceable; he himself was always among the first to advocate their measures, on one hand, while he rode in the foremost ranks of the battle, and hewed down their political adversaries on the other.'[3] A number of anti-Jacobin and pro-government publications flowed from the fruitful union of Gifford and the Pitt Ministry[4] – assorted Crown-and-Anchor pamphlets,[5] translations or edited sets of memoirs related to the French Revolution,[6] and most notably a six-volume *History of the Political Life of the Right Hon. William Pitt*, published in 1809. Gifford is said as well to have become editor in 1796 of two newspapers, one of which his friend John Taylor (q.v.) identified as the *True Briton*.[7] Finally, upon the close of William Gifford's *Anti-Jacobin; or, Weekly Examiner* in July, 1798, John Gifford undertook the direction of the Tory newspaper's successor, the monthly *Anti-Jacobin Review*, which he continued to edit and for which he supplied a large number of articles, until his death in 1818.[8]

That the relationship between John Gifford and the Ministry was of mutual benefit goes without saying. Gifford for his part was appointed to two successive police magistracies,[9] and he seems to have received a pension of £300 per annum as well.[10] It is quite clear, however, that while Gifford's appointments and pension may well have reinforced his allegiance to the Ministry, he was at heart sincerely – even fanatically – loyal to the civil and religious establishments and was already supporting Pitt's government before he first came to the Premier's attention. For evidence of the sincerity of his convictions one has only to note the obvious depth of feeling displayed in Gifford's own writings for the *Anti-Jacobin* – his bitter condemnations of the alleged immorality and irreligion of the German Illuminati, his exposés of the Irish uprising of 1798 as Jacobinism hiding beneath the cloak of separatism and militant Catholicism, his biting characterisation of George Washington as a traitor, Deist, and sympathiser with France,[11] to cite a few examples. In any event the combination of blind resistance to change, an exalted sense of duty, a vitriolic prose style, and a consuming loyalty to Church-and-King principles rendered John Gifford without doubt uniquely qualified to preside over the *Anti-Jacobin Review* during the first twenty of its twenty-three years of life.

Notes

1. *GM*, LXXXVIII-1 (March 1818) 280.
2. According to Gifford's obituary in the *Gentleman's Magazine*, Green 'obtained an introduction to the British Ambassador's retinue [in Paris], where he remained several years, to the delight and admiration of all who had the felicity of his acquaintance, till the violence of that Revolution obliged him to return to England' (ibid.). On the other hand a certain 'A. B.', in a letter to the *Gentleman's* published shortly thereafter, claimed that Gifford resided not in Paris but in Lille and Rouen and that he had already returned to England by early 1788 (*GM*, LXXXVIII-1 [May 1818] 403), a view seconded in the *Annual Biography and Obituary*, III [1819] 313–14. The *DNB* as well supports the latter account of Gifford's Continental years (Leslie Stephen, 'Gifford, John', *DNB*, VII, 1184).
3. *Annual Biography and Obituary*, III (1819) 315.
4. For lists of Gifford's publications see *BLGC* and Gayle Trusdel Pendleton, 'Three Score Identifications of Anonymous British Pamphlets of the 1790s', *Notes and Queries*, n.s. XXVI (June 1979) 210–11, 215.
5. One of them, his *Short Address to the Members of the Loyal Associations*, ran through numerous editions and was said to have sold 100,000 copies (*Annual Biography and Obituary*, III [1819] 316).
6. Most notable were Gifford's translations of Lally-Tollendal's *Defence of the French Emigrants* and Camille Jourdan's *Address . . . on the Revolution of the 4th of September, 1797*.
7. *Annual Biography and Obituary*, III (1819) 322; John Taylor, *Records of My Life* (New York: J. and J. Harper, 1833) p. 386.
8. Gifford also seems to have contemplated founding another periodical, the *Church of England Magazine* – 'its object, the support of the Establishment against the multitude of sectaries and sectarian publications with which the country now swarms, and which, I am concerned to say, daily increase'. He told Richard Polwhele (q.v.) that he was 'thoroughly convinced, that with the Anti-Jacobin Review, and a Magazine such as this, much good may be effected. But if we remain negligent or inert, or even oppose but feeble efforts to the indefatigable exertions of our numerous opponents, we must be ultimately defeated' (John Gifford, letter to Richard Polwhele, 9 August 1799, quoted in R[ichard] Polwhele, *Traditions and Recollections; Domestic, Clerical and Literary* [2 vols; London: John Nichols and Son, 1826] II, 511). The magazine never materialised.
9. He was first appointed a police magistrate in Worship Street,

Shoreditch, and later exchanged the post for a more desirable magistracy in Great Marlborough Street, Westminster. Gifford's office as police magistrate was no sinecure. Cobbett (q.v.) once noted in a letter to Polwhele that Gifford has recently had to help break up a London mob, adding that 'as a magistrate, as well as a writer, . . . [Gifford was] a most vigilant, active, courageous, and persevering man' (William Cobbett, letter to Richard Polwhele, 10 October 1800, quoted in *Polwhele, Traditions and Recollections*, II, 531).

10. Reginald Reynolds, Introduction to William Hazlitt's 'A Letter to William Gifford, Esq.', in George Orwell and Reginald Reynolds (eds), *British Pamphleteers* (2 vols; London: Allan Wingate, 1948–51) II, 72. The Secret Service accounts contain records of several subsidies paid to Gifford: £170 2s. 6d. in 1794; £195 and £15 in 1795; £210 and £30 in 1796 (Chatham Papers [P.R.O. 30/8], vol. 229, pt 2, fols 313a and 314a).

11. The extremism of Gifford's attack upon Washington becomes all the more noteworthy in the light of the generally favourable treatment being accorded Washington by other pro-government journalists, who were praising the dead president as a philosophical conservative like themselves. Compare, for example, Gifford's treatment of Washington in the *AJ*, v (Appendix to January–April 1800) 548, with the very different attitude displayed in the *British Critic*, x (October 1797) 441–2, 445, and 448.

GLASSE, Rev. George Henry (1761–1809)

AJ contributions: II, 219–21; IV, 409–16[?]; V, 75–80, 121–32, 467–72; VI, 455–60[with Polwhele].

George Henry Glasse was a Greek scholar and sermon writer who corresponded frequently with the *Gentleman's Magazine* in addition to supplying occasional reviews for the *Anti-Jacobin*. The son of the Rev. Samuel Glasse, DD, a popular preacher of charity sermons, George Henry Glasse succeeded his father as rector of Hanwell, Middlesex, in 1785 and served in addition as domestic chaplain to the Earl of Radnor, the Duke of Cambridge, and the Earl of Sefton, in that order.[1]

Glasse was an ardent patriot, now preaching in support of the French *émigré* clergy and the widows of British seamen lost in the battle of the Nile, now serving as Honorary Chaplain to the Corps of the Volunteer Armed Association of Hanwell and Ealing, one of the numerous home defence companies formed during the crisis of the French wars. He was in addition a committed anti-Jacobin, who attacked 'the baneful influence of democratical and levelling principles' and delighted in raking over accounts of French Jacobin atrocities.[2]

Despite his potentially valuable connections with various great families, Glasse never managed to rise above the life of clerical mediocrity to which he found himself consigned. His publications included Greek translations of *Samson Agonistes* (1788) and Mason's *Caractacus* (1781), but the bulk of his work consisted of a number of less ambitious sermons on miscellaneous subjects. According to the *Gentleman's Magazine*, 'In person he was short and fat; his face full, and rather handsome, with an expression of benevolence and intelligence.'[3] The heir to a large fortune, Glasse contrived to run through his entire inheritance in sixteen years, whereupon he hanged himself 'in a momentary phrenzy'[4] in the Bull and Mouth inn, London, 30 October 1809.

Notes

1. Alsager Vian, 'Glasse, George Henry', *DNB*, vii, 1299; *Alumni Oxon.*, ii, 528.
2. *AJ*, v (February 1800) 123. See also *AJ*, ii (February 1799) 220, and v (April 1800) 467.
3. *GM*, lxxix-2 (November 1809) 1082.
4. Ibid., p. 1083.

GLEIG, George, Bishop of Brechin (1753–1840)

AJ contributions: iii, 23–7, 259–67; iv, 115–16; v, 297–300, 339, 448–54; vi, 219–28, 265–70, 370–80.

George Gleig, bishop of Brechin and primus (1816–37) of the Scottish Episcopal Church, was a leading supporter of the rights of the Episcopal minority in Presbyterian Scotland and a frequent contributor on political and religious matters to the *Anti-Jacobin Review*. A hard-line Tory of Jacobite ancestry, Gleig received his education at King's College, Aberdeen,[1] winning prizes in mathematics, moral philosophy, and the physical sciences. He took orders in 1773 and embarked shortly thereafter on a campaign to win repeal of the penal laws[2] operating against the Scottish Episcopal Church and to promote closer ties between the Church of England and Scottish Episcopacy.

Gleig's chief rival in the latter movement was John Skinner (q.v.), primus from 1788 to 1816 and undisputed leader of the Episcopal congregations north of the Tweed. Bishop Skinner, though a supporter of a closer association between the Scottish Episcopal Church and the Church of England, opposed the total submersion of Scottish Episcopacy in the Anglican system. Already distrustful of Gleig for personal reasons,[3] Skinner apparently feared that Gleig went too far in his support of the ritual and practices of the English Church. On three occasions – in 1786, 1792, and 1808 – Skinner blocked Gleig's election as bishop of Dunkeld, and in 1808, when Gleig was unanimously chosen bishop-coadjutor of Brechin, Skinner agreed to his elevation only on condition that Gleig bind himself to maintain the Scottish Episcopal Office of Holy Communion. Gleig agreed to the stipulation and was duly consecrated bishop-coadjutor, becoming bishop in his own right in 1810. Six years later Gleig succeeded Skinner as primus of the Scottish Episcopal Church and set about immediately to encourage the adoption of all English rites save Communion by the Episcopal churches of Scotland. In 1828 Gleig presided over the final step in the conversion of Scotland to the English ritual when the General Synod of the Scottish Episcopal Church firmly ordered the adoption of the English liturgy for Morning and Evening Prayer and gave individual bishops the right to require use of the Anglican Communion service in their own dioceses.[4]

Gleig was a frequent contributor to the periodicals, supplying numerous articles for the *Monthly Review*, *Gentleman's Magazine*, *Anti-Jacobin Review*, *British Critic*, and *Scottish Episcopal Magazine*.[5] In addition he wrote the essays on 'Instinct', 'Metaphysics', and 'Theology' for the third edition of the *Encyclopaedia Britannica*, edited volumes XIII–XVIII of the set, and wrote the two supplementary volumes of 1801 almost single-handedly.[6] For the *Anti-Jacobin* he was a steadfast contributor, perfectly in tune with the *Review*'s political philosophy and sharing its commitment to fight Jacobinism in all its forms. The Jacobins, wrote Gleig, had made themselves masters at ideological warfare and could be 'counteracted only by the friends of piety and virtue, and good government, pursuing their aims with equal . . . industry'.[7] Gleig for his part was ever ready to volunteer his services in the cause.

Notes

1. King's College, Aberdeen, eventually accorded him an LL D.
2. For an account of the penal laws restricting Scottish Episcopacy see pp. 144–5.

3. Gordon Goodwin suggests that Skinner was resentful of Gleig's uncomplimentary remarks upon his consecration sermon in the *Gentleman's Magazine*, LV-1 (June 1785) 438 (see Gordon Goodwin, 'Gleig, George', *DNB*, VII, 1302).
4. For a full account of Gleig's dealings with Skinner and his role in the adoption of the English liturgy see George Grub, *An Ecclesiastical History of Scotland, from the Introduction of Christianity to the Present Time* (4 vols; Edinburgh: Edmonston and Douglas, 1861) IV, 99, 124–35, 174–89.
5. Gleig's son, the Rev. George Robert Gleig, carried on the family tradition by becoming a valued contributor to *Blackwood's Magazine* and *Fraser's Magazine* (see George Barnett Smith, 'Gleig, George Robert', *DNB*, VII, 1303–4).
6. Goodwin, 'Gleig', p. 1302.
7. *AJ*, III (July 1799) 260.

GRANT, Rev. Donald (*c.* 1737–1809) [*AJ*: 'Dr. Grant']

AJ contribution: I, 37–41.

Donald Grant – or 'Dr. Grant', as his contemporaries called him[1] – was a London clergyman and Treasury propagandist of some repute in the world of the late eighteenth-century press. While he was of only marginal importance to the *Anti-Jacobin Review*, he played a small but critical role in the history of the *Review*'s predecessor, the *Anti-Jacobin; or, Weekly Examiner*. It was Dr Grant who was Canning's original choice for the editor of the *Anti-Jacobin* weekly newspaper, and it was Grant's sudden illness at the outset of the project that led to the last-minute substitution of William Gifford in the post[2] – an occurrence that not only determined in large measure the character of the *Anti-Jacobin* newspaper but also propelled William Gifford on his way to becoming the future editor of the *Quarterly Review*.

Unfortunately little is known of Dr Grant. The best single source of information concerning him is his highly original epitaph (written in part by Grant himself), which describes him as a Doctor of Divinity, who died 24 April 1809, in London, in his seventy-second year, 'the whole of his ecclesiastical emoluments, during a ministry of 44 years in the Established Church of England, [having] amounted to £743 8s. 5d.!'.[3] Joseph Farington's richly detailed *Diary* supplies a bit more information. Farington, who filled his daily accounts with titbits of gossip concerning the literary and artistic

circles of his time, noted that Grant was a clergyman in the Church
of England, who 'had travelled two or three times as a Tutor to men
of distinction, from [whom] he had annuities'. Despite Grant's bitter
remarks on the inadequacy of clerical salaries, Farington says, he
was able at his death to bequeath about £5000 to the University of
Edinburgh for the establishment of two bursarships. According to
Farington the principal source of Grant's income was his
propaganda writings: 'During Mr. Pitts administration He in some
way was employed by government, probably as a writer in
periodical publications for which He was handsomely paid, as,
when Mr. Pitt resigned in 1801 Dr. Grant sd. *He* lost half His
income.'[4] Farington's statement is borne out by the Secret Service
accounts, which list one 'D. Grant' as the recipient of Treasury funds
on at least two occasions,[5] while University of Edinburgh alumni
records confirm that a Donald Grant of London received the degree
of Doctor of Divinity on 19 June 1775.[6] Aside from these scraps of
information, however, Grant remains a shadowy figure. As for his
connection with the *Anti-Jacobin* newspaper's successor, the *Anti-
Jacobin Review*, the British Library staff copy credits him with only
one article, a critique of Patrick Duigenan's *An Answer to . . . Henry
Grattan*, in which Grant castigated Grattan as a turbulent agitator,
'stimulated by the success of the French regicides and anarchists'
and dangerous to the peace of Ireland.[7]

Notes

1. For the identification of 'Dr. Grant' as the Rev. Donald Grant see Emily
   Lorraine de Montluzin, 'The "Anti-Jacobin's" Elusive Dr. Grant', *Notes
   and Queries*, n.s. XXVI (June 1979) 217–19.
2. [William Gifford Cookesley ('Eponymos')], ['Memoir of William
   Gifford'], in John Nichols, *Illustrations of the Literary History of the
   Eighteenth Century* (8 vols; London: printed for the author, 1817–58) VI,
   5–6.
3. *GM*, n.s. XXXI (April 1849) 338 – see also *GM*, LXXIX (May 1809) 482; and
   the *European Magazine*, LV (May 1809) 409.
4. Joseph Farington, entry for 20 July 1809, in James Greig (ed.), *The
   Farington Diary* (8 vols; London: Hutchinson, 1922–8) V, 209.
5. The Secret Service accounts show that £50 was paid to 'D. Grant' on 2
   January 1794 and again on 9 March 1794 (Chatham Papers [P.R.O. 30/8],
   vol. 229, pt 2, fol. 292a).
6. *A Catalogue of the Graduates in the Faculties of Arts, Divinity, and Law, of
   the University of Edinburgh, Since its Foundation* (Edinburgh: n.p., 1858)
   p. 244.
7. *AJ*, I (July 1798) 38.

GREATHEED, Rev. Samuel (d. 1823)

AJ contributions: II, 97–100, 217–19; III, 84–7; IV, 345–9[?].

Greatheed was a Dissenting minister and editor of the Nonconformist *Eclectic Review* (established 1805) during its first year of operation.[1] Originally from Newport Pagnell, he settled in 1789 in nearby Bedford, where he became a supporter of the Bedford Union, 'an association to promote Nonconformity'.[2] He contributed to the *Evangelical Magazine*, a leading Dissenter and Evangelical publication which enjoyed the widest circulation of any religious miscellany of its day in England.[3] Otherwise Greatheed's publications consisted mainly of sermons, including one preached on the occasion of the death of William Cowper, who was his close personal friend. Greatheed also wrote the memoir of Cowper which appeared in the *Evangelical Magazine* in April and May of 1803.[4]

Greatheed was deeply patriotic and was at great pains to clear his fellow Dissenters of the charge of preaching irreligion and sedition. Noting in a letter to the *Anti-Jacobin* that the Dissenters in *his* neighbourhood prayed for the King and all in civil authority, Greatheed called for any Dissenter discovered advocating disloyalty to be denounced summarily to the authorities.[5] As for the claim that Dissenters sought the overthrow of the Church, Greatheed laid the blame for the charge at the door of Radical atheists, Deists, and Socinians, who were, he assured the *Anti-Jacobin*, erroneously lumped together with 'orthodox' Dissenters to the latter's detriment.[6] On the contrary, he insisted, true Dissenters like himself, by inculcating religious principles and high morals, did 'their utmost in stopping the progress of vice and infidelity' – the vice and infidelity that had ruined France.[7]

Greatheed was a fellow of the Society of Antiquaries and a man of considerable property.[8] John Gifford called him 'a gentleman of respectability among the Dissenters'[9] and in a rare gesture of tolerance printed without critical editorial comment his letters to the *Anti-Jacobin* in defence of Dissent.

Notes

1. Francis E. Mineka, *The Dissidence of Dissent* (Chapel Hill: University of North Carolina Press, 1944) p. 68.
2. Upcott, *Biog. Dict.*, p. 433.
3. Mineka, *Dissidence of Dissent*, p. 65.

4. *BLGC.*
5. *AJ*, ɪɪ (January 1799) 98–9. See also *AJ*, ɪɪ (February 1799) 218–19, and ɪɪɪ (May 1799) 86.
6. *AJ*, ɪɪ (January 1799) 99.
7. Ibid., p. 100.
8. *GM*, xcɪɪɪ-2 (July 1823) 91; Upcott, *Biog. Dict.*, p. 433.
9. *AJ*, ɪɪ (January 1799) 97.

HALDANE, Robert (1764–1842)

AJ contribution: ɪɪɪ, 341–2.

Robert Haldane – Dissenter, democrat, and co-sponsor of the Scottish Congregational churches – was one of a small handful of Radicals accorded space for one reason or another in the pages of the *Anti-Jacobin*.

A man of considerable wealth, Haldane came from a background typical of the propertied, middle-to-upper-class Radicals who figured so prominently in the Scottish reform movement during the early 1790s. Born in 1764 into a well-to-do family and educated at the Edinburgh High School and the University,[1] Haldane settled into a comfortable existence on his estates at Airthrey near Stirling until the French Revolution jolted him out of his uneventful routine and prompted him 'to consider everything anew'.[2] Though far from extreme in his political principles (he opposed civil disorder, levelling, attacks on private property, and what he considered the dangerous tendencies of the Friends of the People[3]) he joined the cause of reform[4] and, more importantly, around 1795 experienced a gradual spiritual awakening. He had earlier considered a career as a minister. Now he plunged into mission work, joining the London Missionary Society and in 1796 broaching a plan to sell his estate, set up a mission fund of £25,000, and go himself to preach in India. The East India Company, however, opposed missionary endeavours in its territory, and any hope Haldane might have had of securing special permission for the work was thwarted by Pitt's Secretary of War, Henry Dundas, who distrusted Haldane's political Radicalism.[5]

Accordingly Haldane turned his energies to the state of religion in Scotland. In 1797 he joined his brother, James Alexander Haldane, and approximately a dozen others in establishing the non-sectarian Society for Propagating the Gospel at Home. The following year

Haldane sold his estate and began to preach, and in 1799 both brothers left the Church of Scotland and set up the first Scottish Congregational tabernacle, James Alexander Haldane serving as its minister. The next dozen years saw Robert Haldane contribute some £70,000 to his newfound cause, financing the establishment of numerous Congregational tabernacles and seminaries to train preachers.[6]

From the very beginning Haldane's career as an unlicensed minister, his zeal for missions, and his reformist politics aroused suspicion on the part of the orthodox clergy.[7] The General Assembly of the Church of Scotland was sufficiently wary of him to circulate a pastoral letter warning against religious innovation and to forbid its ministers to hold communion with unlicensed Congregationalists.[8] In the press, meanwhile, Haldane was denounced by John Robison (q.v.), who linked him with the Freemasons, the Illuminati, and Priestley in the so-called Jacobin plot to subvert the religion, morality, class structure, and Constitution of Britain.[9] The May 1799 number of the *Anti-Jacobin* took up the attack, quoting (from Robison) an alleged statement by Haldane to the effect that the latter was ready 'TO WADE TO THE KNEES IN BLOOD FOR THE PURPOSE OF OVERTURNING EVERY ESTABLISHMENT OF RELIGION'.[10] It was Haldane's angry denial of this accusation that constituted his only contribution to the *Anti-Jacobin Review*.

Haldane's subsequent career was devoted in equal parts to missions[11] and religious controversy, especially after 1808, when his conversion (together with his brother's) to Baptist views aroused a storm of consternation within Congregationalist ranks. He died in 1842 after nearly half a century of vigorous preaching and doctrinal disputes.

Notes

1. In addition, in a departure from the norm, he served from 1780 to 1783 as a midshipman in the Royal Navy, where he saw action against the French.
2. Quoted in Alexander Haldane, *Memoirs of the Lives of Robert Haldane of Airthrey, and of His Brother, James Alexander Haldane* (New York: Robert Carter, 1853) p. 90.
3. Ibid., p. 82.
4. Haldane contrived to win notoriety as a Radical largely thanks to an ill-advised speech he delivered on 1 July 1794, before the freeholders of Stirling. The speech, which attacked the Allied war effort against the French and urged the cause of reform, saddled Haldane with a

reputation for Radicalism which he was not able to shake off for years. In fact it was only in 1800, when he published his *Address to the Public by Robert Haldane concerning his Political Opinions*, that Haldane was finally able to lay the charges against him to rest.

5. Haldane, *Memoirs of Robert Haldane and James Alexander Haldane*, p. 105.
6. Thomas Hamilton, 'Haldane, Robert', *DNB*, viii, 898.
7. Typical of this attitude was a letter from an alarmed Dr Porteous, the staunchly conservative pillar of the Glasgow presbytery, warning the Lord Advocate regarding Haldane: 'Many of us have reason to believe that the whole of this missionary business grows from a democratical root, and that the intention of those who planted it was to get hold of the public mind, and hereafter these societies may employ its energy as circumstances may direct' (The Rev. Dr William Porteous of Glasgow, letter to the Lord Advocate, 24 January 1797, quoted in Henry W. Meikle, *Scotland and the French Revolution* [Edinburgh: James Maclehose and Sons, Publishers to the University, 1912] p. 208). See also a letter from Porteous to the Lord Advocate, 21 February 1798, quoted in Great Britain, Historical Manuscripts Commission, Series 72, pts 1 and 2: *Report on the Laing Manuscripts Preserved in the University of Edinburgh*, ed. Henry Paton (London: His Majesty's Stationery Office, 1914–25) pt 2, pp. 643–4, and a letter from the Duke of Atholl to the Duke of Portland, 20 May 1799, ibid., pp. 676–8.
8. Meikle, *Scotland and the French Revolution*, p. 209.
9. The accusation appeared in the first edition of Robison's *Proofs of a Conspiracy*. Robison withdrew the passage after Haldane heatedly challenged its accuracy.
10. Quoted in the *AJ*, iii (May 1799) 26.
11. In 1816 and for several years thereafter Haldane launched a series of remarkably successful mission tours on the Continent, setting up bases in Switzerland and France and circulating French translations of the Scriptures and of his own theological tracts. (For lists of Haldane's published works see the *BLGC*; Watt, *Biblio. Brit.*, i, 456; the *English Catalogue*, p. 250; and Upcott, *Biog. Dict.*, p. 141.)

HARRAL, Thomas (d. 1853) [*AJ*: 'Harrall']

AJ contributions: iv, 234–6; vi, 52–9, 449–51.

A personal friend of John Gifford,[1] Thomas Harral was the author of several prose and verse accounts of the stage, one novel (*Scenes of Life*, published 1805), and a number of political pamphlets and plays, among them *Church and King and Colour Blue* (1819), *Anne Boleyn and Caroline of Brunswick compared* (1820), *The Demon of the Age: or, signs of the times explained* (1821), *Henry the Eighth and George the Fourth* (1820), and *The Apotheosis of Pitt, . . . a masque* (1822).[2] In addition he was for a time the editor of the *Suffolk Chronicle* (an Ipswich twopenny weekly of liberal views, established 1810)[3] and later of the *Bury Gazette*.[4]

Harral reviewed novels, tales, and plays for the *Anti-Jacobin* and was (in his early manhood, at least) a committed opponent of Jacobinism. His *Scenes of Life* (dedicated to John Gifford) denounced 'novels and romances [which] have of late years been too frequently rendered the vehicles of revolutionary and infidel principles'.[5] Though his particular targets were Rousseau, Godwin, Thomas Holcroft, and Mary Wollstonecraft, Harral seems to have seen the Jacobin threat on all sides. In a review of a set of children's novels he warned his readers that Jacobinism assumed 'various forms . . . to accomplish its atrocious designs' and urged a close inspection even of nursery stories to protect 'the untainted minds of the rising generation from . . . the pestiferous doctrines of the day'.[6]

Notes

1. *AJ*, xxii (September 1806) 72–3.
2. *BLGC; English Catalogue*, p. 256; Upcott, *Biog. Dict.*, p. 146; Watt, *Biblio. Brit.*, i, 467.
3. James Grant, *The Newspaper Press: Its Origin – Progress – and Present Position*, iii (London: George Routledge, n.d.) 290.
4. *GM*, n.s. xxxix (March 1853) 333.
5. Quoted in the *AJ*, xxii (September 1806) 73.
6. *AJ*, vi (May 1800) 56.

HEATH, Dr John (*c.* 1753?–1838?) [*AJ*: 'Dr. Heath']

AJ contributions: iii, 52–3; vi, 184–9.

The British Library's *General Catalogue of Printed Books* lists only two Heaths in the medical profession who lived at the right time to contribute to the *Anti-Jacobin Review* in 1799–1800: first, Joannes Heath, MD, an English medical student at the University of Edinburgh who published his *Dissertatio, quaedam de asthmate spasmodico complectens* in 1787; second, John Heath, surgeon in the Royal Navy, who published a three-volume translation from the French of J. L. Baudelocque's *System of Midwifery* in 1790. It would seem likely that the 'Dr. Heath' who supplied a handful of critiques of medical publications for the *Anti-Jacobin* was the latter, since one of the works he reviewed was related to the field of obstetrics – John Hull's *A Defence of the Cesarean Operation*.[1] If that supposition is correct, then the *Anti-Jacobin's* Dr Heath was an otherwise unknown surgeon in the Royal Navy who died in 1838 at the age of 85.[2]

Notes

1. *AJ*, III (May 1799) 52–3. Dr Heath's other articles in the *Anti-Jacobin* – reviews of Thomas Gibbons's *Medical Cases and Remarks*, Robert Townson's *Tracts and Observations in Natural History and Physiology*, and Benjamin Douglas Perkins's *The Efficacy of Perkins's Patent Metallic Tractors* (all found in the *AJ*, VI [June 1800] 184–9) – are no help in Heath's identification. Neither is the entry for one 'John Heath' on 1 January 1785, in the *General List of the Members of the Medical Society of Edinburgh* (Edinburgh: printed for the Society, 1812) p. 29.
2. *GM*, n.s. IX (June 1838) 666; Upcott, *Biog. Dict.*, p. 151.

HEATH, Rev. William

AJ contributions: III, 37–9, 54–8, 144–6, 164–8; IV, 19–27, 62–7, 76–9, 102–3; V, 23–8, 145–53, 335–8, 424–8, 432–4; VI, 23–7, 88, 159–65, 249–54.

Positive identification of the Rev. William Heath has proved impossible[1] – an unfortunate circumstance since Heath wrote numerous reviews for the *Anti-Jacobin*. Those reviews, most of them of novels, do however provide an excellent insight into Heath's political attitudes. Judging by his articles, Heath was clearly a believer in the supposed Jacobin plot to circulate Radical principles under the cover of literature,[2] and he denounced in his reviews a galaxy of Jacobin and Deistical writers, Godwin, Paine, Gibbon, and Gilbert Wakefield among them.[3] It was, however, the works of the feminist writers of the 1790s that Heath most often singled out for condemnation. The 'Wollstonecraft school', he was convinced, was aiming at nothing less than to turn English women into 'revolutionary agents', not 'dutiful daughters, affectionate wives, tender mothers, and good Christians'.[4] To a loyal anti-Jacobin like Heath, convinced as he was that the morality of English womanhood was the nation's first line of defence against Radicalism and irreligion, the implications of such activities were terrifying. Accordingly he spared no pains in castigating the ideas of the Wollstonecrafts and the Mary Hayses of England, urging feminist writers to give up such 'mischievous' folly and return to their proper sphere in the home. As Heath bluntly put it, *'to your distaff, Mary, to your distaff'*.[5]

Notes

1. Several possibilities exist. Cambridge alumni records list a William Heath of Newcastle, Staffs. (b. *c*. 1751), who matriculated at Magdalene College (BA, 1773; MA, 1776; fellow) and served as curate of Chesterton in Cambridgeshire (1779) and rector of St Michael's, Long Stanton (1781–2). (*Alumni Cantab.*, pt 2, III, 313.) The *Gentleman's Magazine* contains several references to a Rev. William Heath (d. 1830), from 1792 vicar of Inkberrow, Worcs. (*GM*, c-2 [October 1830] 378). There also seems to have been a 'Rev. W. Heath' who was appointed to Calne vicarage, Wilts., in 1828 (*GM*, xcviii-1 [February 1828] 174).
2. See, for example, *AJ*, IV (September 1799) 19.
3. *AJ*, IV (September 1799) 19; V (April 1800) 428.
4. *AJ*, III (May 1799) 55.
5. Ibid., p. 58. The Mary Hays in question was the author of *Memoirs of Emma Courtney* (1796), *Female Biography; or Memoirs of illustrious and celebrated women* (1803), and *Memoirs of Queens, illustrious and celebrated* (1821).

HENSHALL, Rev. J.

AJ contribution: III, 47–9.

All efforts to identify the Rev. J. Henshall have been in vain. Nothing is known of him except for the meagre insight into his opinions afforded by his sole contribution to the *Anti-Jacobin*, a review of a financial pamphlet whose author denounced various members of the Opposition for unpatriotically availing themselves of loopholes in the income tax law. Judging by Henshall's article, he was a Pittite who ranked himself with the pamphleteer as 'a true friend to the constitution, and . . . pure religion'.[1]

Note

1. *AJ*, III (May 1799) 49.

HENSHALL, Rev. Samuel (1764?–1807)

AJ contributions: I, 356–9, 377–9, 398–402, 426–34, 496–9[?], 524–9[?], 579–88, 655–63[?], 678–85[?], 709–12[?], 729–33; II, 17–22, 32–41, 49–53, 79–83, 122–8, 209–12, 241–51, 257–62, 267–72, 339–44; III, 9–16, 241–5, 377–83[?]; IV, 240–1.

Samuel Henshall was a London clergyman[1] and philologist with
pretensions to a specialty in Anglo-Saxon scholarship. He held his
degrees from Brasenose College, Oxford, and in 1800 was an
unsuccessful candidate for the Anglo-Saxon professorship at the
University. His publications included a translation (with
J. Wilkinson) of the *Domesday Book*, an English–Saxon edition of *The
Gothic Gospel of Saint Matthew, The Saxon and English languages
reciprocally illustrative of each other*, and *Specimens and Parts; containing
a history of the County of Kent and a dissertation on the laws from the reign
of Edward the Confessour to Edward the first*.[2]

Samuel Henshall was a prolific writer for the *Anti-Jacobin* and one
of the *Review*'s most dependable political supporters. His reviews
and letters run the gamut of anti-Jacobinism, attacking the Quakers
(for their failure to support the war effort), the Irish rebels (for
collusion with France), popular sovereignty, anarchy, Deism,
Opposition reviews, Whig historians, and, in short 'every
compound of rebellion, dissaffection, and disloyalty, of schism,
irreligion, and atheism'.[3]

Notes

1. Samuel Henshall served as curate of Christ Church, Spitalfields, and,
   from 1802 until his death in 1807, as rector of St Mary Stratford Bow,
   Middlesex (*GM*, LXXVII-2 [December 1807] 1176; Gordon Goodwin,
   'Henshall, Samuel', *DNB*, IX, 583; *Index Eccles.*, p. 84; *Alumni Oxon.*, II,
   646).
2. *BLGC*. See also Gayle Trusdel Pendleton, 'Three Score Identifications of
   Anonymous British Pamphlets of the 1790s', *Notes and Queries*, n.s. XXVI
   (June 1979) 213.
3. *AJ*, IV (October 1799), 241.

HENSHALL, Rev. W.

AJ contributions: I, 561–5[?]; IV, 184–9.

Identification of the Rev. W. Henshall has proven impossible. His
contributions to the *Anti-Jacobin* (two reviews of works pertaining to
a legal dispute involving the College of Physicians of London)
do, however, show him to have been a man of confirmed anti-
Jacobinical opinions. In a review of October 1799, in which he
undertook 'to expose the malignity, Jacobinism, and slander' of one
Dr William Charles Wells, Henshall spoke of the sense of mission

felt by John Gifford's army of contributors. 'As our title is *Anti-Jacobin*', he wrote, 'as we examine with scrupulous eye all *cabals, juntos, affiliated Fraternities,* and innovating associations, any thing that exhibits a revolutionary spirit claims our . . . peculiar attention.'[1] Obviously the Rev. W. Henshall saw himself and his brother reviewers as the *Quarterly Review* would ten years later, as 'literary police'[2] charged with the task of safeguarding the world of letters against the perils of 'Republicans, Reformers and levellers'.[3]

Notes

1. *AJ*, IV (October 1799) 186.
2. [Henry John Stephen and William Gifford(?)], *Quarterly Review*, II (August 1809) 146. Attribution of authorship in Hill Shine and Helen Chadwick Shine, *'Quarterly Review' Under Gifford: Identification of Contributers, 1809–1824* (Chapel Hill: University of North Carolina Press, 1949).
3. *AJ*, IV (October 1799) 184.

HEWIT, G.

AJ contribution: II, 337–9.

Nothing is known of the identity of G. Hewit. Judging by remarks in his sole contribution to the *Anti-Jacobin*, a signed letter to the editor, he does not appear to have been a professional man of letters.[1] Hewit was a political conservative who praised the *Anti-Jacobin*'s press war with the *Critical* and *Monthly* reviews, denounced Godwin, Paine, and the Illuminati, and ranged himself with the *Anti-Jacobin* as an enemy of atheism and social levelling.[2]

Notes

1. 'I have always deemed Reviews and their Authors objects claiming an exclusive deference' (*AJ*, II [March 1799] 337).
2. Ibid., pp. 337, 339.

HUTTON, Rev. George (*c.* 1765–1817)

AJ contribution: II, 433–43.

The Rev. George Hutton, DD, was a parish priest and sermon writer of whom few details are known apart from his academic

achievements and the roster of his clerical appointments.[1] Judging
by his published writings – sermons and pamphlets on religious
matters – he was an avowed defender of the Church of England
against the threat of 'schismatics', especially Deists.[2] His one signed
letter to the *Anti-Jacobin* was written in answer to the *Monthly
Review's* disparaging treatment of his anti-Deist *Appeal to the Nation,
on the Subject of Mr. Gilbert Wakefield's Letter to William Wilberforce,
Esq. M.P.* In the letter Hutton attacked egalitarianism, irreligion,
Godwin's doctrine of perfectibility, and Jacobinical efforts to
overturn the English Church and Constitution – efforts which
Hutton considered an entrée 'for the irruption of the mob, to seize
the reins of government, and erect their own tyranny, exactly
similar to the course of events in France'.[3]

Notes

1. Hutton was an Oxford man – BA, 1785, Magdalen College; fellow,
   1785–97; MA, 1788; BD, 1796; DD, 1808; proctor, 1795 (*Alumni Oxon.*, II,
   723). He served at various times as curate of Plumtree, Notts.; vicar of
   Sutterton, Lincs.; rector of Gate Burton, Lincs.; and rector of Algarkirk
   cum Fosdyke, Lincs. (ibid.; *GM*, LXXXVII-2 [November 1817] 475; *Index
   Eccles.*, p. 95).
2. *BLGC*; Upcott, *Biog. Dict.*, p. 171.
3. *AJ*, II (April 1799) 436, 440.

JONES, Rev. William, of Nayland (1726–1800)

AJ contributions: v, 81–3, 226–9.

William Jones of Nayland looms large in the history of the
eighteenth-century Church chiefly because of his effective
leadership of the High-Church wing of the Establishment. It was the
group around Nayland vicarage that gave rise in the early
nineteenth century to the High-Church Hackney Phalanx,[1] which in
its turn served, indirectly at least, as a link with the Oxford
Movement.

   Jones, like his doctrinal ally John James Watson (q.v.), was a
product of Charterhouse and University College, Oxford,[2] where he
was a friend of Charles Jenkinson, the future Earl of Liverpool (a
fellow Carthusian), and of George Horne, later bishop of Norwich.
Ordained a priest in 1751, Jones set forth upon a highly prestigious
career, receiving a number of preferments in reward for his vigorous

writings in defense of orthodoxy. His long list of ecclesiastical appointments was crowned in 1777 by the perpetual curacy of Nayland, Suffolk, which became his permanent home.[3]

William Jones was an arch-conservative, politically as well as doctrinally. A descendant of one Colonel Jones, the brother-in-law of Oliver Cromwell, he felt a lifelong personal shame for the actions of his ancestor and observed each 30 January as a day of humiliation for his inherited guilt. According to his friend William Stevens (q.v.), it was 'reported, that even while a lad, he [William Jones] so abhorred the sin of rebellion, and so dreaded the judgment of God upon it, that he used to say his family, he feared, would never prosper in the world for the iniquity of his Ancestor, who had been a principal in the murder of the Royal Martyr'.[4]

With the advent of the French Revolution Jones placed his considerable talent for political writing at the services of the Church-and-King party. It was he who in 1792 founded the anti-Jacobinical Society for the Reformation of Principles by Appropriate Literature, which in turn established the *British Critic*.[5] Under its auspices he and William Stevens turned out a series of popular pamphlets[6] directed at a mass audience and aimed at combatting Paine, Joseph Priestley, and other supporters of the French Revolution, which Jones feared would 'lead . . . to the total overthrow of religion and government in this kingdom, perhaps in the whole Christian world'.[7] That Jones verged on the extreme in his pamphleteering even his friend Stevens would admit:

> Mr. Jones was a man of strong attachments, and of strong aversions. In the pursuit of what he considered to be truth, he knew no middle paths, and would listen to no compromises. Such ardent zeal frequently brought on him the charge of bigotry, which perhaps he was the better enabled to bear, as he had to contend with men whose bigotry, in their own way, cannot easily be exceeded.[8]

Jones's most substantial publications were his edition of the *Works* of his friend George Horne, bishop of Norwich, a separate lacklustre biography of Horne, and his celebrated doctrinal work, *The Catholic Doctine of a Trinity proved*. A fellow of the Royal Society, Jones had a keen interest in scientific experimentation, and his writings include (in addition to numerous sermons and political pamphlets) works on such diverse subjects as natural history and musical theory. For the *Anti-Jacobin* he submitted only two contributions, both of them letters defending Anglican orthodoxy against the Calvinist doctrine of predestination.[9]

Notes

1. See p. 159.
2. BA, University College, Oxford, 1749; MA, Sidney College, Cambridge, 1782 (*Alumni Oxon.*, II, 774; *Alumni Cantab.*, pt 2, III, 610).
3. Jones held, in order, the curacy of Finedon, Northants. (1751?); the curacy of Wadenhoe, Northants. (1754); the vicarage of Bethersden, Kent (1764); the rectory of Pluckley, Kent (1765); the perpetual curacy of Nayland, Suffolk (1777); the rectory of Paston, Northants. (*c.* 1781); and the sinecure rectory of Hollingbourne, Kent (1798). He also served as chaplain to his old friend George Horne, bishop of Norwich (*GM*, LXX-1 [February 1800] 183; Chalmers, *General Biographical Dictionary*, XIX, 132–9; John Henry Overton, 'Jones, William, of Nayland', *DNB*, X, 1065).
4. William Stevens, 'The Life of the Author [William Jones of Nayland]', in William Stevens (ed.), *The Theological and Miscellaneous Works of the Late Rev. William Jones, M.A., Minister of Nayland, Suffolk*, I (London: C. and J. Rivington, 1826) ii.
5. There is dispute over whether or not Jones contributed personally to the *British Critic*. His memorialist William Stevens said he did (Stevens, 'Life of the Author', p. xxvii), while J. H. Overton believed he did not (Overton, 'Jones', p. 1065).
6. A[lan] B. Webster, *Joshua Watson: The Story of a Layman, 1771–1855* (London: SPCK, 1954) p. 24. The most notable of this set was Jones's *Thomas Bull to his brother John* (1792), with its several sequels. See also Jones's *The Scholar armed against the Errors of the Time* (1792) and *A Small Whole-Length of Dr. Priestley* (1792).
7. William Jones, *A Letter to the Church of England, Pointing Out Some Popular Errors of Bad Consequence*, p. 29, quoted in *AJ*, I (November 1798) 529.
8. William Stevens, quoted in Chalmers, *General Biographical Dictionary*, XIX, 139.
9. Though only a minor contributor to the *Anti-Jacobin*, Jones heartily supported the *Review*'s principles. 'The *Anti-Jacobin* is in earnest', he wrote, 'and will have the encouragement of the whole honest party, who are now a very great majority' (William Jones of Nayland, letter to the Hon. George Kenyon, 30 November 1798, quoted in Great Britain, Historical Manuscripts Commission, Series 35: *The Manuscripts of Lord Kenyon*, ed. W. J. Hardy [London: Her Majesty's Stationery Office, 1894] p. 550).

KELLY, Patrick (1756–1842) [*AJ*: 'Mr. Kelly master of the Acady. in Finsbury Square']

AJ contributions: III, 161–4; IV, 58–62.

Patrick Kelly was a mathematician and astronomer who occasionally reviewed works on those subjects for the *Anti-Jacobin*. The master for many years of a flourishing private academy, the Mercantile School in Finsbury Square, London, Kelly built up a considerable reputation in the areas of currency and foreign exchange and was frequently called upon for expert testimony in those fields before committees of the Houses of Lords and Commons. He served for many years as mathematical examiner at Trinity House and was for a time treasurer of the Schoolmasters' Society, a benevolent organisation for the relief of schoolmasters' widows and orphans.[1] The University of Glasgow awarded him an LL D in 1813. His publications include *The Universal Cambist, and Commercial Instructor* (1811), which was considered the authority on exchange at the time; *A Practical Introduction to Spherics and Nautical Astronomy* (1796); *Elements of Book-keeping* (1801); *Astronomical Computations* (1812); *Metrology, or an Exposition of Weights and Measures, chiefly those of Great Britain, Ireland, and France* (1816); *Oriental Metrology* (1832); material on commercial and mathematical matters in D. Steel's *The Ship-master's Assistant* (1826); and, in an unusual digression into politics, *Junius proved to be Burke* (1826).[2] Kelly's reviews for the *Anti-Jacobin* were of a technical rather than a polemical nature, though in one rare instance in his review of Margaret Bryan's *A Compendious System of Astronomy* he did note with satisfaction that in that work the reader would 'not find . . . science made the vehicle of infidelity, but the firm support of religion'.[3]

Notes

1. O. F. Christie, note in Joseph Farington, *The Farington Diary*, ed. James Greig (8 vols; London: Hutchinson, 1922–8) III, 35n.
2. *GM*, n.s. XVIII (October 1842) 434–5; Robert Edward Anderson, 'Kelly, Patrick', *DNB*, x, 1245; *BLGC*.
3. *AJ*, IV (September 1799) 58.

KENNEDY, Rev. John

AJ contributions: ii, 91–7; v, 474–6.

John Kennedy was vicar of Teston, Kent ('a respectable Clergyman', the *Anti-Jacobin* called him)[1] and the author of one published work, *The Unsearchable Riches of Christ, . . . a sermon.*[2] No other certain information exists concerning his life, but the series of letters he wrote to the *Anti-Jacobin* in defence of tithes provides ample testimony on the subject of Kennedy's political beliefs and leaves no doubts as to his paranoia on the subject of Jacobinism. '[A]gainst the subtle and designing Infidel and Jacobin, may our rulers and lawgivers be upon their guard',[3] he once exclaimed. It is clear that Kennedy himself saw the Jacobin conspirators' 'subtle designs' everywhere. Certainly opposition to the payment of tithes was in his view all too rarely seen for what it really was, '*rank jacobinism*'.[4] A letter to the *Anti-Jacobin* of late 1800, praising Pitt's treason and sedition acts of 1795, eulogising Louis XVI, and rejoicing in Britain's 'preservation from French fraternity; French requisitions; and all the horrors of a revolution upon French principles',[5] is typical of Kennedy's thought. Without question he believed that Jacobins everywhere were engaged in a concerted plot to undermine the established order in Church and State. 'There never was a moment', he said, 'from the publication of . . . [the] first number [of the *Anti-Jacobin*] to the present day, when the vigilance, zeal, and activity of the friends to religion, order, and law, were more absolutely required, from an *increased necessity* of such zealous and active watchfulness.'[6] Driven underground by government prosecution and the presence of the Volunteer Corps, the Radicals had resorted to plots and were now actively engaged in a covert effort to undermine the political and religious fibre of the nation – an effort which loyal writers everywhere must unite to oppose. As for himself, Kennedy left no doubt as to his own position: 'I have thrown in my mite against Jacobinical attempts, and in defence of what I conceive to be Divine truth. . . . I avow myself an anti-Jacobin in the strictest sense of the word, and, as a friend to religion, order, and law.'[7]

Notes

1. [John Gifford], *AJ*, ii (January 1799) 91.
2. *BLGC*.

3. *AJ*, v (April 1800) 476.
4. Ibid., p. 474.
5. *AJ*, vii (Appendix to September–December 1800) 426.
6. Ibid., p. 425.
7. Ibid., p. 438.

LACHASSAGNE, Jean-Baptiste-Claude de [*AJ*: 'Chevalier de Lachassaigne']

AJ contribution: iii, 489.

The Chevalier de Lachassagne was, like the Comte de Montlosier (q.v.) and the Abbé Tabaraud (q.v.), one of the several thousand French *émigrés* who sought refuge in England during the height of the Terror.[1] Nothing is known of him except what is reported in his official condemnation by the Committee of Public Security of Lyon – that he was a citizen of Lyon (profession: volunteer) and that his property was confiscated on 23 Pluviôse of the Year II [11 February 1794] on the grounds that he was a counter-revolutionary.[2] Lachassagne's name does not appear in the list of survivors of the Terror who were indemnified for their losses by Charles X's government in 1826.[3] He therefore had apparently died before that time.

Lachassagne submitted one contribution to the *Anti-Jacobin*: a signed acrostic written as a 'Tribute of Loyalty and Gratitude' to George III.[4]

Notes

1. *AJ*, iii (August 1799) 489.
2. *Liste Générale des individus condamné[s] par Jugemens, ou mis hors de la Loi par Décrets, et dont les Biens ont été déclarés confisqués au profit de la République*, Liste v [17 Floréal–30 Prairial, Year II] (Paris: L'imprimerie des domaines nationaux, l'an deuxième [1794]) pp. 96–7.
3. *États détaillés des liquidations faites par la Commission d'indemnité à l'époque du 1.ᵉʳ avril 1826 en execution de la loi du 27 avril 1825 au profit des anciens propriétaires ou ayant-droit des anciens propriétaires de biens-fonds confisqués ou aliénés revolutionnairement* (2 pts; Paris: L'imprimerie royale, 1826).
4. *AJ*, iii (August 1799) 489. The offering bears quoting in full as it is excellent evidence of Lachassagne's political principles:

Gouver[n]er ses Etats avec force & sagesse;
Envers tous ses Sujets être bons [*sic*] sans foiblesse;
Offrir à l'Univers l'example des vertus;
Ressembler aux Alfreds, égaler les Titus;
Garder auprès de foi le Conseiller fidèle;
Ecarter le flatteur, soumettre le rebelle;

Terrasser des Tyrans, & relever des Rois: [*sic*]
Rendre aux Fils des Bourbons les soins d'un tendre père;
Ouvrir aux opprimés un asyle prospère;
Intimider l'impie armé contre les lois;
Sauver l'Europe en feu; c'est être GEORGE TROIS.

[To govern one's realms with strength and wise counsel;
To be good to one's subjects without loss of majesty;
To offer all the Universe the example of a virtuous man;
To be a new Alfred, a Titus reborn;
To honour loyal servants and safeguard their goodwill;
To cast out the flatterer and lay the rebel low;

To crush the tyrants and raise up fallen kings;
To cherish the sons of the Bourbons with a father's tender care;
To offer safe refuge to the exiled and oppressed;
To overawe the godless, in arms against the law;
To save a Europe in flames – That is to be GEORGE THE THIRD.]

LAKE, Rev. G.

AJ contributions: IV, 260–8, 392–7[?]; V, 481–4; VI, 516–17.

Efforts to arrive at a positive identification of the Rev. G. Lake have
proved unavailing. A slim possibility exists that he was the Rev.
Gilbert Lake (b. 1718) of Wiltshire, a graduate of Queen's College,
Oxford,[1] vicar of Westport with Charlton, Wilts. (1749) and of
Seagreen, Wilts. (1750). This, however, is mere conjecture. Lake's
several reviews for the *Anti-Jacobin* offer no information about him
except that he was bitterly opposed to the armed aggression of
republican France against the neutral nations of Europe.[2]

Notes

1. BA, 1738; MA, 1741 (*Alumni Oxon.*, III, 809).
2. *AJ*, V (Appendix to January–April 1800) 483–4. See also *AJ*, VI (Appendix
   to May–August 1800) 516–17.

MAVOR, J.

AJ contributions: II, 100–1; III, 207–10.

Nothing is known of Mavor's life except that he was associated in some way with a counting-house, described himself as 'a plain domestic man', and lived in London.[1] The nature of his political principles, on the other hand, is obvious from his letters to the *Anti-Jacobin*. Mavor was a foursquare Tory who saw with alarm the inroads of Jacobinism on all sides, whether political, religious, moral, or social. His first letter to John Gifford found him rejoicing at the *Anti-Jacobin*'s unfavourable review of Alexander Geddes's Deistical commentary on the Bible, a work which Mavor feared would destroy the faith of the vast majority of those who read it.[2] An additional and highly intemperate letter condemned German literature in general and Kotzebue's plays in particular on the grounds that they subtly undermined the social order and exalted female immorality. An excerpt from the latter epistle (describing in part Kotzebue's *Lovers' Vows*) should serve as a revealing example both of Mavor's personality and his principles. *Lovers' Vows*, he said,

is only part of a system adopted by the new philosophy, and assiduously cultivated in every possible way, so as to loosen those bonds which have hitherto so successfully held society together; and we all of us know, by daily experience, how far the seduction of the female mind has that powerful tendency. . . .

My blood boils with indignation when I see my beloved Shakspeare, Otway, Rowe, and all those ornaments of my native country, thrust aside, to make way for the filthy effusions of this German dunce!
   Forbid it Britons! – forbid it common sense!
                            . . . AN ADMIRER OF THE DRAMA.[3]

Notes

1. *AJ*, II (January 1799) 100. Watt, Upcott, and the British Library's *General Catalogue* list one John Maver as a translator of *An Historical View of the Philippine Islands* by Martinez de Zuñiga (1814), but the said John Maver, translator, may have been a retired commander in the Royal Navy who died in 1835 at the age of 90 (*GM*, n.s. IV [July 1835] 99).
2. *AJ*, II (January 1799) 100–1.
3. *AJ*, III (June 1799) 209–210.

MONTLOSIER, François-Dominique de Reynaud [Regnault], Comte de (1755–1838)

AJ contribution: I, 268–80.

Montlosier, a well-known *émigré* journalist and future Napoleonic propagandist, was born in 1755 at Clermont-Ferrand, the twelfth child of an old and noble but impoverished Auvergne family. A gentleman scholar whose interests spanned law, philosophy, history, anatomy, chemistry, and geology, Montlosier was from his earliest days a thoroughgoing eccentric who once, to indulge his passion for geological studies, moved into a rustic manor house in the Auvergne, where he lived for eight years in virtual isolation, reading the Church Fathers, analysing the soil, and writing his *Théorie des volcans d'Auvergne*. It was his fascination for history that led him to become involved in current affairs, and in 1789 he was elected a delegate to France's newly formed Constituent Assembly.[1] Shunning the extremists of Right and Left, Montlosier quickly joined forces with Malouet, Mallet du Pan, and other moderate royalists,[2] seeing in their goal of a limited monarchy France's best hope for the preservation of property and social order tempered with constructive constitutional change.[3]

Montlosier emigrated shortly after the close of the Constituent Assembly. Fearful of the inexorable drift of the government toward Radicalism, he embarked upon a series of wanderings, eventually taking refuge in England.[4] There he held himself aloof from the English, whom he disliked in no small fashion,[5] mingling only with fellow French *émigrés*, whom he also quickly antagonised by his open contempt for their reactionary political principles and their naïve hopes for a wholesale return to the *ancien régime*.[6] Almost penniless when he arrived in England, Montlosier tried his hand at a number of careers, including abortive attempts to qualify as a physician and to practice magnetism,[7] before finally turning his talents to the periodical press. Having established the *Journal de France et d'Angleterre*, he merged the paper in 1797 with the *Courrier de Londres*, an *émigré* newspaper edited by the Abbé de Calonne.[8] With the Abbé's departure for Canada, Montlosier, now sole editor,[9] gradually turned the paper into an outspoken organ of Bonapartist propaganda – a course of action that would reap its due rewards. When Fouché, Napoleon's Minister of Police, and Talleyrand invited him to receive amnesty and return to France as a propagandist for the new regime, Montlosier accepted with alacrity, burning his bridges once and for all with the *émigré* reactionaries with whom he had never felt comfortable.[10]

Montlosier's service to Napoleon was personally disappointing and hardly illustrious. When his newspaper[11] was speedily shut down for daring to criticise various Napoleonic policies, Montlosier took a minor post with the Foreign Ministry, and after the resumption of war with England he was entrusted with publishing a scurrilous anti-English propaganda weekly, the *Bulletin de Paris* – an occupation that even his friends considered dishonourable in light of the hospitality with which England had received him in his *émigré* days.[12] He was finally commissioned by the government to write a history of the French crown – *De la Monarchie française* – in justification of Napoleon's proclamation of the Empire, but Montlosier's stubborn opposition to absolutism displeased Napoleon and precluded publication of the work as long as the Emperor was in power. After this rebuff Montlosier withdrew in large part from public life and immersed himself in writing[13] and geological research. It was only in his last years that he returned to public prominence, when he threw himself into the popular cause of opposition to the Jesuit party at Charles X's court.[14] He died in the Auvergne in 1838, abrasive to the end, locked in a death-bed controversy with the local Ultramontane bishop.[15]

Notes

1. He was elected first as an alternate from the nobility of Riom, then as a full member to replace the Marquis de La Ronzière (Zychlinski, 'Montlosier [François-Dominique de Reynaud, comte de]', *Nouvelle Biographie Générale* [46 vols; Paris: Firmin Didot Frères, Éditeurs, 1853–66] XXXVI, 313).

2. A[génor] Bardoux, *Le Comte de Montlosier et le Gallicanisme*, Études Sociales et Politiques (Paris: Calmann Lévy, Éditeur, 1881) p. 5.

3. Montlosier's political principles were to a large extent those of the old provincial nobility of the Parlements. He was, as a friend described him, at home in 'a society hierarchically ordained [and] classified by graduated rights. . . . He loved orders, corporations, distinct professions, *esprit de corps*, [and] the continuity of interests' ([Amable Guillaume Prosper Brugière] de Barante, 'Montlosier [François-Dominique de Reynaud, comte de]', *Biographie Universelle, Ancienne et Moderne* [85 vols; Paris: Michaud Frères, Imprim.-Libraires, 1811–62] LXXIV, 290).

4. After two initial months with the court in exile at Coblenz, during which time the Ultras regarded him with disfavour because of his moderation, Montlosier returned to Paris. In April 1792 he emigrated a

second time and served as a volunteer with the cavalry in the royalist army of Condé. Once again, however, he soon became disgusted with Ultra politics and intrigue. After a brief stay in Hamburg with a number of other moderate refugees, he took up residence in the Low Countries, where for eighteen months he served as a local military commissioner for Emperor Francis II. He finally settled in England in 1794.

5. Montlosier's *Souvenirs d'un émigré (1791–1798)* (Paris: Librairie Hachette, 1951) contains a number of disparaging remarks on English weather, food, drink, temperament, customs, and so on. As for the two less-than-beautiful sisters with whom he boarded in England, he had only one comment: 'Il faut que Montlosier soit un prince enchanté: il se fait garder par deux monstres' (quoted in Ghislain de Diesbach, *Histoire de l'Émigration, 1789–1814* [Paris: Bernard Grasset, 1975] p. 267).

6. His *Souvenirs d'un émigré* abounds in derogatory comments directed against his fellow exiles and their ultra-conservative 'illusions', as he frequently referred to them. At any event what little rapport Montlosier enjoyed with *émigré* society came to an end with the publication of his *Lettres sur la Modération*, in which he flung down the gauntlet to his ultra-royalist compatriots, charging that they were 'fraught with more crimes than Marat and Robespierre' (quoted in Zychlinski, 'Montlosier', p. 314).

7. While involved in the magnetism experiment 'he fell foul of a jealous husband, for Montlosier was much given to amorous adventures, and risked being thrown out of the country, but was saved through the intervention of an influential friend' (Margery Weiner, *The French Exiles, 1789–1815* [London: John Murray, 1960] p. 119).

8. The Abbé was the brother of Louis XVI's finance minister.

9. Weiner, *French Exiles*, pp. 119–20.

10. Montlosier's dealing with Napoleon began shortly before the Peace of Amiens, when the Count of Artois sent Montlosier on a secret mission to France to offer Bonaparte the throne of Italy in exchange for his support for a Bourbon restoration in France. The mission was a failure, but while in Paris Montlosier met Talleyrand, who convinced him that a Bonapartist government would re-establish the Church, bring back the *émigrés* (returning any of their property that had not already been sold), restore the social order, and destroy the last vestiges of Jacobinism and anarchy. It was precisely the programme that Montlosier, with his allegiance to property and the pre-Revolution social stratification, had long hoped for, and he was swift to accept.

11. After Montlosier's return to France he renamed his newspaper the *Courrier de Londres et de Paris*.

12. Some of Montlosier's anonymous articles for the *Bulletin de Paris* were later collected, without his permission and to his great chagrin, in a volume entitled *Les Anglais ivres d'orgeuil et de bière* (Barante, 'Montlosier', p. 292).

13. For a complete list of Montlosier's publications, which included works on geology, political pamphlets, memoirs, and his anti-Ultramontane *Mémoire à consulter sur un système religieux et politique* (which ran through eight editions in a single year) see the listings in the *BLGC* and the

Catalogue Général des Livres Imprimés de la Bibliothèque Nationale (216 vols; Paris: Paul Catin, Éditeur, 1924–73).
14. Montlosier became (jointly with Bishop Frayssinous) the leading pro-Gallican polemicist of the Restoration (Frederick B. Artz, *Reaction and Revolution, 1814–1832*, Rise of Modern Europe Series, ed. William L. Langer [New York: Harper and Row, 1934] p. 70).
15. According to Barante, Montlosier

> declared to the priest who was confessing him that, if anything in his writings or his conduct had caused scandal and had appeared contrary to the dogmas of the Catholic Church, he would humbly beg pardon from God. The absolution was given to him; but the ecclesiastical authorities demanded a written and formal retraction [of his anti-Jesuit, pro-Gallican writings], of which the terms were prescribed. The dying man refused to sign; [and] . . . he was deprived of the Last Rites and the prayers of his religion (Barante, 'Montlosier', p. 296).

Denied Christian burial by the local Ultramontane bishop, Montlosier's body was carried to the cemetery past the open doors of his parish church.

MOSER, Joseph (1748–1819)

AJ contribution: iii, 221–5.

Joseph Moser was the London-born son of Hans Jacob Moser, a Swiss artist and immigrant to Britain. According to scanty information in the *Gentleman's Magazine*, Moser was apprenticed at an early age to his uncle, one 'G. M. Moser, Esq. late keeper of the Royal Academy, who intended him for the profession of painting in enamel'.[1] Finding the work not to his taste, Moser in 1780 abandoned painting for literature, his numerous publications including poetry, dramas and farces, tales and romances, articles in the periodicals (especially the *European Magazine*), anti-Jacobinical allegories,[2] and 'a great variety of . . . pamphlets and tracts, serious and humorous, at different periods, in support of Government'.[3] After his appointment (*c.* 1794) to the time-consuming post of a commissioner of the peace in Westminster,[4] Moser eventually gave up most of his literary work. He finished his career as a magistrate for the four counties and a Deputy Lieutenant for Middlesex.

Notes

1. *GM*, LXXXIX (Supplement to January–June, 1819) 653.
2. See, for example, his *Lucifer and Mammon, an Historical Sketch of the Last and Present Century; with Characters, Anecdotes, &c.* (London: J. Owen and H. D. Symonds, 1793).
3. *European Magazine*, XLIV (August 1803) 85. See also Gayle Trusdel Pendleton, 'Three Score Identifications of Anonymous British Pamphlets of the 1790s', *Notes and Queries*, n.s. XXVI (June 1979) 209.
4. Upcott, *Biog. Dict.*, p. 244.

MOUNIER, Jean-Joseph (1758–1806)

AJ contribution: V, 339–47.

Jean-Joseph Mounier was a personage of twofold importance to the anti-Jacobin movement in the 1790s. He was in the first place a leader of the moderate-royalist party in the French States-General in 1789 and was one of the first political figures in France to turn against the Revolution. He was in addition the author of an important contemporary study of the French Revolution, his *De l'Influence attribuée aux philosophes, aux francs-maçons et aux illuminés sur la révolution de France* (1801), in which he argued that France's civil upheaval sprang from purely political causes, not from Barruel's international conspiracy of *Philosophes*, Freemasons, and Illuminati.

At thirty-one one of the youngest delegates to take his seat in the States-General, Mounier, a former royal judge,[1] rapidly emerged as a leader of the French reform camp. He supported the reformers' twin demands for voting by head instead of by chamber and for the doubling of the delegates to the Third Estate. In addition it was he who proposed the Tennis Court Oath, by which the delegates to the Third Estate vowed not to disband without the establishment of a new constitution. Yet through all Mounier had deep respect for civil harmony, for property, and for the throne, as well as considerable personal faith in the goodwill of Louis XVI. Perhaps better than any other major French revolutionary figure Mounier exemplified the dual allegiance, to reform and to order, felt by so many moderate politicians in the early days of the revolutionary epoch.[2]

Mounier's influence upon events unfolding in France was destined to be short-lived. Charged with submitting proposals for a new French constitution to the National Assembly, Mounier's committee proposed a thoroughly English-style limited monarchy, steeped in the traditions of Blackstone and Delolme, with a bicameral legislative body and an absolute royal veto. The proposals unleashed a storm of debate in which the radical factions denounced Mounier as 'Monsieur Veto', and Mounier warned his critics that they were 'preparing the way . . . for a long and fatal anarchy in place of the happiness that . . . [France] was expecting from us'.[3] Defeated both on bicameralism and on the veto, Mounier nevertheless was elected president of the National Assembly. He had held that office for barely a week when the crisis of 5–6 October 1789, marked by the bloody dawn attack of revolutionary radicals upon Versailles and the long journey of the now-captive Royal Family back to Paris, brought an effective end to Mounier's role in the direction of the Revolution.[4] Utterly disgusted by the lawlessness of the 'October Days' and by the Assembly's paralysis in the face of it, Mounier resigned office on 8 October, and in May 1790 he fled France to safety in Switzerland.[5]

The rest of Mounier's career could well serve as a study in the uncertainties of *émigré* life. After two years' exile in Switzerland, where he pursued a lacklustre career as a British agent and liaison with counter-revolutionary groups in France,[6] Mounier was forced to flee once more, this time to England. Offered the position of Chief Justice of Canada by his British hosts, he refused, unable to face the prospect of irrevocable separation from France. Returning to the Continent, he settled in Weimar, where, at the behest of the Duke of Saxe-Weimar, he opened an academy in the palace of the Belvedere for training future public officials. It was there that he published his commentary on Barruel, and it was there also that he wrote his only article for the *Anti-Jacobin*, a critique of Kant's philosophy. His exile finally ended by Napoleon's seizure of power in 1799, Mounier died in France in 1806, a member of the Emperor's council of state.[7]

Notes

1. Interestingly enough, Mounier had risen to political prominence by the route of royal patronage. After several youthful false starts, he had settled upon a law career in which he rose swiftly, becoming a royal judge in 1783 at the age of twenty-five. In 1787 and 1788 he had, however, taken a leading role in his province of the Dauphiné in the build-up of agitation for the calling of the States-General.
2. Léon de Lanzac de Laborie, *Un Royaliste Libéral en 1789: Jean-Joseph Mounier, sa vie politique et ses écrits* (Paris: Librairie Plon, 1887).
3. Quoted in Thomas Arthur de Lally-Tollendal, 'Mounier (Jean-Joseph)',

Biographie Universelle, Ancienne et Moderne (85 vols; Paris: Michaud Frères, Imprim.-Libraires, 1811–62) xxx, 319.

4. It was while Mounier was presiding over the National Assembly's session of 5 October 1789 at Versailles that bands of women bread rioters began arriving from Paris. Mounier bravely refused to close the Assembly; and when the rioters appeared at the chamber door demanding bread, they received a trenchant lecture from *M. le président* himself. 'The only way to get bread is to return in orderly fashion', he told them. 'The more you threaten, the less bread you will get' (quoted in ibid., p. 320). The advice fell on deaf ears, as Mounier discovered when he returned from his latest round of talks with the King. As his friend and ally Lally-Tollendal described it, 'Upon returning to the Assembly, he found it delivered over to the most frightful disorder: the mob master of the hall, a woman sitting in the president's chair, insolent shouts, and everywhere scenes of debauched revelry' (ibid., p. 321). In vain Mounier begged his fellow delegates to go in a body to wait upon Louis, believing that only their presence would protect the King from violence. The delegates were, however, either unwilling or too frightened to comply, and in the end it was Mounier who returned alone to the King, posted guards in the palace grounds, and obtained Lafayette's personal assurances for the Royal Family's safety. By this time it was after three o'clock in the morning, and the tubercular Mounier was spitting blood and on the verge of collapse from anxiety and exhaustion. For contemporary – or near-contemporary – accounts of Mounier's role in the events of 5–6 October see J. Chanut, 'Mounier (Jean-Joseph)', *Nouvelle Biographie Générale* (46 vols; Paris: Firmin Didot Frères, Éditeurs, 1853–66) xxxvi, 784–5, and (in abbreviated fashion) 'Mounier', *Biographie Moderne* (4 vols; 3rd edn; Leipzig: Paul-Jacques Besson, Libraire, 1807) iii, 424, as well as the Lally-Tollendal article in the *Biographie Universelle*.

5. After his resignation as president of the National Assembly Mounier became involved in an attempt to raise volunteers in his province of the Dauphiné to march on Paris and liberate the monarchy. The plan was frustrated when Louis XVI, by then in the grip of the factions, was induced to forbid any such rescue attempts. When news arrived from Paris that the revolutionary authorities were charging him with treason for his part in the scheme, Mounier heeded his friends' advice and crossed the border into Switzerland.

6. Mounier in 1793 accepted the Ministry's offer to become a secret agent in Switzerland, answerable to the British *chargé d'affaires*, Lord Robert Stephen FitzGerald. He lost FitzGerald's confidence – and the cabinet's – in 1794, when he revealed his diplomatic naïvety in an abortive series of negotiations with Lafayette's supporters in France. The whole episode left FitzGerald furious with Mounier and with all Frenchmen in general. '[I]f this [French] Revolution has been attended with misery and wretchedness to nations and millions of individuals', FitzGerald wrote, 'it has also been productive of some good in opening the eyes of men on the real character of Frenchmen, and of exhibiting to the world in its true colours that horrid mass of infamy, perfidy, and wickedness of every description, which had been so long concealed under the veil of

politeness and urbanity. . . . They are become like a second race on earth, and it may truly be said that the world is inhabited by two sets of human beings, by men and Frenchmen.' (Lord Robert Stephen FitzGerald, letter to Lord Grenville, 13 January 1795, quoted in Great Britain, Historical Manuscripts Commission, Series 30, pts 1–10: *The Manuscripts of J. B. Fortescue, Esq., Preserved at Dropmore*, ed. Walter Fitzpatrick and Francis Bickley [London: Her Majesty's Stationery Office, 1892–1927] pt 3, p. 7. For a full account of Mounier's failure see letters from various persons quoted in ibid., pt 2, pp. 427, 436, 449, 456, 503, 596, 638, 649, 651–2; and pt 3, pp. 6–7, 486.)

7. For substantial lists of Mounier's published works, mainly political pamphlets, see the *Catalogue Général des Livres Imprimés de la Bibliothèque Nationale* (216 vols; Paris: Paul Catin, Éditeur, 1924–73) and the *BLGC*.

MUNKHOUSE, Rev. Richard (1755–1810)

AJ contribution: v, 108–10.

Richard Munkhouse, sermon writer and translator,[1] contributed only briefly to the *Anti-Jacobin*. A native of Westmorland and a graduate of Queen's College, Oxford,[2] he became vicar of Wakefield in Yorkshire in 1805, serving in that capacity until his death in 1810.[3]

Munkhouse's own publications show him to have been a confirmed political conservative. The notes to his Thanksgiving sermon of 29 November 1798 attack what Munkhouse called '*the licentiousness of the press*' and the spirit of immorality and democracy which he saw fostered by 'the *new-fangled, proud, regenerating philosophy*' of the day.[4] The notes propose accordingly that all reading rooms should be purged of democratic literature. His discourse to the Freemasons of Allmann's Lodge in Yorkshire is written in the same vein, urging British masons to embrace the cause of religion and the Constitution and dissociate themselves from the radicalism of their '*illumined continental brethren*'.[5] Clearly Munkhouse viewed himself, as the *Anti-Jacobin* characteristically described him, as 'a staunch friend to his King and Country'[6] in the full anti-Jacobinical sense of the words.

Notes

1. Munkhouse's publications consist entirely of pulpit oratory and include various single discourses (*A Sermon preached in the Church of St. John Baptist, Wakefield, . . . Nov. 29, 1798 . . . ; A Discourse delivered in the Church of Almondbury, . . . May 16, 1799, at the Constitution and Dedication*

of the *Allmann's Lodge of Free and Accepted Masons;* and so on) plus several collections (*Occasional Discourses on various subjects,* 3 vols [1805]; *Sermons on various subjects, chiefly practical* [1813]; *Sermons on various subjects . . . selected . . . and translated from 'L'Année Évangélique' of F. J. Durand . . . by . . . R. M.* [1802]). (*BLGC; AJ,* II [April 1799] 423–6; *AJ,* IV [December 1799] 535–6.)

2. BA, 1778; MA, 1781; BD and DD, 1795 (*Alumni Oxon.,* III, 997).
3. Ibid.; *Index Eccles.,* p. 124; *GM,* LXXV (December 1805) 1183; *GM,* LXXX-1 (March 1810) 288. Sources of information concerning Munkhouse are very scanty. The British Library does possess a rare copy of a funeral tribute to Munkhouse (M[artin] J[oseph] Naylor, *A Sermon, preached . . . on occasion of the death of the Rev. Richard Munkhouse, D.D. . . .* [Wakefield: printed by R. Hurst, 1810]), but this work, though attesting to Munkhouse's exemplary character, contains very little biographical data.
4. Richard Munkhouse, *A Sermon preached in the Church of St. John Baptist, Wakefield, . . . Nov. 29, 1798* (London: Rivingtons, 1799), quoted in the *AJ,* II (April 1799) 424.
5. Richard Munkhouse, *A Discourse delivered in the Church of Almondbury, . . . May 16, 1799, at the Constitution and Dedication of the Allmann's Lodge of Free and Accepted Masons* (London: Hurst, 1799), quoted in the *AJ,* IV (December 1799) 536.
6. *AJ,* II (April 1799) 425.

O'HALLORAN [or HALLORAN], 'Rev.' Lawrence Hynes (1766–1831)

AJ contribution: V, 111.

O'Halloran, 'apparently a native of Ireland'[1] and a self-styled Doctor of Divinity, was only briefly an *Anti-Jacobin* contributor. He was a part-time schoolmaster, cleric, and poet[2] whose chequered career encompassed service as a Royal Navy chaplain at Trafalgar and eventual transportation to the penal colony in New South Wales for forgery.

Fresh from an uneventful term as master of an academy at Alphington near Exeter, O'Halloran became chaplain of HMS *Britannia,* the flagship of Admiral the Earl of Northesk at Trafalgar. It was this eventuality which led to the publication of O'Halloran's *Sermon on Occasion of the Victory off Trafalgar* (1805) and *The Battle of Trafalgar, a Poem* (1806). Shortly thereafter he removed to South Africa to become Chaplain to the Forces and rector of the Cape Town grammar school. There in 1810 he fell foul of the colonial government for championing the cause of two British officers who were under court martial for engaging in a duel. As the *Gentleman's Magazine* reported,

> His conduct was highly disapproved by Lieut.-Gen. the Hon. H. G. Grey, who ordered his removal to an outpost called Simon's Town. The Doctor resigned his office of Chaplain, but gave vent to his anger in 'Cap-Abilities, or South African characteristics, a Satire,' for which a suit was commenced against him, and he was sentenced to be banished from the colony, and to pay costs.[3]

Upon his return to England O'Halloran ingratiated himself into the confidence of the Rev. Richard Warner of Bath, who was apparently captivated by the enterprising 'doctor's' commanding appearance and impressive sermon delivery. 'His large black eye was intelligent, but fierce; and not rendered less so, by the broad brow of the same hue, which surmounted it. His strongly-marked features indicated capacity of mind, and force of understanding', Warner recalled. 'I ought to have been warned by his physiognomy; and certainly, *si mens non laeva fuisset*, should never have admitted the *horse* within the *walls*.'[4] After a period as Warner's curate, during which time O'Halloran enjoyed a large degree of fame as the clerical prodigy of Bath, he was exposed as an imposter, with no higher orders than those of deacon, and forced to leave the city, whence he travelled eventually to the smaller parish of Wotton-under-Edge in Gloucestershire, 'playing the same game, under a borrowed name', until the congregation began to entertain doubts of his respectability.[5]

The year 1818 found O'Halloran in the dock at the Old Bailey, sentenced to seven years' transportation to Australia for the crime of 'forging a frank, by which he defrauded the revenue of 10*d*. . . . It was surmised that the charge would not have been brought, had he not quarrelled with his correspondent, the Rector whose church he was serving. He pleaded guilty; and it may be presumed that he was not unwilling to resume his migratory and colonial habits.'[6] He died in New South Wales in 1831, the rector of a flourishing school in Sydney.[7]

Notes

1. *GM*, CI-2 (November 1831) 476.
2. His publications include *Odes, Poems and Translations* (1790), *Poems on Various Subjects* (1791), *Lacrymae Hibernicae, or the Genius of Erin's*

Complaint (1801), and *The Female Volunteer* (1801), the last being a drama published under the name of 'Philo-Nauticus' – see Upcott, *Biog. Dict.*, p. 143.
3. *GM*, cɪ-2 (November 1831) 477.
4. Richard Warner, *Literary Recollections* (2 vols; London: Longman, Rees, Orme, Brown, and Green, 1930) ɪɪ, 292.
5. Ibid., p. 296.
6. *GM*, cɪ-2 (November 1831) 477 – see also 'Occurrences in London and Its Vicinity (entry for 16 October 1818)', *GM*, ʟxxxvɪɪɪ (November 1818) 462.
7. *GM*, cɪ-2 (November 1831) 476–7.

PEARS, Charles (b. *c.* 1760?)[1]

AJ contributions: ɪɪɪ, 323–33; vɪ, 254–65, 386–98, 430–1.

Charles Pears, physician and writer of medical treatises, was best known to conservative circles in his day for his assistance in the campaign to circulate anti-Jacobin literature among the English poor. Pears began his career as an apothecary in Newington, Surrey, taking his degree as a physician some years later after his return to England from South America.[2] While still in Newington he helped establish the Endeavour Society for the Relief and Instruction of the Poor, serving as its treasurer and apothecary. The Endeavour Society, officially endorsed by the *Anti-Jacobin* and by the Church-and-King Rivington brothers, was typical of the numerous organisations established in England during the French revolutionary era to inoculate the lower orders against the writings of Thomas Paine. Dedicated to relieving the material needs of the poor through the supply of medical services, child-bed linen, small business loans, and charitable donations, the Society was 'equally vigilant in instilling sound principles of religious and civil duty', maintaining a free library of simplified theological studies and circulating tracts and printed prayers among the poor for this purpose.[3]

While Pears's own publications were chiefly medical,[4] from time to time he too branched out into the field of conservative politics, considering it his 'duty to expose to public reprehension every opinion which we hold dangerous to the religion, the law, and the morality of this country, or which seems at all to further the dark designs of Jacobinism'.[5] Accordingly he contributed articles to both the *Orthodox Churchman's Magazine* and to the *Anti-Jacobin Review*, supplying for the latter several reviews viciously attacking the Quakers, whom he detested for their 'disloyal' refusal to contribute to the British war effort.

Notes

1. A Charles Pears, son of Charles Pears, Sr, of Hackney, matriculated at Queen's College, Oxford, 13 February 1778, aged 18 (*Alumni Oxon.*, III, 1084). There is no conclusive evidence as to whether or not this was the Charles Pears who wrote for the *Anti-Jacobin*.
2. Upcott, *Biog. Dict.*, p. 266.
3. See [John Gifford], *AJ*, VI (June 1800) 228.
4. His writings include miscellaneous articles in the *Medical Journal*; *Cases of Phthisis, Pulmonalis, successfully treated upon the Tonic plan* (1801); *Observations on the Prevention and Cure of Consumptions* (1814); and *The Case of a full grown Woman, in whom the Ovaria were deficient* (1805), the last being a paper presented to the Royal Society (Watt, *Biblio. Brit.*, I, 739; *Philosophical Transactions of the Royal Society of London*, XCV [London: W. Bulmer, 1805] 225; Upcott, *Biog. Dict.*, p. 266).
5. *AJ*, III (July 1799) 323. Though the portion of the July number containing this review is missing from the British Library staff copy, internal evidence proves conclusively that Pears was indeed the author.

POLWHELE, Rev. Richard (1760–1838)

AJ contributions: III, 120–32, 155–61, 180, 185–8, 216–20, 279–82, 297–303, 307–9; IV, 327–30; V, 28–37, 56–64, 71–5, 179–82, 241–63, 295–7, 300–1, 361–4, 431–2, 435–7, 443–4, 454–7; VI, 1–12, 45–7, 109–18, 132–41, 156–9, 173–7, 191–3, 215–16, 218–19, 274–81, 302–6, 315–20, 435–8, 455–60[with Glasse].

One of the *Anti-Jacobin*'s most frequent contributors was Richard Polwhele, a country clergyman[1] and well-known Cornish poet and historian.[2] Though his modern fame – or rather notoriety – rests almost exclusively on his blatantly anti-feminist poem, *The Unsex'd Females*[3] (in which he attacked the moral and religious views of Mary Wollstonecraft, Helen Maria Williams, and Mary Hays), in his own day Polwhele enjoyed a considerable reputation as a local historian, pouring out poems, histories, topographical studies, works on divinity, and memoirs in ever-increasing numbers.[4] He was a prolific contributor to the periodicals, and in addition to supplying dozens of reviews to the *Anti-Jacobin* between 1799 and 1805,[5] he wrote material for the *Gentleman's Magazine* throughout his lifetime, besides contributing occasionally to the *Literary Gazette*,[6] the *European Magazine*, the *Orthodox Churchman's Magazine*, and the *British Critic*[7] as well.

While John Wilson Croker could describe him as a man of 'very little worldly wisdom',[8] Polwhele in fact thrived in an atmosphere of religious and political controversy. 'He was a laborious working man, with no low opinion of himself', Cyrus Redding noted, 'never offensive except to a methodist, whom he could not tolerate.'[9] His literary duel with the Rev. Dr Hawker, a Methodist preacher who had strayed into Polwhele's parish of Manaccan, was particularly acrimonious and provided an unsavoury insight into the vindictiveness of Polwhele's character. In politics Polwhele was a staunch supporter of the Church-and-King party, 'ever ready to come forward on all loyal and other occasions with his person and his pen'.[10] He served for a number of years as a magistrate, and the national emergency of January 1793 saw him presiding over a meeting of the leading citizens of the parishes of Kenton and Powderham, held 'to avow their allegiance to their Sovereign, and their reverence for the Constitution', to formulate means of stamping out '*treasonable*' and 'inflammatory' writings, and to urge moral instead of political reform.[11] Polwhele's anti-Jacobinical opinions are especially prominent in a number of reviews he wrote for John Gifford, slashing criticisms of the whole gamut of writers who 'muttered sedition from their lurking-holes, and scattered, in dark corners, the seeds of anarchy'.[12]

'I am still zealous in the cause of my King and Country', Polwhele wrote in 1803,[13] and thirty years later his opinions had not altered. The Reform Bill crisis of 1832 found him locked in combat with the reformist editor of the Truro *West Briton*, who had criticised a fiery sermon Polwhele had preached, attacking from the pulpit upper-class Radicals for stirring up incendiaries and announcing (as the disgusted *West Briton* summarised it) 'that he regarded the visitation of the Cholera as a token of the displeasure of Heaven towards this once happy land'.[14] 'I glory in those anti-revolutionary principles with which the Editor of that paper has charged me', wrote Polwhele to the Bishop of Exeter. 'In those principles have I lived (as my forefathers have lived), and in those principles I hope to die.'[15] Polwhele did die loyal to his principles, and deep in the composition of his memoirs, at Truro in 1838, one of the last survivors of the band of Jacobin-hunters who had flocked to John Gifford's standard forty years before.

Notes

1. After leaving Christ Church, Oxford, without a degree, Polwhele was appointed, in order, curate of Lamorran in Cornwall and of Kenton in Devonshire (1782), curate of Exmouth and vicar of Manaccan, near Helston (both in 1794), curate of Kenwyn (*c.* 1806), vicar of St Anthony in Meneage (1809), and vicar of Newlyn East (1821).
2. Polwhele, who spent his life in and around his native city of Truro, was a descendant of a distinguished West Country family whose members included several knights of the shire, a royalist major in the army of Charles I, and one Drogo de Polwhele, chamberlain to the Empress Mathilda.
3. See Janet M. Todd's 'The Polwhelean Tradition and Richard Cobb', *Studies in Burke and His Time*, xvi (Spring 1975) 271–7, which places modern historiographical trends in Wollstonecraft scholarship in the context of the long tradition of hostility toward Wollstonecraft epitomised by Polwhele's *Unsex'd Females*.
4. The best known of Polwhele's works are his three-volume *History of Cornwall, civil, military, religious, architectural, agricultural, commercial, biographical and miscellaneous* (1803–8); a three-volume *History of Devonshire* (1793–1806); *The Old English Gentleman, a poem* (1797); three sets of biographical sketches and memoirs, namely, *Biographical Sketches in Cornwall* (1831), *Traditions and Recollections* (1826), and *Reminiscences, in Prose and Verse* (1836); and *The Unsex'd Females* (1798) (*BLGC*).
5. William Prideaux Courtney, 'Polwhele, Richard', *DNB*, xvi, 73.
6. William Jerdan, *The Autobiography of William Jerdan* (4 vols; London: Arthur Hall, Virtue, 1852–3) ii, 236.
7. It was his West Country neighbour (and, later, fellow *Anti-Jacobin* contributor) John Whitaker who brought Polwhele to the attention of the *British Critic*'s co-editor, Archdeacon Nares (John Nichols, *Illustrations of the Literary History of the Eighteenth Century* (8 vols; London: printed for the author, 1817–58) vii, 680n; John Whitaker, letter to Richard Polwhele, 16 October 1797, quoted in R[ichard] Polwhele, *Biographical Sketches in Cornwall* [3 vols; Truro: printed by W. Polyblank, 1831] iii, 124–5). Nares in turn seems to have recommended Polwhele as his successor on the staff of the *British Critic*, though nothing ever came of the suggestion (Robert Nares, letter to Richard Polwhele, 13 March 1812, quoted in Nichols, *Illustrations*, vii, 614). Polwhele also tried, unsuccessfully, to offer his services as a contributor to the *Quarterly Review*, this time through the introduction of Walter Scott, although this effort too proved fruitless – Walter Scott, letter to Richard Polwhele, 21 July 1808, in H. J. C. Grierson (ed.), *The Letters of Sir Walter Scott* (12 vols; centenary edn; London: Constable, 1932–7) ii, 81–2. Neither Hill Shine and Helen Chadwick Shine's *The 'Quarterly Review' Under Gifford* nor the *Wellesley Index* lists any contributions to the *Quarterly Review* by Polwhele.
8. John Wilson Croker, Diary for 5 March 1820, quoted in Louis J. Jennings (ed.), *The Croker Papers* (3 vols; London: John Murray, 1884) i, 165.
9. Cyrus Redding, *Fifty Years' Recollections, Literary and Personal* (3 vols; London: Charles J. Skeet, 1858) i, 139–40.

10. [John Bowyer Nichols], *GM*, n.s. ix (May 1838) 547.
11. The quotations are taken from the resolution of the citizens' meeting
    of 2 January 1793, reprinted in R[ichard] Polwhele, *Traditions and
    Recollections; Domestic, Clerical, and Literary* (2 vols; London: John
    Nichols and Son, 1826) i, 162. They are typical of resolutions proposed
    at hundreds of similar meetings nationwide in the wake of the
    establishment of John Reeves's Crown and Anchor Association in
    November 1792.
12. [Richard Polwhele] *AJ*, iii (June 1799) 185.
13. Richard Polwhele, letter to General Simcoe, 8 November 1803, quoted
    in Polwhele, *Traditions and Recollections*, ii, 542.
14. Quoted in R[ichard] Polwhele, *Reminiscences, in Prose and Verse* (3 vols in
    1; London: J. B. Nichols and Son, 1836) ii, 28.
15. Richard Polwhele, letters to the Bishop of Exeter, 31 March 1832, quoted
    in ibid., p. 27.

PRINCE, Rev. John (*c.* 1753–1833)

AJ contributions: vi, 196–7, 444–5.

The Rev. John Prince was vicar of Enford, Wilts. (1793–1833) and a
sermon writer of minor importance.[1] He was chiefly known in his
own day for his service for forty-three years as chaplain to the
Magdalen Hospital, Lambeth.[2]

The best available portrait of Prince the man is an oblique
reference to him found in James Allan Park's *Memoirs of William
Stevens*, Prince's friend and fellow *Anti-Jacobin* reviewer (q.v.).
According to Park, 'Mr. Prince was [for a time] Curate of St. Vedast,
Foster Lane, where Mr. S[tevens] used frequently to attend the
weekly prayers.' Prince at first assumed from Stevens's 'black
clothes, and . . . bushy clerical wig' that the latter was a clergyman
too and was amazed to learn that the pious Stevens was in fact a
layman. Prince accordingly made inquiries at the Rivington
bookshop and discovered Stevens's name, whereupon the two
formed a firm friendship. 'Certainly', Park added, 'if congeniality of
sentiments, if sound orthodox opinions, if unfeigned piety, if the
warmest benevolence, could endear men to each other, never were
two persons better suited for such mutual and affectionate regard
than Mr. Stevens and Mr. Prince.'[3]

Prince was an infrequent contributor to the *Anti-Jacobin*, in which
he reviewed works on divinity. He described himself by means of
the usual patriotic formula as a 'true friend to his King and
country'.[4]

Notes

1. *Alumni Oxon.*, III, 1153; Upcott, *Biog. Dict.*, p. 284. Prince was a product of Christ's Hospital and Oriel College, Oxford (BA, 1775).
2. *GM*, LX-1 (June 1790) 578.
3. James Allan Park, *Memoirs of William Stevens, Esq. Treasurer of Queen Anne's Bounty* (4th edn; London: C. & J. Rivington, 1825) pp. 39–40.
4. *AJ*, VI (August 1800) 445.

PYE, Henry James (1745–1813)

AJ contribution: I, 210–1.

'The poetical Pye', in Sir Walter Scott's inimitable phrase[1] – perhaps the least respected, if not the most universally scorned, versifier ever to occupy the office of Poet Laureate of England – was one more of the army of occasional contributors upon whom John Gifford could rely for anti-Jacobinical filler. The main facts of Pye's career are well known. A descendant of what the *Gentleman's Magazine* rather pretentiously called 'a very antient and respectable family',[2] dating from the Conquest and encompassing a Jacobean auditor of the Exchequer and several Members of Parliament, Pye was a typical example of a country gentleman of a literary turn of mind. A gentleman commoner at Magdalen College, Oxford, he received the honorary degree of MA in 1766 and in 1773 was made Doctor of Laws after the installation of Lord North as chancellor.[3] He spent his early manhood in the country, 'dividing his time between his studies, the duties of a magistrate, and the diversions of the field, to which he was remarkably attached'.[4] He also served for a time in the Berkshire militia. He sat in Parliament as a Member for Berkshire from 1784 to 1790 and from 1792 served as a magistrate for Westminster. He was named Poet Laureate in 1790, probably as a reward for his support of Pitt during his term in the House of Commons.[5] The appointment was greeted with universal contempt by the literary world, a contempt which only grew deeper with each passing year, as one ponderous birthday ode, prolix elegy, or stillborn tragedy followed another and enshrined the hard-working but woefully deficient Laureate in the ranks of mediocrity.[6] Pye held the position until his death in 1813, when he was succeeded by the equally earnest and inept Robert Southey, Walter Scott having wisely refused the dubious honour of the laurel wreath and tierce of canary.

Notes

1. Quoted in Sidney Lee, 'Pye, Henry James', *DNB*, xvi, 512.
2. *GM*, lxxxiii-2 (September 1813) 293.
3. *Alumni Oxon.*, iii, 1166.
4. *GM*, lxxxiii-2 (September 1813) 293.
5. Lee, 'Pye', p. 511.
6. See for example Byron's comment in *The Vision of Judgment*:

> The monarch, mute till then, exclaim'd 'What! what!
> Pye come again? No more – no more of that!'

RANDOLPH, Rev. Francis (1752–1831)

AJ contributions: i, 409–15; iv, 213–25; vi, 270–4.

The Rev. Dr Francis Randolph, sermon writer, pamphleteer, and divine, brought to the *Anti-Jacobin* an expertise in fighting Socinian heresy and an unsavoury reputation for involvement in Palace intrigue. Randolph, a King's scholar at Eton and fellow of King's College, Cambridge,[1] resided for a number of years in Germany, perfected the language, and was subsequently engaged as private tutor of English to the Duke of York's German-speaking duchess. William Upcott claimed that it was to this circumstance that Randolph owed his advancement in the Church,[2] in which he rose rapidly to become chaplain to the Duke of York, prebendary of Bristol, and proprietor of Laura Chapel, Bath.[3]

In 1795 Randolph fell under suspicion for having become involved in a particularly dishonourable bit of Court intrigue. As Robert Huish later reconstructed the incident,

> In the month of August, 1795, whilst residing at Brighton, the Princess [of Wales, Caroline of Brunswick] committed to the care of Dr. Randolph a packet of letters to convey to Brunswick, as he expressed his intention of visiting Germany. Those letters were private and confidential: they contained strictures on the character of the Queen [George III's queen, Charlotte, mother-in-law of the Princess of Wales], and one of them had been imprudently laid about by her Royal Highness, after she had written it. That letter was perused by Lady Jersey, and to the Queen she determined to convey it, with those which constituted the remainder of the packet. The letters never reached their destination, and were afterwards possessed by Queen Charlotte.[4]

Whether Randolph was the innocent victim in this unedifying piece of bedchamber politics, or whether for self-serving motives he was actually a conspirator in the plot to disclose the letters to Queen Charlotte, has never been satisfactorily established.[5] Lady Jersey denied the charge that she had given the letters to the Queen, seeking to lay the blame instead on Randolph. The latter insisted meanwhile that he was innocent, having (as he said) returned the packet of letters to the Princess upon cancelling his travel plans for Germany.[6] Princess Caroline's followers for their part charged that Randolph had been enticed into surrendering the letters to the Queen with the promise of a bishopric.[7] Whatever the truth of the charges, Randolph, though never receiving a bishopric, suffered no permanent ill effects from the scandal. If anything, he went from strength to strength in his ecclesiastical career following the incident.

When not embroiled in Palace intrigue, Randolph occupied himself with sermon writing, political pamphleteering, fighting heresy, and urging schemes for reducing the national debt.[8] He contributed occasionally to the *Anti-Jacobin*, where he proved himself a political and religious conservative, denouncing 'atheism, and the . . . propagation of those licentious and infidel principles, which have for their object the subversion of every government, and the dissolution of every moral and religious tie'.[9]

Notes

1. Fellow of King's College, 1775; BA, 1777; MA, 1780; DD, University of Dublin, 1806 (*Alumni Cantab.*, pt 2, v, 242).
2. Upcott, *Biog. Dict.*, p. 287.
3. Randolph did indeed enjoy a prestigious career in the Church. He was appointed, in order, vicar of Broad Chalke, Wilts., 1786; incumbent of Chenies, Bucks., 1788; chaplain to the Duke of York and prebendary of Bristol, 1791; proprietor of Laura Chapel, Bathwick, Bath, 1796; rector of Aston, Herts.; rector of Watton-at-Stone, Herts., 1804; vicar of Banwell, Somerset, 1809 (reappointed 1817); and rector of St. Paul's, Covent Garden, 1817. However, some of these livings were in the gift of the Duke of Bedford, not the Crown (*Index Eccles.*, p. 147; *GM*, ci-1 [Supplement to January–June 1831] 648; Upcott, *Biog. Dict.*, p. 287; Gerald le Grys Norgate, 'Randolph, Francis', *DNB*, xvi, 716; *The Times*, 20 June 1831, p. 2).
4. Robert Huish, *Memoirs of George the Fourth* (2 vols; London: T. Kelly, 1830) i, 383.
5. Whatever his position in 1795, Randolph was quite clearly a partisan of Caroline's in later years. The Sunday following the Prince of Wales's coronation as George IV in 1821 Randolph preached a daring sermon in

Bristol cathedral, taking as his text 'Belshazzar the King made a great feast' and including a pointed reference to royal mistresses (*Alumni Cantab.*, pt 2, v, 242).

6. Francis Randolph, *The Correspondence between the Earl and Countess of Jersey, and the Rev. Dr. Randolph, upon the subject of some letters belonging to H. R. H. the Princess of Wales, of late so much the topic of public conversation* (London: Richard White, 1796).

7. Robert Huish, *Memoirs of Caroline, Queen Consort of England from the Earliest Period of Her Eventful Life* (2 vols; London: T. Kelly, 1821) I, 62–3; Norgate, 'Randolph', p. 716.

8. His writings include *A Letter to the Right Hon. William Pitt, . . . on the proposed Abolition of the African Slave Trade* (1788); *Arm, arm, ye Brave! or, a Serious address to the people of England, By a lover of his king and country* (on the threatened Napoleonic invasion; 1803?); *Scriptural Revision of Socinian Arguments, in a letter to . . . Dr. Priestley* (1792); *Scriptural Revision of Socinian Arguments vindicated, against the reply of B. Hobhouse* (1793); and *A Few Observations on the present state of the Nation* (on the national debt; 1808).

9. *AJ*, I (October 1798) 411.

REEVES, John (1752–1829)

AJ contributions: I, 381–7; II, 1–3, 224–6; III, 43–5, 276–9, 283–6.

One of the most significant of John Gifford's contributors, in terms of the wider context of the entire anti-Jacobin movement, was John Reeves, career civil servant, legal scholar, and founder of the Crown and Anchor Association, whose pivotal role in English anti-Jacobinism has already been discussed. A product of Eton, Oxford,[1] and the Middle Temple, Reeves, after being called to the Bar in 1780, embarked upon a dual career in the civil service and in legal scholarship, where he built up an impressive reputation as an historian of the common law.[2] His record of civil service appointments was formidable to say the least, beginning in 1780, when he was named a commissioner of bankrupts, and continuing over the next several decades as he was appointed, in order, law clerk to the Board of Trade (1787), chief of the Standing Committee of the Mint, receiver to the police, Chief Justice of the Court of Judicature in Newfoundland (1791), High Steward of the Manor and Liberty of the Savoy (1793), joint patentee of the office of King's Printer (1800), and joint Superintendent of the Alien Office (1803). In addition he found time to establish the anti-Jacobin Association for Preserving Liberty and Property against Levellers and Republicans (the Crown and Anchor Association) and to organise a massive campaign to circulate counter-revolutionary pamphlets under its auspices, efforts that led William Jerdan to dub him 'the Magnus Apollo' of patriotic propaganda.[3]

Though Reeves's civil service career was exceedingly profitable[4] and though at least some of his appointments were bestowed as overt rewards for his support of the Ministry's anti-Jacobin policies, it would be a mistake to dismiss Reeves as an idle sinecurist and paid government propagandist. In the first place, Reeves's government posts were by no means all sinecures, popular stereotypes of the eighteenth-century civil service to the contrary.[5] In the second place, Reeves was no subservient ministerial apologist, blindly turning out Pittite propaganda in exchange for a Treasury dole. He was, rather, a sincere anti-Jacobin, honestly concerned for the safety of the Constitution and of political order. He 'was through life distinguished for zealous loyalty', his fellow contributor John Taylor (q.v.) noted,[6] and he saw English Jacobinism as an attack upon loyalty – an insidious campaign to prey upon the minds of the lower orders and seduce them from their native patriotism by sowing discontent.[7] The genuine alarm which prompted Reeves to establish the Crown and Anchor Association during the crisis weeks of late 1792 – and the zeal with which he masterminded the Association's efforts to ferret out sedition nationwide – speak volumes for the sincerity of Reeves's conservative views. In fact, the almost reactionary awe in which he held the institution of monarchy and which he displayed in his 1795 *Thoughts on the English Government* involved him in an acrimonious legal action with the House of Commons and almost led to a breach with Pitt,[8] whose policies Reeves had always so assiduously supported.[9] Finally, it is useful to note that, his horror of Jacobinism notwithstanding, Reeves discharged his highly demanding duties as Superintendent of Aliens (1803–14) with a humaneness, an independence, and a rigorous insistence on the principles of British justice that lost him much goodwill among the hard-liners in government.[10]

As far as volume of production is concerned, Reeves's connection with the *Anti-Jacobin Review* was slight, his major efforts in the cause of anti-Jacobinism falling in the early 1790s before the *Review*'s establishment. Ever a scholarly man and a long-time fellow of the Royal Society and of the Society of Antiquaries, Reeves devoted his last years to the study of classical languages and his duties as a treasurer of the Literary Fund. He died in 1829 at the age of 77, without living to see the Reform Bill, whose passage he would surely have regarded as marking the 'fall' of the Constitution.

Notes

1. BA, 1775, Merton College; fellow, 1777, and MA, 1778, Queen's College (*GM*, xcix-2 [November 1829] 468; *Alumni Oxon.*, iii, 1185).
2. Reeves's most substantial work was his multi-volume *History of the English Law, from the time of the Romans to the end of the reign of Elizabeth.* His other publications included *A Chart of Penal Law* (1779); *Considerations on the Coronation Oath . . .* (1801); *The Law of Shipping and Navigation, from the time of Edward III. to the end of the year 1806* (1807); *Legal Considerations on the Regency, as far as it regards Ireland* (1789); *Two Tracts shewing, that Americans, born before the Independence, are, by the law of England, not aliens* (1814); *An Enquiry into the Nature of Property and Estates as defined by the Laws of England* (1779); and the celebrated *Thoughts on the English Government . . .* (1795–1800).
3. William Jerdan, *The Autobiography of William Jerdan* (4 vols; London: Arthur Hall, Virtue, 1852–3) i, 118. For the titles of some of Reeves's own counter-revolutionary pamphlets, published anonymously, see Gayle Trusdel Pendleton, 'Three Score Identifications of Anonymous British Pamphlets of the 1790s', *Notes and Queries*, n.s. xxvi (June 1979) pp. 209, 213–15.
4. 'The *Star* claimed (30 Nov. 1792) that his offices were worth £1000 a year' (Austin Mitchell, 'The Association Movement of 1792–3', *Historical Journal*, iv [1961] 59, n. 18).
5. During his tenure at the Board of Trade, for example, Reeves dealt with a formidable array of disputes over commercial policy and was so assiduous in the preparation of reports that his health nearly failed as a result of physical exhaustion (*Annual Biography and Obituary*, xiv [1830] 282). Reeves's most demanding service to the Board of Trade came in 1791–2, when he held the highly responsible post of Chief Justice of the Court of Judicature in Newfoundland and presided over that body's campaign to bring dissident elements in the powerful Newfoundland fishing industry more firmly under Crown control.
6. John Taylor, *Records of My Life* (New York: J. and J. Harper, 1833) p. 357.
7. John Reeves, *Thoughts on the English Government, Addressed to the Quiet Good Sense of the People of England, In a Series of Letters: Letter the First* (London: J. Owen, 1795) pp. 74–7.
8. In 1795 when Reeves published the first part of his *Thoughts on the English Government*, asserting that the Crown was the trunk of the constitutional tree and the Houses of Parliament mere insignificant branches, an offended Pitt joined with Sheridan and the Opposition in voting to charge the author with a seditious libel on the House of Commons. Reeves was brought to trial before Lord Kenyon on 20 May 1796 and found not guilty of criminal intent in his metaphor of the constitutional tree. However, he continued to press the point in further instalments of his *Thoughts on the English Government* – a stand which

could not have won him much favour with Pitt, a stalwart House of Commons man.

9. On other occasions Reeves took pains to consult Pitt ahead of time, submitting pro-government, counter-revolutionary pamphlets, resolutions, and addresses for Pitt's approval before publishing them. See John Reeves, letter to William Pitt, 7 November 1795, Chatham Papers (P.R.O. 30/8), vol. 170, pt 2, fols 255b–256a; Reeves, letter to Pitt, 10 November 1795, ibid., fol. 257; Reeves, letter to Pitt, 18 November 1795, ibid., fols 265–6; Reeves, letter to Pitt, 27 December 1797, ibid., fols 273–4.

10. Patrick Polden, 'John Reeves as Superindendent of Aliens, 1803–14', *Journal of Legal History*, iii (May 1982) 31–51.

REID, William Hamilton (d. 1826)

AJ contributions: vi, 354–6, 468–72.

The career of William Hamilton Reid offers the unusual spectacle of a man who went through two political metamorphoses – from enthusiasm for the French Revolution, to intense allegiance to Church and King, and back again. Reid was the child of domestic servants in the household of the Duke of Hamilton. Orphaned at an early age and taken in by a parish officer, he 'was subsequently apprenticed to a silver-buckle-maker near Soho, and from that period he commenced his literary studies. All his pocket-money was expended in books, and, after a long day of severe labour, half of the short period allotted for his repose was frequently spent in reading, particularly history and poetry'.[1] When the silver-buckle trade declined as a result of changes in fashion, Reid applied himself more and more to literature, writing miscellaneous poems for the newspapers and magazines. He had received a smattering of education as a child, thanks to the generosity of the Duke of Hamilton. Now he set about to learn French, in which he quickly became proficient enough to translate French news items for one of the daily papers. By any standard his facility for languages must have been tremendous, for he subsequently taught himself Italian, Spanish, German, Portuguese, Latin, Greek, and Hebrew and was studying the northern dialects when he died. His taste, though, did not stop with languages. He undertook the study of topography, biography, and the antiquities of London, as well as being, by one account, 'a mere bookworm in divinity ever since the age of 16'.[2]

Reid came to the notice of the Ministry in 1800 when he published

The Rise and Dissolution of the Infidel Societies in this Metropolis, in which he accused the London Corresponding Society and other Radical groups of disseminating atheistical or Deistical propaganda. According to William Upcott, Reid in the early days of the French Revolution had been 'a zealous advocate of the republican doctrines, with no small tinge of infidelity. After some time, however, he wavered, and, for a short space, was such a determined friend to orthodoxy, that the late Bishop of London, Dr. Porteus, it is said, offered him ordination, which he . . . declined.'[3] His stridently anti-Jacobinical *Rise and Dissolution of the Infidel Societies* was in effect a recantation of his former revolutionary principles, principles which he now renounced with all the zealotry of a new convert. So devoted did Reid become to his new-found loyalty that, by his own account, he 'hazarded his personal safety by his repeated exposure of Jacobin principles, particularly in 1800 and 1801'.[4] Certainly his letters to the *Anti-Jacobin*, written at this time, bear all the hallmarks of a personal crusade to rescue his fellow Britons from the errors of anarchy and republican levelling.

Reid, however, was to undergo yet another philosophical metamorphosis, this time in religion. He had early in his career written letters to the *Gazetteer* under the name Philo-Veritas, attacking a Methodist contributor who had criticised the Established Church.[5] He had in his *Rise and Dissolution of the Infidel Societies* condemned the Deistical or atheistical writings of Paine and the French *Philosophes*. Now he abandoned his orthodox religious views for Dissent. 'After editing for a little while a periodical work devoted exclusively to the support of the church establishment', Upcott reported, 'he avowed himself an Unitarian',[6] to the distress of his conservative admirers. The Church-and-King party could, however, take comfort in the fact that by the time William Hamilton Reid so ostentatiously turned his coat, the period of the greatest Radical threat to the Establishment was already past.

Notes

1. *GM*, xcvi-2 (August 1826) 184.
2. The phrase was erroneously printed 'every since'. *GM*, lviii (July 1788) 594.
3. Upcott, *Biog. Dict.*, p. 291. Reid's widow said that it was 'his objection to subscribe to the Articles of Faith, and a strong inherent love of independence' that persuaded him to refuse ordination. She added that the only patronage Reid ever received was a present of £5 from Canning (*GM*, xcvi-2 [August 1826] 185).

4. *GM*, LXXXI-2 (September 1811) 233.
5. *GM*, LVIII (July 1788) 594.
6. Upcott, *Biog. Dict.*, p. 291.

RIVERS, Rev. David

AJ contribution: II, 214–15.

Rivers described himself in his *Literary Memoirs* as a 'Dissenting Minister of a small congregation at Highgate'.[1] He published, in addition to the *Literary Memoirs* (a two-volume literary biographical dictionary), several sermons including *A Discourse on Patriotism, or the Love of our Country*, a *Sermon against Popery*, and his vehemently anti-French-revolutionary *The Gospel a Law of Liberty*.[2] According to his own memoir he was as well

> the author of several anonymous Pamphlets; was a very frequent correspondent with the newspaper called the World, while it was under the direction of Captain Topham, signing his pieces MARCUS ANTONINUS; and . . . had a principal share in conducting the Sunday Reformer and the Sunday Recorder, newspapers. He, moreover, edited 'The Beauties of Saurin,' a duodecimo volume, published in 1797.[3]

In 1798 Rivers broke with the Dissenters over their alleged disloyalty to the State. His personal recantation of his former principles took the form of a pamphlet, *Observations on the Political Conduct of the Protestant Dissenters, . . . In Five Letters to a Friend*, which sought to survey Dissenter disaffection from the time of Calvin to the 1790s, paying special attention to Dissenter involvement in the Wilkes movement, in English Jacobinism, and in the Irish rebellion. It was this pamphlet that gave rise to Samuel Greatheed's (q.v.) series of letters to the *Anti-Jacobin* in vindication of the Dissenters, which in its turn provoked Rivers's retaliatory letter to the *Anti-Jacobin*, reaffirming his contention that '*as a body*, . . . [the Dissenters] are, and ever have been, enemies to the constitution'.[4]

Notes

1. David Rivers, *Literary Memoirs of Living Authors of Great Britain* (2 vols; London: R. Faulder, 1798) II, 202.

2. Ibid., pp. 202–3; *BLGC*; David Rivers, *Sermons on Interesting Subjects* (London: printed for the author, 1801). See also Gayle Trusdel Pendleton, 'Three Score Identifications of Anonymous British Pamphlets of the 1790s.', *Notes and Queries*, n.s. xxvi (June 1979) 212.
3. Rivers, *Literary Memoirs*, ii, 203.
4. *AJ*, ii (February 1799) 215.

ROBISON, John (1739–1805)

AJ contribution: vi, 342.

John Robison was a writer of scientific treatises and professor of natural philosophy at the University of Edinburgh. He was probably best known to the British reading audience of the 1790s as the author of the sensationally anti-Jacobinical and highly controversial *Proofs of a Conspiracy against All the Religions and Governments of Europe, Carried on in the Secret Meetings of Free Masons, Illuminati, and Reading Societies*. In this work Robison, who was himself a Freemason, joined the Abbé Barruel in claiming the existence of a conscious conspiracy of *Philosophes*, Freemasons, and German Illuminati organised to undermine the religious and political allegiance of the population of Europe.[1]

Aside from his one spectacular foray into political pamphleteering, Robison's life was largely confined to military and scientific pursuits. Born into a well-to-do Glasgow merchant family, Robison took an arts degree from the University of Glasgow and in 1759 became tutor to the son of Admiral Charles Knowles. When his pupil, a lieutenant in the Royal Navy, was sent to Canada to take part in the British campaign against Quebec, Robison enlisted as a midshipman and accompanied him. He saw active military service in Canada and was among the party in General Wolfe's boat when the latter made his midnight voyage down the St Lawrence to attack Quebec.[2]

After the war Robison's interest focused more and more on science. He had helped survey the St Lawrence for the British forces and in 1762 had taken part in an expedition to the West Indies to conduct experiments with Harrison's chronometer for the Board of Longitude. He now returned as a student to the University of Glasgow where in 1766 he was elected lecturer in chemistry.[3] Four years later, in 1770, he journeyed to St Petersburg as private secretary to Admiral Knowles, who had been appointed president of the Russian Board of Admiralty. Robison enjoyed great favour in Russia, especially with General Kutusoff, and in 1772 he was appointed colonel and professor of mathematics in the imperial academy for training noble cadets for the Russian navy. The following year, after rising to the post of inspector-general of the corps, he returned to Scotland and a professorship at the University of Edinburgh.

Henry Cockburn's *Memorials of His Time* contains a striking portrait of Robison the scientist and teacher:

> John Robison, the Professor of Natural Philosophy, . . . made himself remarkable, like others of his class at that time, by humouring his own taste in the matter of dress. A pig-tail so long and so thin that it curled far down his back, and a pair of huge blue worsted hose without soles, and covering the limbs from the heel to the top of the thigh, in which he both walked and lectured, seemed rather to improve his wise elephantine head and majestic person. A little hypochondria, induced by the frequent use of laudanum, . . . heightened the interest with which we gazed on a person who we knew combined such profound philosophy with such varied active life.[4]

When not lecturing on mechanics, hydrodynamics, astronomy, optics, electricity, and magnetism, Robison spent his time writing scientific articles for the third edition of the *Encyclopaedia Britannica*, which his friend George Gleig (q.v.) was putting together, or discharging his duties as general secretary of the Royal Society of Edinburgh.[5] His *Proofs of a Conspiracy* was his only political publication.

Notes

1. See pp. 16–17.
2. John Playfair, 'Biographical Account of the late John Robison, LL.D. F.R.S. Edin. and Professor of Natural Philosophy in the University of Edinburgh', *Transactions of the Royal Society of Edinburgh*, vii (Edinburgh: Archibald Constable, 1815; London: Cadell and Davies, 1815) 499. Robison's account of that night contains a number of valuable details of the hours before the battle. It was Robison, for example, who reported that Wolfe whiled away the time during the slow trip down the river by reciting Gray's 'Elegy' to his officers.
3. Robison's tenure at the University was not without incident. While serving as a lecturer in chemistry he 'was fined in 1769 for his share in a

squabble with . . . [David Woodburn], who was expelled' (*The Matriculation Albums of the University of Glasgow*, ed. W. Innes Addison [Glasgow: James Maclehose, 1913] p. 44).
4. Henry Cockburn, *Memorials of His Time*, ed. Karl F. C. Miller, Classics of British Historical Literature, ed. John Clive (Chicago: University of Chicago Press, 1974) p. 51.
5. Robison received honorary LL Ds from the College of New Jersey and from the University of Glasgow, as well as a membership in the Russian imperial academy of sciences, before dying in 1805.

SKINNER, John, Bishop of Aberdeen (1744–1816)

AJ contributions: IV, 336–41[?], 375–86[?]; V, 9–16, 101–6, 137–45.

John Skinner, bishop of Aberdeen and primus (1788–1816) of the Scottish Episcopal Church, was the central figure in the late eighteenth-century renaissance of Scottish Episcopacy. After their ill-fated support of the Jacobite rebellions of 1715 and 1745 the Episcopal churches in Scotland had gone into eclipse, their congregations divided, their leadership in disarray, and their freedom of worship severely restricted by a stringent retaliatory penal code enacted by the governments of George I and George II. Skinner as a youth had experienced the weight of religious repression,[1] and it was to free Scottish Episcopacy from those restrictions and to lift the Church in Scotland out of its depressed state that he dedicated himself. Ordained a priest in 1764 and consecrated bishop-coadjutor of Aberdeen in 1782,[2] Skinner launched a lifelong campaign to unite the Episcopal congregations of Scotland, win repeal of the penal laws operating against them, and bring the Scottish Episcopal Church into communion with the Church of England.

Skinner's energetic crusade met with immediate success. Under his leadership the synod of bishops and deans that met in Aberdeen on 24 April 1788 (in the wake of the death of the Young Pretender), resolved unanimously to order the Scottish Episcopal clergy to pray for George III as king according to the Anglican rite. The following year Skinner and a delegation of two other Scottish bishops journeyed to London to assure John Moore, then archbishop of Canterbury, of their allegiance to the English liturgy and to negotiate with the Ministry for a repeal of the penal laws. After an unsuccessful first attempt, and following a vigorous campaign led in

Scotland by Skinner and in London by (among others[3]) the noted Anglican philanthropist William Stevens (q.v.), the Scottish relief bill passed both Houses of Parliament and received the royal assent on 15 June 1792. By this Act the position of the Scottish Episcopal clergy was legalised in exchange for a requirement that the clergy take an oath abjuring their past loyalty to the Jacobite cause. In addition the Act lifted all penal restrictions from the congregations that prayed for the Hanoverian house.[4]

Skinner, who enjoyed complete authority over the Scottish Episcopal congregations during his lifetime,[5] was influential in determining the direction to be taken by the Church on the other side of the Atlantic as well. The American Revolution had left the Episcopal congregations in America cut off from the Church of England and without a bishop to ensure the continuance of the apostolic succession. When delegates of the American congregations encountered delays from the English clergy in their negotiations to secure the ordination of an American bishop, they turned to Skinner and the clergy of Scotland instead. On 14 November 1784, Skinner joined with Bishops Kilgour and Petrie in consecrating Samuel Seabury as bishop of Connecticut. The next day Skinner and the Scottish clergy met with Seabury to draw up a concordat cementing ties between the Anglican communion of Scotland and the new diocese of Connecticut, first in the United States.[6]

Skinner published little save sermons, and his few contributions to the *Anti-Jacobin* concerned only theological works. He was, however, loyal to the political principles of the *Anti-Jacobin*, as evidenced by a declaration he signed in 1793 in the name of the Episcopal clergy of Aberdeen, pledging 'their grateful and inviolable attachment to the King and Constitution of Great Britain' and promising to 'make it their constant study to counteract the insidious operation of all seditious and inflammatory publications, tending to alienate the affections of the people from the Government'.[7]

Notes

1. Skinner had shared the imprisonment of his father, the Rev. John Skinner, an Episcopal priest who had officiated for his congregation in defiance of the penal code (John Skinner, *Annals of Scottish Episcopacy, from the Year 1788 to the Year 1816, Inclusive* [Edinburgh: A. Brown, 1818] p. 4).

2. Skinner was ordained deacon in 1763 and priest in 1764. He was consecrated bishop-coadjutor of Aberdeen in 1782 and bishop in his own right in 1786, and two years later he was elected primus of the Scottish Episcopal Church (Alexander Gordon, 'Skinner, John', *DNB*, xviii, 344–5).
3. Sir James Allan Park, the author of the Scottish relief bill, was, with Stevens, Skinner's principal London ally during the campaign.
4. Gordon, 'Skinner', p. 345; George Grub, *An Ecclesiastical History of Scotland, from the Introduction of Christianity to the Present Time* (4 vols; Edinburgh: Edmonston and Douglas, 1861) iv, 103ff.; Fred D. Schneider, 'Scottish Episcopalians and English Politicians: The Limits of Toleration', *Historical Magazine of the Protestant Episcopal Church*, xlv (September 1976) 285–7.
5. Skinner's work in reshaping the Scottish Episcopal Church was completed in 1804 when a synod meeting in Laurencekirk voted in favour of the unification of all the Episcopal congregations north of the Tweed. Skinner's only reservation with regard to the proceedings seems to have been his fear that in their zeal to promote close ties with the Church of England (a cause to which he still completely adhered), the congregations would sacrifice their historic and distinctly Scottish Communion rite. As a result Skinner for the rest of his life vigorously campaigned against the adoption of the English Office of Holy Communion, requiring Scottish candidates for bishop (including George Gleig [q.v.]) to promise to uphold the Scottish order of the Eucharist before being consecrated.
6. Gordon, 'Skinner', p. 345.
7. Quoted in Skinner, *Annals of Scottish Episcopacy*, p. 263.

STEVENS, William (1732–1807)

AJ contributions: iii, 99; iv, 471–2[?]; v, 106[?], 347–8.

William Stevens, London hosier and philanthropist, was one of the leading lay members of the High-Church and Evangelical wings of Anglicanism in the late eighteenth century. Born in Southwark the son of a tradesman, he was the boyhood friend and school companion of his cousin George Horne, the future bishop of Norwich, until the latter was sent to Oxford. Stevens for his part was apprenticed at the age of fourteen to one Hookham, a hosier and the grandfather of John Hookham Frere. Stevens rose in the trade, was made a partner in his master's business, and eventually emerged as a man of considerable wealth, which he devoted in large part to religious and charitable purposes.[1]

Stevens was a self-educated man with a consuming interest in theology and a reputation for intense piety. In order to prepare himself for his extensive private reading in dogma, he taught himself French, Latin, Greek, and Hebrew. Such was his proficiency that 'whenever he went to visit in the country, he carried with him his Hebrew Bible and Greek Testament – and uniformly read the lessons for the day, before he left his chamber in their original languages'.[2] He was a constant churchgoer, and his faithful attendance on the services, coupled with his 'black clothes, and . . . bushy clerical wig', misled at least one person, the Rev. John Prince (q.v.), into thinking that Stevens was a clergyman.[3]

Stevens's acquaintances included several fellow *Anti-Jacobin* contributors, namely, the above John Prince, John Skinner, Francis Randolph, William Jones of Nayland, and Jonathan Boucher. It was, however, chiefly in philanthropical and Evangelical circles that Stevens moved. He was a leading figure on the boards of several benevolent societies,[4] and when Scottish Bishop John Skinner (q.v.) undertook negotiations with the Pitt Ministry in 1789 to secure the repeal of the penal laws that operated against Episcopal congregations in Scotland, Stevens served on Skinner's London liaison committee and helped eventually steer the relief bill successfully through Parliament.

As Stevens's friend and biographer Park noted, 'Government he regarded as the ordinance of God, for the benefit of man; and was therefore a steady friend to our admirable constitution in Church and State.'[5] The French Revolution, with its levelling principles and militant de-Christianisation campaign, filled Stevens with horror and led him to speculate that perhaps the tribulations of the Jacobin era had been sent by God as punishment for a Europe that had abandoned religion.[6] Ever anxious to do his part in helping to stem the revolutionary tide, Stevens assisted William Jones of Nayland in the establishment of the latter's anti-Jacobinical Society for the Reformation of Principles by Appropriate Literature. Together the two men produced a set of Church-and-King pamphlets for mass consumption, attacking Paine, Priestley, and all other 'Jacobins, anarchists, regicide republicans, fratricide aristocrats, fanatics, . . . British crops [i.e. cropped heads], United Irishmen, Wakefieldean sectaries, Tookean brawlers, [and] Godwinean philosophers'.[7]

In addition to his political pamphlets and doctrinal studies, Stevens published a memoir of William Jones of Nayland and edited a twelve-volume set of Jones's collected writings, plus three volumes of Bishop Horne's sermons. Always a retiring man,

Stevens never published under his own name, entitling even his own volume of collected writings *OὙΔΕΝὸΣ ΕΡΓΑ* (*The Works of Nobody*).[8] Likewise printed unsigned were his contributions to the *Anti-Jacobin* – an anti-Fox comic poem, a letter facetiously attacking French and English Jacobins, and a tribute to William Jones of Nayland.[9]

Notes

1. For the best account of Stevens's early life see James Allan Park's *Memoirs of William Stevens, Esq. Treasurer of Queen Anne's Bounty*, published in 1825 for the Society for Promoting Christian Knowledge. The work, written in cloying, hagiographical style, is an expanded version of Park's obituary article for Stevens which appeared in the *GM*, LXXVII-1 (February 1807) 173–5.
2. Park, *Memoirs of William Stevens*, p. 41.
3. Ibid., p. 39.
4. He served variously as the treasurer of Queen Anne's Bounty (for approximately thirty years); as steward to the Feast of the Sons of the Clergy; and as a governor of Christ's Hospital, of Bridewell, of Bethlehem Hospital, and of the Magdalen Charity. He was a contributor to the Corporation of the Widows of the Clergy and to the Clergy Orphan School and was a member of the Corporation for Promoting the Gospel in Foreign Parts and of the Society for Promoting Christian Knowledge.
5. Park, *Memoirs of William Stevens*, p. 21.
6. William Stevens, quoted in ibid., p. 107.
7. [William Stevens(?)], *AJ*, V. (January 1800) 106.
8. The title gave rise to the Nobody's Club, which some thirty friends of Stevens's, including 'several members of both Houses of Parliament, and some of the most distinguished characters in the church, the law, in medicine, and in other respectable walks of life', formed in his honour (Samuel Egerton Brydges, *Censura Literaria* [10 vols; London: T. Bensley, 1805–9] IV, 223).
9. Stevens also appears to have written a letter to the editor of the *Anti-Jacobin*, IV (December 1799) 471–2.

STEWART, Rev. Charles Edward (*c.* 1748–1819)[1]

AJ contributions: I, 351–2, 598.

The Rev. Charles Edward Stewart – 'A Suffolk Freeholder' as he signed himself – was a Tory pamphleteer of some repute in the 1790s and a committed opponent of two of the *Anti-Jacobin*'s special foes, the *Critical Review* and the *Monthly Review*, which latter periodical he attacked in his 1795 *Letter to Mr. Sheridan . . . To Which Is Added, A*

Short Answer to the Monthly Reviewers and his 1795 *Reply to the Monthly Reviewers.* Stewart was a product of both Oxford and Cambridge universities[2] and a recipient of several Church appointments, culminating in his presentation in 1807 to the rectory of Rede in Suffolk, which he held until his death.[3] His publications, in addition to those already cited, included political poems (*The Regicide*; *The Foxiad*; *Charles's Small-Clothes: a National Ode* [a satirical treatment of Charles James Fox]), several volumes of *Trifles in Verse*, and assorted patriotic addresses and sermons, of which his *Obedience to Government, Reverence to the Constitution, and Resistance to Bonaparte, A Sermon* is typical.[4]

Notes

1. Possible birth dates range from 1748 to 1751, depending on the source.
2. BA, Christ's College, Cambridge, 1771; MA, Magdalen College, Oxford, 1773 (*Alumni Cantab.*, pt 2, VI, 37). (The *Alumni Oxon.*, IV, 86, erroneously reports that he received his BA from St. John's College, Cambridge.)
3. Stewart's first parish was that of Courteenhall, Northants., where he was named rector in 1773. He was presented to the rectory of Wakes Colne, Essex, in 1795, and to that of Rede, Suffolk, in 1807, holding both until his death in 1819 (*Alumni Oxon.*, IV, 86; *Index Eccles.*, p. 166).
4. *BLGC*; *GM*, LXXXIX-2 (October 1819) 382.

TABARAUD, Mathieu-Mathurin (1744–1832) [*AJ*: 'l'Abbé Taboureau']

AJ contributions: IV, 570–80[?]; V, 153–62[with John Gifford].

Tabaraud, like Lachassagne (q.v.) and Montlosier (q.v.), was an *émigré* residing in London during the extremist phase of the French Revolution. A native of Limoges, he had been a leading spirit in the Congregation of the Oratory and an avid participant in religious controversy, especially with the rival Jesuit order. Tabaraud had for a number of years taught theology, Greek, Hebrew, and the humanities in several of the Congregation's houses before being appointed superior, first of the *Collège* of Pézénas (1783) and then of the *Collège* of La Rochelle (1787). He was serving as superior of the congregational house of Limoges when the French Revolution broke out.

Like many others in France in 1789 Tabaraud at first took a positive view of the Revolution, hoping for moderate and useful reforms in Church and State.[1] When however it became obvious that the leaders of the Constituent Assembly were intent on sweeping changes, Tabaraud turned against the revolution. His refusal to take the required oath to the newly enacted Civil Constitution of the Clergy,[2] coupled with his pamphlets defending the monarchy and attacking the Assembly's Church policy, rendered him suspect in the eyes of the radicals. Denounced before the Jacobin club of Paris, he took refuge in Rouen, whence he fled to England after the September Massacres.[3]

Tabaraud lived in exile in London for ten years, supporting himself by writing for the press. He supplied material for the *Oracle* and occasionally for the *Anti-Jacobin Review*,[4] and he was said to have edited the political section of *The Times*.[5] In addition he wrote a French translation of John Bowles's *Reflections submitted to the Consideration of the Combined Powers*, complete with his own introduction and notes.

Apparently Tabaraud was beginning to lean toward the Bonapartist camp during his last years in England.[6] In any event he lost no time in returning to France after Napoleon made his peace with the papacy in the Concordat of 1802. Although he served briefly as chief governmental censor during the Napoleonic regime (a position secured with the help of his old friend Fouché, the Minister of Police), Tabaraud devoted most of his remaining years to the writing of pamphlets on controversial religious issues. His works range from defences of Gallicanism and Jansenism to attacks upon the Jesuit order to disputatious analyses of Napoleon's divorce and the civil law of marriage.[7] A lover of argument and a man of a 'habitually warlike temperament',[8] as one memorialist put it, he died in 1832 amid predictable controversy, after tricking his pro-Jesuit confessor into giving him absolution in exchange for a largely meaningless recantation of his Jansenist principles.[9]

Notes

1. F., 'Tabaraud (Mathieu-Mathurin)', *Biographie des Hommes Vivants* (5 vols; Paris: L. G. Michaud, Imprimeur-Libraire, 1816–19) v, 421. The *Nouvelle Biographie Générale* offers some conflicting evidence on this point, claiming that at the beginning of the revolution Tabaraud's congregation in Limoges was divided on the question of reform, part of the house favouring the Church reforms being proposed by the Constituent Assembly, part (including Tabaraud) opposing any changes whatsoever (A. Taillandier, 'Tabaraud [Matthieu-Mathurin]', *Nouvelle Biographie Générale* (46 vols; Paris: Firmin Didot Frères, Éditeurs, 1853–66)

XLIV, 751). This statement would appear to be correct as a representation of Tabaraud's later opinion, after the first flush of optimism over the French Revolution had worn off.

2. The Civil Constitution of the Clergy (1790) provided among other things that the clergy were to be elected by the voters and salaried by the State. Although a substantial number of the lower clergy took the required oath to the Civil Constitution, many abjured their oaths when the document was officially condemned by the papacy. The debate over the Civil Constitution and the problem of non-juror clergy became a moot point after the Jacobins seized control of the Revolution and launched their de-Christianisation campaign in earnest.

3. Tabaraud's older brother, who was also a member of the clergy, was not so fortunate. He was killed by the Revolutionists while attempting to escape from France (Badiche, 'Tabaraud [Matthieu-Mathurin]', *Biographie Universelle, Ancienne et Moderne* [85 vols; Paris: Michaud Frères, Imprim.-Libraires, 1811–62] LXXXIII, 118n).

4. He wrote one or two articles in collaboration with John Gifford condemning the Jacobin government and the French wars of aggression.

5. Badiche, 'Tabaraud', p. 118; F., 'Tabaraud', p. 421.

6. Badiche, 'Tabaraud', p. 130.

7. Tabaraud also wrote articles for the *Biographie Universelle*. For lists of his publications see the above articles in the *Biographie des Hommes Vivants*, the *Nouvelle Biographie Générale*, and the *Biographie Universelle* (which is particularly useful for its analysis of Tabaraud's doctrinal works), plus the *BLGC* and the *Catalogue Général des Livres Imprimés de la Bibliothèque Nationale* (216 vols; Paris: Paul Catin, Éditeur, 1924–73).

8. Badiche, 'Tabaraud', p. 123.

9. Tabaraud, when required by the attending curé to abjure his Jansenist views and specifically his opinions on the sacrament of marriage, referred his confessor to a formal recantation supposedly contained in his will. The will, however, was later found to include only a very vague prayer for forgiveness in the event that any of his writings should have offended the Church.

TAYLOR, John (1757–1832)

AJ contributions: v, 304–8[with John Gifford], 435; vi, 100–3, 281–7, 381–6.

John Taylor was a journalist and writer of numerous incidental works for the theatre, including prologues and epilogues, occasional verses, theatrical addresses, and a dramatic tale entitled *Monsieur Tonson*.[1] Though he was originally intended to follow in the path of his father and grandfather[2] as Court oculist, Taylor's abilities as a verse maker, his desire for more rapid advancement, and above all his inordinate interest in the theatre led him to concentrate his energies instead upon a career in the press. As William Jerdan noted, Taylor's 'whole being was entranced upon the stage, in the theatre and theatrical doings and gossip, and in the actors and actresses, with nearly all of whom he lived in intimacy'.[3] To be sure, his list of friends, whose company he so enjoyed at the Turk's Head coffee-house and the Keep the Line club[4] and in the green-rooms of the London theatres, reads like the literary and theatrical *dramatis personae* of the age, including in its ranks Sarah Siddons, John Kemble, David Garrick, Sheridan, William Gifford, John Gifford, Peter Pindar, John Bowles, Boswell (whom he is said to have advised on last-minute corrections in the *Life of Johnson*), John Reeves, Henry James Pye, Horne Tooke, and Byron.

Taylor was connected, to varying degrees, with four newspapers during his fifty-odd years as a journalist. An early role in the conduct of the *Morning Herald*[5] gave place to a more significant involvement with the *Morning Post* in the 1780s. After serving the *Morning Post* as drama critic for two years, Taylor succeeded William Jackson as editor during the midst of the regency crisis, when the Carlton House faction purchased the *Morning Post* and appointed Taylor editor. According to one account Taylor was given the position 'in order that he might forward the cause of . . . [the Carlton House] clique at Court in return for a substantial bribe'.[6] In any case, in the resultant staff reorganisation aimed at converting the *Morning Post* into an Opposition mouthpiece, Taylor was dismissed. At about the same time, he entered the service of the government as a paid Treasury writer at the modest starting salary of £3 3s. per week.[7]

Taylor's later career as a journalist was centred around the Pittite wing of the press. He was associated for a time with the *True Briton* (first as drama critic, then as proprietor), after which time he sold his shares in the *True Briton* and bought part ownership in the *Sun*, succeeding William Jerdan as editor in 1817.[8] Taylor was a Tory in his politics and a useful acquisition for the Treasury's stable of salaried journalists and pamphleteers. In the assessment of Lucyle Werkmeister, 'he was loyal to the point of fanaticism: there was almost nothing he would not do for money'.[9] It is true that, as the *Oracle* reported on 17 July 1792, Taylor was once arrested and brought to trial for inciting Jacobin riots in Edinburgh, only to be acquitted on the grounds that he had been acting as a government *provocateur*.[10] It is also true that during the first half of 1794 Taylor operated as a government spy at LCS meetings and at John Thelwall's lectures, turning in more than sixty reports to the Home Office.[11] Probably, though, Taylor by and large wrote his political propaganda from his own personal convictions.[12] In his *Records of My Life* he declared himself 'not ashamed of my attachment to the political principles and judicious administration of the glorious William Pitt',[13] and additional passages in the same work and in his reviews in the *Anti-Jacobin* further attest to his sincere support of Pitt and abhorrence of Jacobinism and 'all the bloody horrors of the French revolution'.[14]

Notes

1. Taylor's other published works include *Verses on various occasions* (1795) and *Poems on several occasions: consisting of sonnets, miscellaneous pieces, prologues and epilogues, tales, imitations, etc.* (1811) (*BLGC*).
2. His grandfather was the so-called Chevalier John Taylor (1703–72) of European renown, who served as Court oculist to George II. Taylor's father (John Taylor, 1724–87) continued the Chevalier's profession and was appointed oculist to George III. The *Anti-Jacobin*'s John Taylor (1757–1832), third of the name, was named (with his brother Jeremiah) to succeed his father as Court oculist in 1790 but soon gave up the profession for journalism.
3. William Jerdan, *The Autobiography of William Jerdan* (4 vols; London: Arthur Hall, Virtue, 1852–3) II, 72.
4. Charlotte Fell-Smith, 'Taylor, John', *DNB*, XIX, 445.
5. Taylor was associated with the *Morning Herald* during the tenure of the Rev. Bate Dudley as editor ([Alexander Chalmers], *GM*, CII-2 [July 1832] 90).
6. H. R. Fox Bourne, *English Newspapers: Chapters in the History of Journalism* (2 vols; London: Chatto and Windus, 1887) I, 224. Taylor's own guarded and fuzzy version of the events indicates that Carlton House used Taylor as a go-between to secure the purchase of the newspaper, after the *Morning Post* began printing rumours of the Prince of Wales's marriage to Mrs Fitzherbert (John Taylor, *Records of My Life* [New York: J. and J. Harper, 1833] pp. 382–3). See also Lucyle Werkmeister, *The London Daily Press, 1772–1792* (Lincoln: University of Nebraska Press, 1963) pp. 99–104, for a detailed account of the incident.
7. A[rthur] Aspinall, *Politics and the Press, c. 1780–1850* (London: Home and Van Thal, 1949) p. 164 and n. 5; Werkmeister, *London Daily Press*, p. 343. See also the entry in the Secret Service accounts recording the payment on 17 May 1791 of £100 to Taylor (Chatham Papers [P.R.O. 30/8] vol. 229, pt 2, fol. 276a).
8. By 1817 Taylor was the majority stockholder in the *Sun* and in perpetual conflict with its editor, William Jerdan, who owned one share to Taylor's nine but would allow the latter no part in the conduct of the paper. That year Taylor succeeded at last in buying out Jerdan's share,

as well as his 900-year contract as editor, and the paper remained under Taylor's exclusive control until he sold it in 1825 (Joseph Farington, *The Farington Diary*, ed. James Greig [8 vols; London: Hutchinson, 1922–8] VIII, 121–2 [entries for 15 April and 18 April 1817]; Fell-Smith, 'Taylor', p. 445).

9. Lucyle Werkmeister, *A Newspaper History of England, 1792–1793* (Lincoln: University of Nebraska Press, 1967) p. 30.
10. Ibid., p. 102.
11. Clive Emsley, 'The Home Office and Its Sources of Information and Investigation, 1791–1801', *English Historical Review*, XCIV (July 1979) 548. Taylor was unmasked as a spy when he testified for the government at the treason trials of Robert Watt and David Downie in Edinburgh in September 1794 (see *State Trials*, XXIII, 1238, and XXIV, 24).
12. His reviewer in the *Gentleman's Magazine* concurs with this opinion ([James Boaden], *GM*, CII-2 [July 1832] 544).
13. Taylor, *Records of My Life*, p. 386.
14. Ibid., p. 406. See also pp. 78, 99, 356–8, 364, 387, and 451 in the same work and two notable reviews in the *Anti-Jacobin*, V (March 1800) 304–8, and VI (May 1800), 100–3.

THOMAS, Rev. George Andrew (1767–1804)

AJ contribution: II, 329–30.

George Andrew Thomas, rector of Wickham, Hants., submitted one contribution to the *Anti-Jacobin Review*, a signed letter in defence of the religious Establishment. Apart from his university achievements[1] and an impressive list of Church preferments,[2] little information exists concerning his short life. He is known to have edited the pulpit oratory of his uncle, Thomas, Bishop of Rochester, in addition to publishing several sermons of his own,[3] generally under the auspices of the Church-and-King firm of Rivingtons and chiefly concerning patriotic themes.[4]

Notes

1. Scholar, St John's College, Cambridge, 1785; BA, 1789; MA, 1793; LL D, 1803 (*Alumni Cantab.*, pt 2, VI, 152).
2. Thomas, who was ordained a deacon in 1789 and a priest in 1791, served as curate of Whinburgh, Norfolk, 1789–91; rector of Woolwich, Kent, 1791–1800; rector of Wickham, Hants., 1800–04; and rector of Deptford, Kent. He was made prebendary of Lichfield in 1797 (ibid.; *Index Eccles.*, p. 172).
3. *BLGC*; *AJ*, I (October 1798) 459–61; *AJ*, I (December 1798) 671–2; *AJ*, II (March 1799) 298–9; *GM*, LXXIV-2 (November 1804) 1074.

4. See, for example, his *Consequences of a French Invasion*, describing the over-running of Venice by the French Republic's 'worse than Gothic destroyers' and quoted in the *AJ*, ɪ (October 1798) 460.

VOLNEY, Constantin-François Chasseboeuf, Comte de (1757–1820)

AJ contributions: ɪɪ, 331–4, 443–6.

The French politician and historian Volney was only tangentially associated with the *Anti-Jacobin Review*. A Deist and a proponent of moderate political reforms, he had already earned the condemnation of the Church-and-King camp with his controversial *Les Ruines, ou Méditations sur les révolutions des empires* (1791), an essay on comparative religion and Utopian politics, combined with an attack upon priestcraft and the established orders.[1] Accordingly his 'contributions' to the *Anti-Jacobin Review* are only excerpts from one of his minor works, chosen for their uncomplimentary content.[2]

Volney (born Constantin-François Chasseboeuf[3]) was already a figure of considerable repute by the time the *Anti-Jacobin* undertook to reprint him. His first publication (an examination of Herodotus's system of chronology [1781]) had catapulted him into fame and given him an entrée to the *salons* of the *Philosophes*. His second major effort, a travel account of his romantic wanderings in Egypt and Syria, had won him a decoration from Catherine the Great.[4] With the coming of the French Revolution, Volney fixed his sights on politics, winning election as a delegate to the Third Estate from Anjou. From the start a dedicated reformer of the moderate stamp, he spoke in defence of popular sovereignty, urged a reduction of royal authority (especially in the power to make peace and war), and vigorously supported the seizure and sale of Church and royal lands.[5] Volney's moderation, though, made him suspect in the eyes of the Jacobins; and after their seizure of power in 1793, he was imprisoned during the Girondist purge and lived for ten months in constant danger of execution.

Released at the end of the Reign of Terror, Volney left prison and, after a brief term as professor of history in the newly organised national normal school, embarked for America. There he was warmly received by George Washington and roundly denounced by a fellow immigrant and religious dissident, Joseph Priestley, who, in a vicious attack upon Volney's *Les Ruines*, called the Frenchman among other things 'an atheist, an ignoramus, a Chinaman, and a Hottentot'.[6] Though Volney was rapidly becoming involved in more serious difficulties with the American government – he was accused of helping plot a French take-over of Louisiana – the savagery of Priestley's attack probably played a large part in Volney's decision to return to France. He left America in 1798 when war between that nation and France loomed likely, thoroughly disgusted with his attempt to find 'repose beyond the seas'.[7]

Volney returned to a France on the verge of the Bonapartist seizure of power. Feeling that the general would be preferable to anarchy,[8] he supported *faute de mieux* the *coup d'état* of Brumaire. He soon drifted into the anti-Bonapartist faction, however, and though he would receive numerous honours at the hand of Napoleon – a seat in the senate (1799), the appointment of commander of the Legion of Honour (1804), and the title of count (1808) – he remained a foe of Napoleon's absolutist policies throughout the regime. His last years were devoted mainly to literature, especially studies in ancient history and Oriental languages,[9] and he closed his career as a member of the Chamber of Peers under the restored monarchy.

Notes

1. Note that cheap excerpts from *Les Ruines* would later enjoy a wide circulation among British artisans in the nineteenth century (E. P. Thompson, *The Making of the English Working Class* [New York: Random House, 1963] pp. 98–9).
2. The excerpts the *Anti-Jacobin* reprinted were from Volney's published reply to Priestley. The *Anti-Jacobin* was quick to note that it was printing Volney's defence 'not from any concurrence with the opinions which it contains, but from the consideration that a controversy between an *infidel philosophist* [Volney], and an *Unitarian philosopher* [Priestley], has something novel and curious in it' (*AJ*, ii [March 1799] 331).
3. He acquired the title of Comte de Volney in 1808.
4. Volney prepared for his travels by a vigorous programme of exercise and by a stay of several months in a Coptic monastery in order to familiarise himself with Arabic.
5. 'Volney (C.-F. Chasseboeuf de)', *Biographie Moderne* (4 vols; 3rd edn; Leipzig: Paul-Jacques Besson, Libraire, 1807) iv, 478; *Annual Biography and Obituary*, v (1821) 461.
6. Quoted in Durozoir, 'Volney (Constantin-François Chasseboeuf, comte de)', *Biographie Universelle, Ancienne et Moderne* (85 vols; Paris: Michaud Frères, Imprim.-Libraires, 1811–62) xlix, 445.
7. *Annual Biography and Obituary*, v (1821) 463.
8. M. Avenel, 'Volney (Constantin-François Chasseboeuf, comte de)',

Nouvelle Biographie Générale (46 vols; Paris: Firmin Didot Frères, Éditeurs, 1853–66) XLVI, 350.

9. For lists of Volney's publications see the *Catalogue Général des Livres Imprimés de la Bibliothèque Nationale* (216 vols; Paris: Paul Catin, Éditeur, 1924–73) and the *BLGC*.

WALKER, James, Bishop of Edinburgh (1770?–1841)

AJ contributions: v, 568–80; vi, 343–9, 494–8, 562–76[?], 578–80.

James Walker, deacon and eventually bishop and primus of the Scottish Episcopal Church, was a short-term but fanatically zealous contributor to the *Anti-Jacobin Review*. His efforts for the cause of anti-Jacobinism grew out of a verbal duel in which he became embroiled as a young man with the German archaeologist Karl Augustus Boettiger (q.v.). At the time of their exchange of letters Walker, who had recently taken his degrees at Cambridge,[1] was employed as tutor to Sir John Hope and was travelling on the Continent as Hope's companion. During the course of his travels Walker spent considerable time in Weimar, where he studied metaphysics and acquired a horror of the moral and political principles of the German literati. When Boettiger's *New German Mercury* denounced Walker's friend John Robison (q.v.) and the Abbé Barruel for proposing that the literati and Illuminati were Jacobin conspirators, Walker was quick to leap to Robison's defense.

Walker's articles on 'The Literati and Literature of Germany' and his miscellaneous letters to the editor on the same subject must certainly rank among the most fanatical ever printed in the *Anti-Jacobin Review*. In part they were the product of an extreme form of literary chauvinism: Walker overflowed with anger at the current enthusiasm for German literature in England and the bare suggestion (made by certain misguided Britons and, of course, by Germans) that such 'foreign trash' was worthy of praise.[2] However, the more important consideration in Walker's mind was the danger that such works – Schiller's *Mary Stuart* for example – might corrupt the morals of uncritical British readers.[3] After noting the various methods whereby authors might seduce their readers, Walker concluded that it was 'by such means that men, like Voltaire, D'Alembert, Diderot, &c. under the amiable names of philosophy, moderation, progress of letters, and perfectionment of human nature, conceal . . . [their true aims] and, under the resemblance of virtue, indulge in themselves, and intice [*sic*] others into, every vice'.[4] Walker hesitated to go quite so far as Barruel and contend that the Illuminati were *all* Jacobins or that 'the writings and conduct of so many German scribblers and pretended philosophers, . . . [were] the effects of a formal conspiracy'. However, he concluded, 'so extensive and so uniformly dangerous' were their works that, premeditated or not, 'the consequences to the public must be the same'.[5]

In his later life Walker enjoyed a prestigious career in the Scottish Episcopal Church, rising from deacon (1793), to priest (1805), to bishop of Edinburgh and Pantonian Professor at the Episcopal Theological College in Edinburgh (1830–41), to primus of the Scottish Episcopal Church (1837–41), in which position he succeeded the retiring George Gleig, himself a fellow *Anti-Jacobin* contributor (q.v.). In addition he found time to serve as sub-editor (under Gleig) of the third edition of the *Encyclopaedia Britannica*, for which he wrote the article on Kant. He died in 1841 at about the age of seventy-one.[6]

Notes

1. BA, St. John's College, 1793; MA, 1796; DD, 1826 (*Alumni Cantab.*, pt 2, VI, 318).
2. *AJ*, v (Appendix to January–April 1800) 568.
3. Ibid.; *AJ*, VI (Appendix to May–August 1800) 498.
4. *AJ*, VI (Appendix to May–August 1800) 566.
5. Ibid., p. 575. Walker's interest in the Illuminati also led him to translate J. J. Mounier's treatise *On the Influence attributed to Philosophers, Freemasons, and to the Illuminati on the Revolution of France* (1801).
6. Brief summaries of Walker's life and publications are to be found in Edward Irving Carlyle, 'Walker, James', *DNB*, xx, 525; *GM*, n.s. xv (May 1841) 551; George Grub, *An Ecclesiastical History of Scotland, from the Introduction of Christianity to the Present Time* (4 vols; Edinburgh: Edmonston and Douglas, 1861) IV, 129, 180–1, 187–92, 245; and the *BLGC*.

WATSON, Rev. John James (1767–1839)

AJ contributions: I, 310–3; II, 63–71, 298–9; v, 464–6.

John James Watson, DD, archdeacon of St Albans, prebendary of St Paul's, rector of Hackney,[1] and sometime *Anti-Jacobin* reviewer, was a figure of considerable significance for the history of the Victorian Church. Educated at Charterhouse and University College, Oxford,[2] where he was a contemporary of the second Earl of Liverpool and made the acquaintance of a number of future Church leaders, Archdeacon Watson became one of the chief supporters of the early nineteenth-century High-Church party that would later figure prominently in the rise of the Oxford Movement.[3]

Together with his layman brother, Joshua Watson (1771–1855),[4] and his curate, Henry Handly Norris (1771–1850), Archdeacon Watson turned his rectory in Hackney into the centre of operations for the High-Church party, though his own health obliged him to turn over the actual direction of activities to Joshua Watson and Norris. The roster of members and allies of the 'Hackney Phalanx', as it came to be called, contained a remarkable number of prominent figures of the day – Archbishop Manners-Sutton; four colonial bishops (Middleton of Calcutta, Inglis of Nova Scotia, Broughton of Australasia, and Selwyn of New Zealand); William Van Mildert, bishop of Durham; William and Christopher Wordsworth; Charles Daubeny, archdeacon of Salisbury; Thomas Bowdler (nephew of the Thomas Bowdler who edited *The Family Shakespeare*); Robert Southey; Sir James Allan Park; and John Bowles (q.v.).[5] After 1811 the chief mouthpiece of the Phalanx became the *British Critic*, which Joshua Watson and Norris purchased in that year 'in order to restore it to its original lines as the organ of the high-church party, from which it had somewhat diverged'.[6]

The members of the Hackney Phalanx were uniformly members of the Pittite–Peelite mainstream of the Tory party and thus, while not reactionaries, were cautious of change and incontrovertibly opposed to Radicalism,[7] as John James Watson's reviews in the *Anti-Jacobin* clearly demonstrate. A friend of *Anti-Jacobin* contributors William Stevens and John Bowles and the former curate of Jonathan Boucher at Epsom, Archdeacon Watson shared his associates' anti-Jacobinical political views to the full. His reviews for the *Anti-Jacobin* followed the orthodox Tory line, denouncing the French Revolution, praising the vigilance of the Volunteer associations, opposing any proposals of parliamentary reform during times of civil unrest, and applauding all efforts 'to stem the torrent of anarchy and irreligion which still threatens the unresisting nations of Europe'.[8]

160 *The Anti-Jacobins*

Notes

1. Watson was also rector of Digswell, Herts. (*GM*, n.s. xii [July 1839] 209; *Index Eccles.*, p. 185).
2. BA, 1790; MA, 1793; BD and DD, 1808 (*Alumni Oxon.*, iv, 1511).
3. It should be noted that while John James Watson and his brother Joshua served as a link with the Oxford Movement, they did not entirely approve of the direction in which the Tractarians eventually led the Church (John Henry Overton, 'Watson, Joshua', *DNB*, xx, 930).
4. Joshua Watson, a wine merchant and the younger brother of John James Watson, was a devout churchman and committed Evangelical. He was a member of the Society for the Propagation of the Gospel and was joint treasurer of the Society for Promoting Christian Knowledge. He helped establish the National Society (for the education of the poor), the Additional Curates' Society, and the Church Room Society (later the Church Building Society), as well as serving as a royal commissioner for church building. He was treasurer of the Clergy Orphan School and secretary of the fund established for the relief of German victims of the Napoleonic Wars. He was the friend of a number of colonial bishops and was active in promoting missions, serving as a liaison between the missions and the Church societies at home. In 1828 he was one of the men instrumental in establishing King's College, London, as an orthodox Church of England alternative to the new and non-sectarian University of London. For full accounts of the activities of Joshua Watson see A[lan] B. Webster, *Joshua Watson: The Story of a Layman, 1771–1855* (London: S.P.C.K., 1954); Edward Churton (ed.), *Memoir of Joshua Watson* (2 vols; Oxford: J. H. and Jas. Parker, 1861); and Overton, 'Watson', pp. 928–30.
5. Webster, *Joshua Watson*, pp. 26–7, 34; Overton, 'Watson', pp. 928–9.
6. Overton, 'Watson', p. 929.
7. Webster, *Joshua Watson*, p. 23. Joshua Watson for one was so alarmed at the possible consequences of the 1832 Reform Act 'that . . . he invested money abroad in Louisiana shares, only to lose heavily ten years later when Louisiana stopped payment' (ibid.).
8. *AJ*, i (September 1798) 311.

WHITAKER, Rev. John (1735–1808)

AJ contributions: i, 693–6; iii, 16–23, 27–33, 181–5, 424–32; iv, 227–34, 369–74; v, 16–23, 132–7, 382–91; vi, 12–23, 33–45, 89–100, 121–32, 142–6, 241–9, 336–42, 361–70.

John Whitaker, clergyman, antiquarian, and author of *The History of Manchester*, was a frequent contributor to the *Anti-Jacobin*. Born in Manchester, the son of an innkeeper, and educated at Oxford,[1] Whitaker held a number of clerical appointments[2] culminating in the valuable rectory of Ruan Lanihorne, Cornwall, to which he was presented in 1777 by Corpus Christi College and where he remained, preaching, writing, and caring for his parish, until his death.[3] It was not as a cleric but as an antiquarian that Whitaker made his reputation, however, and he turned out a series of enthusiastic but factually shaky productions,[4] of which *The History of Manchester* is best known. Notwithstanding his scholarly deficiencies, he was duly elected to the Society of Antiquaries of London and of Scotland, and he regularly wrote the antiquarian reviews for the *British Critic*[5] from 1797 to 1801, 'when a refusal to admit his opinions on the subject of Ossian, caused a separation between [him and the editors]'.[6]

Whitaker was a man of intensely held feelings and explosive temperament, and his highly charged emotions frequently coloured his religious and political attitudes.[7] In his own parish Whitaker was a veritable lightning rod for controversy, alienating his parishioners to such a degree over his demands for tithes that the congregation lodged a complaint with his bishop. As his friend Polwhele (q.v.) reported of this occasion,

> On his own ground at Ruan Lanyhorne [*sic*], he . . . (literally) laid low the sturdiest of his parishioners, with the Squire at the head of them! And at a special sessions at Truro he . . . incurred the indignation of the Bench (who were on the point of committing him), by threatening, with a clenched fist an insolent antagonist.[8]

A political conservative and implacable foe of Dissenters,[9] he envisioned himself as a champion of Church and Constitution, locked in a life-or-death struggle with 'French anarchy and French Atheism'.[10] Whitaker's conservatism should not, however, be misconstrued as evidence that he was a political reactionary. While he regarded the French Revolution with horror, and while he hated Paine and opposed a regicide peace, Whitaker did not equate constructive change with revolution and did not reject the possibility of some repairs to the British Constitution in later, less-troubled times.[11] Certainly he did not envision himself as one disgruntled literary opponent did – 'half-cracked with ultra-loyalty'.[12]

As for Whitaker the man, no portrait would be complete without the sketch of him drawn by his old friend Polwhele:

Hard featured, with a dark complexion and with light-coloured eyes (rather greenish) in repose; but sparkling when kindled up in conversation, or flashing fire . . . or melting in tenderness . . . he had a strong muscular frame of body, that well answered to his powerful mind. That he had an eye of glass and teeth of ebony, was the common report. I can vouch for a squint at least in one eye; and I am sure he used false teeth, 'upon occasions' as we say. When attiring himself for company, he would take from a little case (which he was not shy in shewing to his friends) a sett [*sic*] of dusky teeth – which he called ebony. To a young lady, who asked him, why he preferred ebony to ivory, he once jocularly said: 'ivory would ill suit the gravity of an antiquary!'[13]

Notes

1. After entering Brasenose College, Oxford, as a school exhibitionist, he migrated to Corpus Christi College, where he proceeded scholar, BA, MA, fellow, and BD in rapid order (*Alumni Oxon.*, IV, 1536).
2. The details of Whitaker's ecclesiastical career are sketchy. He is known to have served as curate first of Newton Heath chapel near Manchester and then of Bray in Berkshire. For a brief four months during the winter of 1773–4 he held the morning preachership at Berkeley chapel in London, leaving as a result of a dispute with his patron. Otherwise nothing is known of his ecclesiastical career until his presentation to Ruan Lanihorne in 1777.
3. Though Whitaker acquired a lively enthusiasm for the history and antiquities of Cornwall, he never lost his interest in Manchester. In 1777, the year of his departure to Ruan Lanihorne, he helped raise a Manchester regiment intended for service in America; and in 1787 'in a contest . . . between the lord of the manor of Manchester and the inhabitants, [he] . . . was singularly instrumental in the assertion of the rights of the town against the assumed powers of the lord' (Edward Baines, *The History of the County Palatine and Duchy of Lancaster*, ed. John Harland [2 vols; rev. edn; London: George Routledge, 1868–70] I, 411). Whitaker never managed to attain one goal, however – the wardenship of Manchester College. (James Crossley [ed.], *The Diary and Correspondence of Dr. John Worthington*, II, pt 1, Chetham Society, Remains, XXXVI [n.p.: Chetham Society, 1855] 237, n. 1. See also Whitaker's obsequious letter of 1 January 1794 to Pitt asking for the post [Chatham Papers (P.R.O. 30/8), vol. 189, fols 18–19].)
4. Among his publications were *The genuine history of the Britons asserted, in a . . . refutation of Mr. Macpherson's Introduction to the History of Great Britain and Ireland* (1772), *The Course of Hannibal over the Alps ascertained* (1794), various writings on Cornish history, and *The Life of St. Neot*, on which he was at work when he died. He was, in Cyrus Redding's opinion, 'one of those writers of the old school, who would indite a whole volume upon a topic which any body else to do would have

required some actual knowledge of localities' (Cyrus Redding, *Yesterday and To-day* [3 vols; London: T. Cautley Newby, 1863] I, 74). Even his *History of Manchester* was roundly attacked by his contemporaries as being more imagination than fact, a lovingly written pseudo-history that was, as an unappreciative Samuel Johnson put it, 'all a dream ' (James Boswell, *The Life of Samuel Johnson, LL.D.*, ed. John Wilson Croker [5 vols; London: John Murray, 1831] IV, 194).

5. In addition to the *Anti-Jacobin* and the *British Critic* Whitaker also supplied contributions to the *English Review*.

6. Robert Nares, letter to Richard Polwhele, quoted in R[ichard] Polwhele, *Biographical Sketches in Cornwall* (3 vols; Truro: printed by W. Polyblank, 1831) III, 68, n. 2.

7. See John Britton's comment that to Whitaker 'a sentiment, a liberal or approving term of any political or religious person, or subject, not in unison with those of the reviewer, were pronounced to be Jacobinical, and consequently vile and bad' (John Britton, *The Autobiography of John Britton* [2 vols; London: printed for the author, 1849–50] I, 216).

8. R[ichard] Polwhele, *Traditions and Recollections; Domestic, Clerical, and Literary* (2 vols; London: John Nichols and Son, 1826) I, 159n.

9. Though he abhorred Dissenters of other varieties, Whitaker disapproved of Polwhele's attack upon the Methodists (John Whitaker, letters to Samuel Drew, 29 May 1800, and 25 August 1800, quoted in Jacob Halls Drew, *The Life, Character, and Literary Labours of Samuel Drew, A.M.* [New York: Harper, 1835] pp. 94, 96–7).

10. John Whitaker, letter to Richard Polwhele, 14 November 1794, in Polwhele, *Biographical Sketches*, III, 95.

11. John Whitaker, letter to Sir Christopher Hawkins, 6 January 1793, *quoted in* R[ichard] Polwhele, *Reminiscences, in Prose and Verse* (3 vols in 1; London: J. B. Nichols and Son, 1836) I, 84.

12. Richard Warner, *Literary Recollections* (2 vols; London: Longman, Rees, Orme, Brown, and Green, 1830) II, 127.

13. Polwhele, *Biographical Sketches*, III, 69–70.

WHITE, Rev. R.

AJ contribution: III, 63–72.

Positive identification of the 'Rev. R. White', as the British Library staff copy styles him, has proven impossible. He may have been Richard White of Emmanuel College, Cambridge,[1] a native of Essex, vicar of Shalford, Essex, from 1810 to 1840 and rector of Alkerton, Oxon., from 1821 to 1835.[2] White submitted one contribution to the *Anti-Jacobin*, a letter to the editor signed 'Scrutator' and consisting of a running criticism of the *Monthly Review* of February 1799, peppered with oblique denunciations of Godwin, Thomas Paine, the French Jacobins, and Bonaparte.

Notes

1. Admitted pensioner, 1778; BA, 1783; MA, 1787.
2. *Alumni Cantab.*, pt 2, VI, 439; *Index Eccles.*, p. 188; *GM*, LXXX-1 [May 1810] 483. A second possibility is the Rev. Richard Walton White, MA, rector (in order) of Wootton, Isle of Wight (1808); of Marksbury, Somerset (1816); of Up Cerne, Dorset (1828); and of Marksbury once again (1828) (*Index Eccles.*, p. 188).

WILLICH, Anthony Florian Madinger (d. 1804)

AJ contributions: II, 530–7[?]; IV, 512–33[?]; V, 502–13.

According to John Nichols, virtually the sole source of information on Willich, the latter was an 'eminent German physician' who practiced medicine in London for a time and 'died at Charkof, in Russia, in 1804, shortly after his arrival. He had been appointed professor of physic there'.[1] It is clear that he had also resided for a time in Edinburgh, for he tutored Walter Scott and several of Scott's friends in German there.[2] Willich co-edited (with T. Bradley) the *Medical and Physical Journal* (*Physisch-Medicinisches Journal nach Bradley und Willich für Deutschland*), established 1799; translated Adelung's *Three philological Essays* (1798) and Struve's *Treatise on the Education of Children*; and published in his own right *The Domestic Encyclopaedia, or, a dictionary of facts and useful knowledge* (1802), *Lectures on diet and regimen* (1799), and *Elements of the Critical Philosophy: containing a concise account of its origin and tendency; a view of all the works published by its founder, I. Kant, and a glossary for the explanation of terms and phrases* (1798). He wrote one review for the *Anti-Jacobin*, a multipart critique of P. S. Pallas's *Remarks on a Journey to the Southern Provinces of the Russian Empire*. Willich's private secretary was Francis William Blagdon, a fellow reviewer for the *Anti-Jacobin* (q.v.).[3]

Notes

1. John Nichols, *Illustrations of the Literary History of the Eighteenth Century* (8 vols; London: printed for the author, 1817–58) VIII, 333 and n. Cf. *GM*, LXXIV-2 (July 1804) 690, and *The Times*, 26 May 1804, p. 2.
2. Edgar Johnson, *Sir Walter Scott: The Great Unknown* (New York: Macmillan, 1970) I, 96.
3. *GM*, LXXXIX-2 (July 1819) 88.

Anti-Jacobin Review and Magazine, vols I–VI

(*Note*: 'NA' signifies no attribution in British Library copy.)

Volume I, July 1798

'Prefatory Address to the Reader', i–viii.   John Gifford.
'Prospectus', 1–6.   John Gifford.
'*The Republican Judge . . .*', 7–17.   John Gifford.
'*Thoughts on Mr. Fox's Secession . . .*', 17–21.   John Gifford.
'*Letter of Thomas Paine . . .*', 21–5.   John Gifford.
'*Considerations upon . . . Public Affairs . . .*', 25–33.   John Bowles.
'*The Crisis . . .* [by Maurice]', 34–7.   John Gifford.
'*An Answer to . . . Henry Grattan . . .*', 37–41.   Donald Grant.
'*A Journal of the Occurrences at the Temple . . .*', 42–51.   John Gifford.
'*Knave or Not . . .*', 51–4.   Robert Bisset.
Prefatory remarks, 55.   NA.
'To the Editor . . .', 56–62.   John Brand.
Headnote to '*Letters of the Ghost of Alfred . . .*', 62.   NA.
'*Letters of the Ghost of Alfred . . .*', 62–72.   Jonathan Boucher.
'*A Reply to . . . the Bishop of Landaff's* [sic] *Address . . .*', 72–8.   John
    Gifford.
'*An Answer to an Address . . . by the Bishop of Landaff* [sic] *. . .*',
    78–82.   John Gifford.
'*An Examination of Mr. Wakefield's Reply . . .*', 83–91.   John Gifford.
'*Maria, or the Wrongs of Woman . . .*', 91–3.   Robert Bisset.
'*Memoirs of the Author of the Vindication of the Rights of Woman . . .*',
    94–102.   Robert Bisset.
Headnote to monthly list of publications, 103.   NA.
'The Anti-Gallican', 107–8.   John Gifford.
'The Rise, Progress, Operations, and Effects of Jacobinism in these
    Realms', 109–11.   Robert Bisset.
'To the Editor . . .', 112.   John Bowles.
'Fragment, from a work published in 1755', 113.   NA.
'The Theatre', 114.   John Gifford.

'Explanation of the . . . Print ["New Morality"]', 115–16.   John
   Gifford.
'The Progress of Liberty . . .', 116.   Anonymous.
'A Congratulatory Ode . . .', 117.   Anonymous.
'The United Irishman . . .', 117–18.   NA.
'Summary of Politics Foreign and Domestic', 119–31.   John Gifford.
'To Correspondents', 131.   John Gifford.
'Deaths', 132.   NA.

Volume I, August 1798

'*Considerations upon . . . Public Affairs . . .*', 133–40.   John Bowles.
'*Letter of Thomas Paine . . .*', 140–6.   John Gifford.
'*Copies of Original Letters . . . to Dr. Priestley . . .*', 146–51.   John
   Gifford.
'*A Letter to Sir John Scott . . .*', 151–7.   John Gifford.
'*The Causes of the Rebellion in Ireland . . .*', 158–60.   John Gifford.
'*Walsingham . . .*', 160–4.   Robert Bisset.
'Prefatory Observations on Reviewers . . .', 165–71.   John Brand.
'*Tableau Historique et Politique . . .*', 171–6.   John Gifford.
'*Edmund Oliver . . .*', 176–80.   Robert Bisset.
'*Address from Camille Jordan . . .*', 180–3.   Robert Bisset.
'*A short Address to the . . . Loyal Associations . . .*', 183–6.   Robert
   Bisset.
'*The Young Philosopher . . .*', 187–90.   Robert Bisset.
'*A Chapter to the English Multitude . . .*', 190–1.   John Gifford.
'*Arminius . . .*', 191–3.   Robert Bisset.
'*Reform or Ruin . . .*', 193–5.   Robert Bisset.
'*Sound an Alarm . . .*', 196–7.   Robert Bisset.
'Copies of Original Letters, &c', 197–8.   John Gifford.
'Detection of the *Monthly Magazine*', 198–201.   John Gifford.
'Monthly List of Publications . . .', 202–3.   NA.
Prefatory material on the *Courier*, Earl Moira, and the Duke of
   Portland, 203–7.   John Gifford.
'The Queen of France', 207–8.   John Gifford.
'Madame Liebaud du Fief', 209.   John Gifford.
'On the Volunteer Corps, 210–11.   Henry James Pye.
'Political Anecdotes', 211–12.   John Gifford.
'To the Editor', 212–13.   Anonymous.

'To the Editor', 213–17.   Anonymous. [The author describes herself as 'the daughter of a country gentleman of considerable fortune' (p. 213). However, it appears that the whole account is fiction, possibly written by a man.]
'The Illuminati', 217–20.   Anonymous article 'extracted from a German publication' (p. 217). ['The paper which we now present to our readers has been in our possession upwards of two years. . . . It was brought over to this country by an *illustrious personage*, who has been an object of proscription and persecution to the general plunderers of Europe' (p. 217). British Library copy notes that the article was 'sent by Mr Luke Gilbert Franklyn Esq.' from the Stadtholder'.]
'To the Editor . . .', 220–1.   Anonymous.
'American Buildings', 222–3.   NA. ['Extracted from an American publication, printed at Philadelphia' (p. 222).]
'The Rise, Progress, and Effects of Jacobinism', 223–7.   Robert Bisset.
'The Wanderings of Iapis . . .', 228–32.   NA.
'To the Editor . . .', 233.   NA.
'An Address to a Premier Peer . . .', 233–4.   Anonymous.
'A Jacobin Council', 235.   William Thomas Fitzgerald.
'Lines . . .', 236.   Anonymous.
'The Ages of Reason', 236–7.   Anonymous.
'Epistle to Nathaniel Lister . . . by Miss Anna Seward . . .', 237–9. [Prefatory note states that 'the following little poem is extracted from the first Volume of the Rev. S[tebbing] Shaw's folio History of Staffordshire'.]
'Summary of Politics Foreign and Domestic', 240–6.   John Gifford.
'Jacobin Prints', 247–8.   Robert Bisset.
'*False and True* . . .', 248–9.   Robert Bisset.
'Marriages, Births, Deaths, &c', 249–51.   NA.
'To Correspondents', 252.   NA.

Volume I, September 1798

'*Aristotle's Ethics and Politics* . . .', 253–63.   Robert Bisset.
'*Considerations upon . . . public Affairs* . . .', 263–8.   John Bowles.
'*Fragmens sur Paris* . . .', 268–80.   François-Dominique de Reynaud, Comte de Montlosier.
'*Remonstrance* . . .', 280–4.   John Gifford.

'*Evidence to Character* . . .', 284–92.   John Gifford.
'*Report from the Committee of Secrecy of the House of Commons* . . .',
    292–6.   John Gifford.
'*Report from the Committee of Secrecy of the House of Lords* . . .',
    297–300.   John Gifford.
'*Strictures on the late Motions of the Duke of Leinster* . . .', 300–2.   John
    Gifford.
'*The Warning* . . .', 303.   John Gifford.
'*The Duty of Loving our Country* . . .', 303–5.   Jonathan Boucher.
'*A Sermon* . . . *on the General Fast* . . .', 306.   Jonathan Boucher.
'*On the present Crisis of Affairs* . . .', 306–8.   Jonathan Boucher.
'*A Sermon* [by Richard Munkhouse] . . .', 308–9.   John Gifford.
'*A Charge* . . . *to the Clergy of* . . . *Landaff* [sic] . . .', 310–13.   John
    James Watson.
'Prefactory Observations on Reviewers', 314–24.   John Brand[?]
    ['Rev. J. B.'; probably John Brand, who did the prefatory remarks
    to the *Reviewers Reviewed* section in the October 1798 number.]
'*The Spirit of the Public Journals* . . .', 324–31.   John Gifford.
'*An Examination of* . . . *Godwin's* . . . *Political Justice* . . .', 331–
    6.   Robert Bisset.
'*The Question as it stood in March 1798* . . .', 336–41.   John Gifford.
'*The Constitution of a perfect Commonwealth* . . .', 341.   John Gifford.
'*A Bone to gnaw for the Democrats* . . . ; *A Rod for the Backs of the
    Critics* . . .', 342–9 [?].   [British Library copy attributes this review
    to John Gifford. It would, however, have been very unlikely for
    Gifford to have reviewed his own work (*A Rod for the Backs of the
    Critics*).]
'The Suffolk Freeholder . . .', 350–1.   John Gifford.
'To the Editor . . . [signed "A Sussex Freeholder"]', 351–
    2.   Charles Edward Stewart ['Sussex' is a misprint for 'Suffolk'].
'Monthly List of Publications . . .', 352–4.   NA.
'Counsellor Ego', 355.   John Gifford.
'The Quakers' Loyalty . . .', 356–9.   Samuel Henshall.
'The Rise, Progress, and Effects of Jacobinism', 359–62.   Robert
    Bisset.
'A Medicine for the Times . . .', 362–3.   John Gifford. [Gifford's
    name is listed for the introduction of this selection in the British
    Library copy. Apparently the name is meant to apply to the entire
    selection.]
'The Political Fantoccini . . .', 364.   Anonymous.
'The Anarchists. – An Ode', 365–7.   Anonymous.

'Summary of Politics Foreign and Domestic', 368–76.   John Gifford.
'Jacobin Prints, Speeches, &c.', 376–9.   John Gifford (p. 376) and
    Samuel Henshall (pp. 377–9).
'Correspondence', 380.   Anonymous.
'Answers to Correspondents', 380.   NA.

Volume I, October 1798

'*The Saxon and English Languages* . . .', 381–7.   John Reeves.
'Dr. Gillies's Translation of Aristotle', 387–98.   Robert Bisset.
'*A Letter to the Church of England* . . .', 398–402.   Samuel Henshall.
'*Mercure Britannique* . . .', 403–9.   John Gifford.
'*A Letter to the Bishop of Salisbury* . . .', 409–15.   Francis Randolph.
'*Cambro-Britons* . . .', 415–17.   Robert Bisset.
'*Derwent Priory* . . .', 417–18.   Robert Bisset.
'*Laura* . . .', 418–20.   Robert Bisset.
'*A Narrative of the Sufferings and Escape of Charles Jackson* . . .',
    420–1.   Robert Bisset.
'*Speech of R. Goodloe Harper* . . .', 421–3.   Robert Bisset.
'*An Account of the late Insurrection* . . .', 424–6.   John Gifford.
'*A Sermon* [by the Rev. L. H. Halloran] . . .', 426–8.   Samuel
    Henshall.
'*A Sermon* [by Ralph Churton] . . .', 428–31.   Samuel Henshall.
'*A Discourse* [by Richard Munkhouse] . . .', 431–2.   Samuel
    Henshall.
'*A Sermon* [by George Smith] . . .', 432–4.   Samuel Henshall.
'Prefatory Observations on Reviewers', 434–44.   John Brand.

*(Remainder of the October 1798 number missing from the British Library
copy.)*

*'Porcupiniana; or, Scraps from *Porcupine's Gazette*', 479.   William
    Cobbett. [Article consists of an excerpt from Cobbett's American
    periodical, *Porcupine's Gazette*, prefixed by an introductory note
    from one 'Adolescens'.]
*'Summary of Politics Domestic and Foreign', 483–95.   John
    Gifford[?] [entire series is by John Gifford].
*'Jacobin Prints, Speeches, &c. [Cont.]', 496–9.   John Gifford
    and/or Samuel Henshall[?][*v. AJ*, I, 376–9].

Volume I, November 1798

(*Entire November 1798 number missing from the British Library copy.*)

*'M. Mallet du Pan's historical Essay . . .', 501–15. John Gifford[?][*v. AJ*, I, 403–9].

*'Dr. Gillies's Translation of Aristotle', 515–23. Robert Bisset[?] [*v. AJ*, I, 387–98].

*'A Letter to the Church of England . . .', 524–9. Samuel Henshall[?][*v. AJ*, I, 398–402].

*'Oratio Anniversaria . . .', 561–5. W. Henshall[?][*v. AJ*, IV, 184–9].

*'Detection of the *Monthly Magazine*', 569–74. John Gifford[?][*v. AJ*, I, 198–201].

*'Henshall to some Writers in the Gentleman's Magazine, and the Analytical Review', 579–88. Samuel Henshall [signed letter].

*'Dr. Bisset's Reply . . .', 588–91. Robert Bisset [signed letter].

*'Porcupiniana; or, Scraps from *Porcupine's Gazette*', 591–3. William Cobbett [entire article is an excerpt from *Porcupine's Gazette*].

*'To Lady Nelson . . .', 598. Charles Edward Stewart [signed letter].

*'Summary of Politics, Foreign and Domestic', 605–11. John Gifford[?][entire series is by John Gifford].

*'To the Editor . . . [signed "Oxoniensis"]', 612. Joshua Cooke[?][Cooke used this signature in *AJ*, v, 457–9].

Volume I, December 1798

(*Entire December 1798 number missing from the British Library copy.*)

*'A View of the Causes and Consequences of English Wars . . .', 613–20. Jonathan Boucher[?][*v. AJ*, II, 3–10].

*'British public Characters of 1798 . . .', 634–6. Robert Bisset[?][*v. AJ*, II, 57–63].

*'ΕΠΕΑ ΠΤΕΡΟΕΝΤΑ, or the Diversions of Purley . . .', 655–63. Samuel Henshall[?][*v. AJ*, II, 37–41; III, 9–16].

*'View of the Causes and Consequences of the American Revolution . . .', 674–8. John Bowles[?][*v. AJ*, II, 83–90].

*'A Second Letter to the Hon. Thomas Erskine . . .', 678–82. Samuel Henshall[?][*v. AJ*, II, 209–12].

*'*Arthur Fitz-Albini* . . .', 683–5. Samuel Henshall[?][*v. AJ*, II, 79–83].

*'*Vaurien* . . .', 685–90. Robert Bisset[?][*v. AJ*, III, 196].

*'*An Oblique View of the Grand Conspiracy against Social Order* . . .', 691–2. John Gifford[?][*v. AJ*, II, 75–9, 203–9].

*'Reflections suggested by the present State of Europe', 693–6. John Whitaker [review attributed to Whitaker in the *Palatine Note-book*, I, 80].

*'Detection of the Quakers', 709–12. Samuel Henshall[?][*v. AJ*, I, 356–9].

*'The Rise, Progress, and Effects of Jacobinism', 712–18. Robert Bisset[?][entire series is by Bisset].

*'Peter Porcupine's Will', 725–8. William Cobbett [entire article is an excerpt from *Porcupine's Gazette*].

*'Henshall's Reply', 729–33. Samuel Henshall [signed letter].

*'Summary of Politics, Foreign and Domestic', 734–9. John Gifford[?][entire series is by John Gifford].

Volume I, Appendix

(*Entire appendix missing from the British Library copy.*)

Volume II, January 1799

'Preface', i–iv. NA.

'*An Abridgement of Cases* . . .', 1–3. John Reeves.

'Robinson's *View of the Causes* . . .', 3–10. Jonathan Boucher.

'*The Retrospect* . . .', 10–17. John Gifford.

'*Eight Sermons* . . .', 17–22. Samuel Henshall.

'*Report of the Committee of the House of Commons* . . .', 22–6. John Gifford.

'*State of the Country* . . .', 26–8. John Gifford.

'*A Short Account of the Principal Proceedings of Congress* . . .', 29–32. John Gifford.

'*A Day at Rome* . . .', 32. John Gifford.

'*History of Great Britain* . . .', 32–7. Samuel Henshall.

'Tooke's *Diversions of Purley*', 37–41. Samuel Henshall.

'*An Address to the People* . . .', 42–9. John Gifford.

'*Travels through* . . . *North America* . . .', 49–53. Samuel Henshall.

'*Substance of Mr. Canning's Speech* . . .', 54–6.   John Gifford.
'*Ode to Lord Nelson* . . .', 56–7.   John Gifford.
'*British Public Characters*', 57–63.   Robert Bisset.
'*A Sermon* [by George Henry Glasse] . . .', 63–7.   John James Watson.
'*A View of* . . . *Public Fasts* . . .', 67–8.   John James Watson.
'*Ignorance productive of Atheism* . . .', 68–71.   John James Watson.
'*Remarks on the Conduct of Opposition* . . .', 71–5.   Robert Bisset.
'*An Oblique View of the Grand Conspiracy* . . .', 75–9.   John Gifford.
'*Arthur Fitz-Albini* . . .', 79–83.   Samuel Henshall.
'Boucher's *View of the Causes and Consequences* . . .', 83–90.   John Bowles.
'Tithes', 90–7.   John Gifford (pp. 90–1) and John Kennedy (pp. 91–7).
'An Attempt to Justify the Conduct of the Dissenters', 97–100.   John Gifford (introductory paragraph, p. 97) and Samuel Greatheed (pp. 97–100).
'To the Editor . . .', 100–1.   J. Mavor.
'Defence of the Quakers', 102–4.   NA. [Article consists of remarks written by one 'Examiner' in December 1798 and supplied to the *Anti-Jacobin*.]
'Summary of Politics, Foreign and Domestic', 104–12.   John Gifford[?][NA. Article undoubtedly written by John Gifford, who is listed as the author of all but one – also unattributed – of the other articles in the 'Summary of Politics' series.]

Volume II, February 1799

'*The History of Scotland* . . .', 113–22.   Robert Bisset.
'*The History* . . . *of Winchester* . . .', 122–8.   Samuel Henshall.
'Bowles's *Retrospect* . . .', 128–33.   John Gifford.
'*History of Sir George Warrington* . . .', 133–6.   Robert Bisset.
'*The Vagabond* . . .', 137–40.   Robert Bisset.
'*A Discourse on the* . . . *Law of Nature and Nations* . . .', 140–6.   Robert Bisset.
'*A Collection of Trifles in Verse* . . .', 146–9.   John Gifford.
'*Critical Trifles* . . .', 149–51.   John Gifford.
'*The Battle of the Nile* . . .', 151–5.   John Gifford.
'*A Sermon* [by Colin Milne] . . .', 155–6.   Robert Bisset.
'*A Sermon* [by John Farrer] . . .', 157–8.   Jonathan Boucher.

'*The Favour of God the only Security* . . .', 159–60.   Jonathan Boucher.
'*The Probability* . . . *of an Union.* . . . By . . . Dennis Taaffe . . .', 160–2.   John Gifford.
'The Second Part of Taaffe's Reflections . . .', 163–5.   John Gifford.
'*An Union neither necessary or (nor) expedient for Ireland* . . .', 165–8.   John Gifford.
'*Strictures on a Pamphlet* . . .', 168–9.   John Gifford.
'*An Union to be Subjection* . . .', 169–70.   John Gifford.
'*Observations on a Pamphlet* . . .', 170.   John Gifford.
'*An Answer to the Pamphlet, entitled, Arguments for and against an Union* . . .', 171–3.   John Gifford.
'*An Address to the People of Ireland* . . .', 174–5.   John Gifford.
'*An Answer to some of the many Arguments* . . .', 175–6.   John Gifford.
'*A Memoire* . . . *respecting the* . . . *Union* . . .', 176–9.   John Gifford.
'*A Letter to Theobald M'Kenna* . . .', 180–2.   John Gifford.
'*Impartial Remarks on the Subject of an Union* . . .', 182.   John Gifford.
'*To be or not to be, a Nation?* . . .', 183.   John Gifford.
'*A Letter addressed to the Gentlemen of England and Ireland* . . .', 183–6.   John Gifford.
'*An Argument for Independence* . . .', 186–8.   John Gifford.
'*Some Observations on the* . . . *Union* . . .', 189–90.   John Gifford.
'*Reasons against an Union* . . .', 190.   John Gifford.
'*Ireland Sabinized* . . .', 190.   John Gifford[?][NA. Undoubtedly written by John Gifford, who reviewed all the other publications on the Union.]
'*Strictures on an Union* . . .', 191.   John Gifford.
'*Letter to Joshua Spencer* . . .', 191–3.   John Gifford.
'*A Loyal Subject's Thoughts on an Union* . . .', 193–4.   John Gifford.
'*The probable Consequences of an Union* . . .', 194.   John Gifford.
'*Verbum Sapienti* . . .', 194.   John Gifford.
'*Letter from a Retired Barrister* . . .', 195.   John Gifford.
'*Union or not?* . . .', 195–7.   John Gifford.
'*A Few Thoughts on an Union* . . .', 197.   John Gifford.
'*Ireland profiting by Example* . . .', 197–9.   John Gifford.
'*Reasons for adopting an Union* . . .', 199–203.   John Gifford.
'*An Oblique View of the Grand Conspiracy* . . .', 203–9.   John Gifford.
'Gifford's *Second Letter to Erskine, &c.*', 209–12.   Samuel Henshall.
Editorial paragraph appended to the end of the Reviewers Reviewed section (beginning 'The great length . . .') 213.   NA.
'Description [of the Nelsonian medal]', 213–14.   W[illiam?] Bridges.

'To the Editor . . .', 214–15.   David Rivers [signed letter].
'To the Editor . . . [signed "X."]'. 215–17.   Anonymous.
'To the Editor . . . [signed "G."]', 217–19.   Samuel Greatheed.
'Essay on the Use of Polysyllables . . .', 219–21.   George Henry
  Glasse.
'To James Mackintosh, Esq.', 222–4.   John Bowles.
'To the Editor . . . [signed "Strafford"]', 224–6.   John Reeves.
'Summary of Politics, Foreign and Domestic', 227–31.   John
  Gifford.
'Correspondence', 231–2.   NA.

Volume II, March 1799

'*Essays on . . . Ireland . . .*', 233–41.   John Gifford.
'Weld's *Travels through North America*', 241–7.   Samuel Henshall.
'Milner's *History of Winchester*', 247–51.   Samuel Henshall.
'*Proceedings of the Association for promoting the Discovery of . . .
  Africa . . .*', 252–7.   Robert Bisset.
'*Memoirs of the Kings of Great Britain . . .*', 257–62.   Samuel
  Henshall.
'Pinkerton's *History of Scotland*', 262–7.   Robert Bisset.
'*The Art of floating Land . . .*', 267–72.   Samuel Henshall.
'*The Nurse . . .*', 272–5.   John Gifford.
'Mackintosh on the *Law of Nature and Nations*', 275–80.   Robert
  Bisset.
'*The Shade of Alexander Pope . . .*', 280–5.   John Gifford.
'*The Patriot . . .*', 286.   John Gifford.
'*The Irish Boy . . .*', 286–7.   John Gifford.
'*The Equality of Mankind . . .*', 287–9.   Jonathan Boucher.
'*The Present State of Ireland . . .*', 289–91.   John Gifford.
'*The Consequences of the proposed Union . . .*', 291.   John Gifford.
'*Necessity of an Incorporate Union . . .*', 292–3.   John Gifford.
'*Thoughts on an Union . . .*', 293–4.   John Gifford.
'*Letters on the Subject of Union . . .*', 294–7.   John Gifford.
'*Christian Patriotism . . .*', 297–8.   Jonathan Boucher.
'*A Sermon* [by G. A. Thomas] . . .', 298–9.   John James Watson.
'*The Excellency of the Church of England . . .*', 299.   John James
  Watson.
'*A Sermon* [by John Woodrow] . . .', 299–300.   Jonathan Boucher.

(*Remainder of the March 1799 number missing from the British Library copy.*)

*'The Beauties of the Anti-Jacobin, or Weekly Examiner . . .', 302–4. John Gifford[?][*v. AJ*, iii, 192–4].

*'To the Editor . . .', 326–7. Robert Farren Cheetham [signed letter].

*'To the Editor . . .', 329–30. George Andrew Thomas [signed letter].

*'Volney's Answer to Dr. Priestley', 331–4. Constantin-François Chasseboeuf, Comte de Volney [the article is a signed contribution by Volney].

*'To the Editor . . .', 337–9. G. Hewit [signed letter].

*'Henshall's Reply', 339–44. Samuel Henshall [signed letter].

*'Summary of Politics, Foreign and Domestic', 344–52. John Gifford[?][entire series is by John Gifford].

Volume II, April 1799

(*Entire April 1799 number missing from the British Library copy.*)

*'The History of Great Britain, during the Reign of Queen Anne . . .', 353–61. Robert Bisset[?][*v. AJ*, iii, 33–7; iv, 49–58].

*'A Voyage of Discovery . . .', 372–80. Robert Bisset[?][*v. AJ*, iii, 138–43].

*'Mackintosh on the *Law of Nature and Nations*', 388–93. Robert Bisset[?][*v. AJ*, ii, 140–6, 275–80].

*'Lines suggested by the Fast . . .', 428–33. Robert Bisset[?][*v. AJ*, i, 176–80; iii, 188–92].

*'To the Editor . . .', 433–43. George Hutton [signed letter].

*'The Wrangling Philosophers', 443–6. Constantin-François Chasseboeuf, Comte de Volney [signed letter].

*'Summary of Politics, Foreign and Domestic', 457–64. John Gifford[?][entire series is by John Gifford].

Volume II, Appendix

(*Entire appendix missing from the British Library copy.*)

*'Tableau Historique et Politique . . .', 519–35. John Gifford[?][*v. AJ*, i, 171–6].

Volume III, May 1799

'Preface', vi–viii.   NA.
'*The Holy Bible . . . faithfully translated . . .*', 1–8.   George Croft.
'Tooke's *Diversions of Purley*', 9–16.   Samuel Henshall.
'*Specimens and Parts . . .*', 16–23.   John Whitaker.
'*The Importance of Religious Establishments . . .*', 23–7.   George Gleig.
'*The Unsexed Females . . .*', 27–33.   John Whitaker.
'Somerville's *Reign of Queen Anne*', 33–7.   Robert Bisset.
'*Ellinor . . .*', 37–9.   William Heath.
'*The False Friend . . .*', 39–42.   Robert Bisset.
'*The Epiphany . . .*', 42–3.   Jonathan Boucher.
'*The Speech of Lord Minto . . .*', 43–5.   John Reeves.
'*Substance of the Speech of Lord Auckland . . .*', 45.   John Gifford.
'*The Wrangling Philosophers . . .*', 46–7.   John Gifford.
'*Considerations upon Frauds on the Revenue . . .*', 47–9.   J. Henshall.
'*Union or Separation*. By R. Farrell . . .',49.   [?] [British library copy
   is signed 'Farrell', but this appears to be an error. It is unlikely that
   Farrell should have reviewed his own work and far less probable
   that he should have condemned his own writing style as
   'factious', as the reviewer did.]
'*An Examination into the . . . Discontents in Ireland . . .*', 50–1.   John
   Gifford.
'*The Sword of the Lord and of Gideon . . .*', 51.   John Gifford.
'*A Sermon* [by J. Howlett] . . .', 52.   John Gifford.
'*A Defence of the Cesarean Operation . . .*', 52–3.   John Heath.
'*Dancing Masteriana . . .*', 53.   John Gifford.
'*The Sizar . . .*', 54.   William Heath.
'*Memoirs of Emma Courtney . . .*', 54–8.   William Heath.
'To the Editor . . . [signed "Clericus Anglicanus"]', 58–63.   NA.
'To the Editor [signed "Scrutator"]', 63–72.   R. White.
'Schism and Schismatics [introductory remarks]', 73–4.   John
   Gifford.
'To the Editor [signed "Clericus"]', 74–5.   Anonymous.
'To the Editor [signed "A Friend to the Church of England"]',
   75–6.   Anonymous.
'To the Editor [signed "A Friend to the Establishment"]', 76–
   7.   William Agutter.
'To the Editor [signed "T. Countermine"]', 77–9.   Anonymous.
'To the Editor [signed "Clericus"]', 79–82.   Anonymous.
'To the Editor [signed "W. A."]', 82–4.   William Atkinson.

'To the Editor [signed "G."]', 84–7.   Samuel Greatheed.
'On the late Charge of Jacobinical Principles . . .', 87–90.   Arthur Cayley.
'To the Editor . . . [signed "W."]', 90.   NA.
'The Rise, Progress, and Effects of Jacobinism', 91–6.   Robert Bisset.
'To the Editor . . .', 96–8.   Robert Bisset.
'The Night Mare', 99.   William Stevens.
'The Literary Fund', 100–3.   John Gifford [article includes an 'Address' by William Thomas Fitzgerald, printed in full on pp. 101–3].
'France. An Elegy', 103–5.   Anonymous.
'Summary of Politics', 105–11.   John Gifford.
'To Correspondents', 112.   NA.
'Literary Intelligence', 112.   NA.

Volume III, June 1799

'Pinkerton's *History of Scotland*', 113–20.   Robert Bisset.
'*Joan of Arc* . . .', 120–8.   Richard Polwhele.
'*Considerations on the . . . Lord's Supper* . . .', 128–32.   Richard Polwhele.
'*Sermons* [by Charles Henry Hall] . . .', 133–7.   NA.
'Vancouver's *Voyage of Discovery* . . .', 138–43.   Robert Bisset.
'*A Letter to the Women of England* . . .', 144–6.   William Heath.
'Somerville's *Reign of Queen Anne*', 146–50.   Robert Bisset.
'*What is She?* . . .', 150–5.   John Gifford.
'*The Reconciliation* . . .', 155–61.   Richard Polwhele.
'*A Course of Mathematics* . . .', 161–4.   Patrick Kelly.
'*Illustrations of Sterne* . . .', 164–8.   William Heath.
'*A Proposal for restoring the ancient Constitution of the Mint* . . .', 168–71.   Jonathan Boucher.
'*The Old English Gentleman* . . .', 171–4.   William Lisle Bowles.
'*Sketches in Verse* . . .', 174.   William Lisle Bowles.
'*Neutrality of Prussia* . . .', 175–6.   NA.
'*Tax upon Income* . . .', 176–7.   John Gifford.
'*A Sermon on Death* . . .', 177–9.   Anonymous.
'*A Sermon* [by David Williams] . . .', 179–80.   Jonathan Boucher.
'*Morning and Evening Prayers* . . .', 180.   Richard Polwhele.
'*Devotional Exercises and Contemplations* . . .', 180–1.   John Gifford.

'*A Letter to a College Friend* . . .', 181–5.   John Whitaker.

'*The Lawfulness of Defensive War* . . .', 185–8.   Richard Polwhele.

'Lloyd's *Letter to the Anti-Jacobin Reviewers* . . .', 188–92.   Robert Bisset.

'*The Beauties of the Anti-Jacobin, or Weekly Examiner*', 192–4.   John Gifford.

'*The Libertines* . . .', 194–6.   Robert Bisset.

'*Romances* . . .', 196–8.   Robert Bisset.

'To the Editor [signed "Metellus"]', 198–207.   John Brand.

'Remarks on Kotzebue's *Pizarro*', 207–10.   J. Mavor.

'To the Editor [signed "Misofanaticus"]', 211–12.   George Croft.

'To the Editor [signed "X."]', 212–14.   Anonymous.

'To the Editor [signed "Examiner"]', 215–16.   Anonymous.

'To the Editor [signed "Fatidicus"]', 216–20.   Richard Polwhele.

'The Rise and Decline of the Empire of the Mameloucs. By Joseph Moser, Esq.', 221–5.   Joseph Moser [signed contribution].

'The Rise, Progress, and Effects of Jacobinism', 225–30.   Robert Bisset.

'Summary of Politics, Foreign and Domestic', 231–9.   John Gifford.

'Literary Intelligence', 240.   NA.

'To Correspondents', 240.   NA.

Volume III, July 1799

'*An authentic Account of the Embassy of the Dutch East India Company* . . .', 241–5.   Samuel Henshall.

'Pinkerton's *History of Scotland*', 246–59.   Robert Bisset.

'*The Rise, Progress, and Consequences of the New Opinions* . . .', 259–67.   George Gleig.

'*Voyages to the East-Indies* . . .', 267–76.   Robert Bisset.

'*Two Biographical Tracts* . . .', 276–9.   John Reeves.

'*Six Essays upon Theological . . . Subjects* . . .', 279–82.   Richard Polwhele.

'*Remarks on the Eastern Origination of Mankind* . . .', 283–4.   John Reeves.

'*Conjectures on the Egyptian Original of the Word* Πυρ . . .', 284–6.   John Reeves.

'*Bubble and Squeak* . . .', 286–91.   John Gifford.

'*Crambe Repetita* . . .', 292–4.   John Gifford.

'*The Caldron* . . .', 294–6.   John Gifford.

'*Four occasional Poems* . . .', 296–7.   John Gifford.
'*Goetz, of Berlichingen* . . .', 297–301.   Richard Polwhele.
'*The Votary of Wealth* . . .', 301–3.   Richard Polwhele.
'*Substance of the Speech of . . . Addington* . . .', 303–4.   John Gifford.
'*A Letter . . . to a Member of the Irish Parliament* . . .', 305–6.   John Gifford.
'*Observations on the Speech of . . . Foster* . . .', 306.   John Gifford.
'*A Letter to the Pope* . . .', 306–7.   John Gifford.
'*Family Lectures* . . .', 307–9.   Richard Polwhele.
'*A Sermon* [by George Hutton] . . .', 309–11.   John Gifford.
'*A Sermon* [by John Hayter] . . .', 311–12.   John Gifford.
'*Two Sermons* [by the Bishop of Winchester] . . .', 313–16.   John Gifford.
'*The Days of Visitation* . . .', 316–17.   John Gifford.
'*Letters on Subjects of Importance* . . .', 317–18.   John Gifford.

(*Remainder of the July 1799 number missing from the British Library copy.*)

*'*Elements of Geography, and of Natural and Civil History*. By John Walker . . .', 323–33.   Charles Pears. [Pears (*AJ*, VI, 255) refers to 'John Walker, Author of the Elements of Geography, which we had occasion to expose in a former volume'. The review of the *Elements of Geography* also condemns the Quakers, as Pears does in the *AJ*, VI, 254–65.]
*'To the Editor', 341–5.   Robert Haldane (pp. 341–42) [signed letter; pp. 342–5 consist of unidentified editorial comment].
*'To the Editor [signed "Miso Fanaticus"]', 349–51.   George Croft [Croft used this signature in *AJ*, III, 211–12, to which letter he refers].
*'To the Editor', 356–7.   Isaac D'Israeli [signed letter].

Volume III, August 1799

(*Entire August 1799 number missing from the British Library copy.*)

*'Somerville's *Reign of Queen Anne*', 369–76.   Robert Bisset[?][*v. AJ*, III, 33–7; IV, 49–58].
*'Tooke's *Diversions of Purley*', 377–83.   Samuel Henshall[?][*v. AJ*, II, 37–41; III, 9–16].

*'The History of . . . the Roman Republic . . .', 413–21. Robert Bisset[?][v. AJ, IV, 39–49, 174–84].

*'Domesday . . .', 424–32. John Whitaker [attributed to Whitaker in the *Palatine Note-book*, I, 80].

*'Historical and Political Survey . . .', 446–9. John Gifford[?][v. AJ, I, 171–6; II, 519–35].

*'A Letter to the Rev. Robert Hawker . . .', 451–7. John Gifford[?][v. AJ, IV, 97–102; VI, 440–3].

*'The New Annual Register . . .', 461–7. John Gifford[?][v. AJ, IV, 106–11].

*'Tribute of Loyalty and Gratitude', 489. Jean-Baptiste-Claude de Lachassagne [the poem is a signed contribution].

*'Summary of Politics, Foreign and Domestic', 489–96. John Gifford[?][entire series is by John Gifford].

Volume III, Appendix

(*Entire appendix missing from the British Library copy.*)

*'Bemerkungen auf einer Reise in die Südlichen Statthalterschaften des Russischen Reichs . . .', 530–7. Anthony Florian Madinger Willich[?] [v. AJ, V, 502–13].

Volume IV, September 1799

'Preface', vi–xvi. John Gifford.

'The History and Antiquities of Staffordshire . . .', 1–11. Samuel Egerton Brydges [British Library copy attributes the article to 'M! Bridges, author of Fitz-Albini'].

'Travels in the Interior . . . of Africa . . .', 12–18. Robert Bisset.

'Family Sermons . . .', 19–27. William Heath.

'Journal of a Tour . . .', 27–33. Jonathan Boucher.

'Observations on the . . . present Times . . .', 33–5. Jonathan Boucher.

'A Letter to the Reverend John Milner . . .', 36–9. Jonathan Boucher.

'Ferguson's History of . . . the Roman Republic [Cont.]', 39–49. Robert Bisset.

'Somerville's Reign of Queen Anne', 49–58. Robert Bisset.

'A Compendius System of Astronomy . . .', 58–62. Patrick Kelly.

'*The Castle of Montval* . . .', 62–7.   William Heath.
'*Travels in Africa, Egypt, and Syria* . . .', 67–76.   Robert Bisset.
'*Gleanings, after Thomson* . . .', 76–9.   William Heath.
'*A concise Account of the* . . . *Rebellion* . . .', 79–86.   John Gifford.
'*A Letter from Benjamin Bousfield* . . .', 86–9.   John Gifford.
'*Observations on Mr. Bousfield's Letter* . . .', 89–90.   John Gifford.
'*A Warning against Schism* . . .', 90–2.   Jonathan Boucher.
'*The Love of Mankind* . . .', 92–3.   Jonathan Boucher.
'*A Sermon* [by William Knox] . . .', 93–5.   Jonathan Boucher.
'*A Sermon* [by William Knox] . . .', 95–6.   Jonathan Boucher.
'*A Sermon* [by Thomas Armistead] . . .', 96–7.   Jonathan Boucher.
'Polwhele's *Letter to Dr. Hawker*', 97–102.   John Gifford.
'*Letters from Lausanne* . . .', 102–3.   William Heath.
'The Peckham Frolic . . .', 103–4.   Robert Bisset.
'*The Stranger* . . .', 104–5.   Robert Bisset.
'*The New Annual Register* . . .', 106–11.   John Gifford.
'*Who were the Aggressors?* . . .', 111–12.   John Gifford.
'*National Gratitude* . . .', 112–15.   John Gifford.
'To the Editor . . .', 115–16.   George Gleig [signed letter].
'To the Editor . . .', 117–18.   Anonymous.
'Summary of Politics, Foreign and Domestic', 119–28.   John
    Gifford.
'Literary Intellig[e]nce', 128.   NA.
'To Correspondents', 128.   NA.

Volume IV, October 1799

'*Eight Sermons* . . .', 129–33.   George Croft.
'*Histoire des Campagnes* . . .', 133–8.   NA.
'*The Annual Hampshire Repository* . . .', 138–50.   John Gifford.
'*Travels in Africa, Egypt, and Syria* . . .', 150–60.   Robert Bisset.
'*Travels in the Interior* . . . *of Africa* . . .', 161–70.   Robert Bisset.
'Shaw's *History and Antiquities of Staffordshire*', 171–4.   Samuel
    Egerton Brydges [British Library copy attributes this to 'Wm.
    Brydges', but this is obviously an error for Samuel Egerton
    Brydges, who wrote the first part of the review (*AJ*, IV, 1–11)].
'Ferguson's *History of* . . . *the Roman Republic*', 174–84.   Robert
    Bisset.
'*Oratio in Theatro Collegii Regalis Medicorum Londinensis* . . .', 184–
    9.   W. Henshall.

'*Strictures on . . . Female Education . . .*', 190–9. Jonathan Boucher.
'*Thoughts on the English Government . . .*', 200–5. John Gifford.
'*Speech of the Right Honourable Sylvester Douglas . . .*', 205–7. John Gifford.
'*Strictures on the proposed Union . . .*', 207–8. John Gifford.
'*Union, a Plague . . .*', 208–10. John Gifford.
'*Constitutional Objections . . .*', 210–12. John Gifford.
'*Biographical Anecdotes . . .*', 212–13. John Gifford.
'The Wanseian Controversy', 213–25. Francis Randolph.
'*A Sermon* [by E. P. Waters] . . .', 225–6. John Gifford.
'*Sermons on various Subjects . . .*', 227–34. John Whitaker.
'Bicheno's *Glance at the History of Christianity . . .*', 234–6. Thomas Harral.
'*Letter to a County Member . . .*', 236–40. John Gifford.
'To the Editor [signed "Ormond"]', 240–1. Samuel Henshall.
'Summary of Politics, Foreign and Domestic', 241–8. John Gifford.
'Literary Intelligence', 248. NA.
'To Correspondents', 248. NA.

Volume IV, November 1799

'*Reflections on . . . Popery . . .*', 249–53. Jonathan Boucher.
'*A Letter to Mrs. Hannah More . . .*', 253–6. Jonathan Boucher.
'*An Apology for Brotherly Love . . .*', 256–60. Jonathan Boucher.
'*Memoirs of the Courts of Berlin, Warsaw, and Vienna . . .*', 260–8. G. Lake.
'*Thoughts on the English Government . . .*', 269–82. John Gifford.

(*Remainder of the November 1799 number missing from the British Library copy.*)

*'*Original Sonnets . . .*', 327–30. Richard Polwhele [attributed to Polwhele by John Gifford, letter to Richard Polwhele, 24 September 1799, quoted in R[ichard] Polwhele, *Traditions and Recollections; Domestic, Clerical, and Literary* (2 vols; London: John Nichols and Son, 1826) II, 512].
*'*A Guide to the Church . . .*', 336–41. John Skinner[?][v. *AJ*, v, 9–16, 137–45].
*'To the Editor . . . [signed "G."]', 345–9. Samuel Greatheed[?][v. *AJ*, II, 97–100, 217–19; III, 84–7].

Volume IV, December 1799

(*Entire December 1799 number missing from the British Library copy.*)

*'A Short Commentary . . . on . . . Dr. Paley and Mr. Gisborne . . .',
369–74.   John Whitaker. [*v. AJ*, v, 16–23, 132–7. This review is
also attributed to Whitaker in the *Palatine Note-book*, I, 80.]

*'Daubeny's *Guide to the Church*', 375–86.   John Skinner[?][*v. AJ*, v,
9–16, 137–45].

*'Memoirs of the Courts of Berlin, Warsaw, and Vienna . . .', 392–
7.   G. Lake[?][*v. AJ*, IV, 260–8].

*'Gleanings through Wales, Holland, and Westphalia . . .', 409–16
[misnumbered as 509–16].   George Henry Glasse[?][*v. AJ*, v,
75–80 (Glasse); VI, 455–60 (Glasse and Richard Polwhele)].

*'A Brief Vindication . . .'; 'Thoughts on the English Government . . .',
420–7 [misnumbered as 520–7].   John Gifford[?][John Gifford
reviewed *Thoughts on the English Government* in *AJ*, IV, 200–5,
269–82].

*'To the Editor [signed "Z."]', 471–2.   William Stevens[?][Stevens
used the signature 'Z.' in *AJ*, v, 347–8].

*'Summary of Politics, Foreign and Domestic', 473–88.   John
Gifford[?][entire series is by John Gifford].

Volume IV, Appendix

(*Entire appendix missing from the British Library copy.*)

*'Systeme Maritime et Politique . . .', 489–503.   John Andrews[?][*v.
AJ*, VI, 481–94].

*'Remarks on a Journey . . .', 512–33.   Anthony Florian Madinger
Willich[?][*v. AJ*, v, 502–13].

*'Coup d'Oeil sur le Continent . . .', 570–80.   Mathieu-Mathurin
Tabaraud and/or John Gifford[?][*v. AJ*, v, 153–62].

Volume V, January 1800

'Elements of Christian Theology . . .', 1–9.   George Croft.
'An Appendix to the Guide to the Church . . .', 9–16.   John Skinner.
'A Short Commentary . . . on . . . Dr. Paley and Mr. Gisborne',
16–23.   John Whitaker.

'*St. Leon* . . .', 23–8.   William Heath.

'*Observations on the Western Parts of England* . . .', 28–37.   Richard Polwhele.

'*The Annual Necrology* . . .', 37–46.   John Gifford.

'*A Letter to the Rev. C. Daubeny* . . .', 46–8.   William Agutter.

'*Annals of the French Revolution.* . . . By A. F. Bertrand De Molville [*sic*] . . .', 48–56.   [?] [British Library copy is signed 'M. de Moleville', but this appears to be an error. For Bertrand de Moleville to have reviewed his own work would have been unlikely. In addition the tone of the review suggests that another person was the author.]

'*Critical Disquisitions* . . .', 56–64.   Richard Polwhele. [Note that Polwhele does not appear to have written the first part of the review (*AJ*, III, 397–403). See John Gifford, letter to Richard Polwhele, 24 September 1799, quoted in R[ichard] Polwhele, *Traditions and Recollections; Domestic, Clerical, and Literary* (2 vols; London: John Nichols and Son, 1826) II, 512.]

'*A Fair Representation of* . . . *Ireland* . . .', 64–71.   John Gifford.

'*An Epistle to a Friend* . . .', 71–5.   Richard Polwhele.

'*Gleanings in England* . . .', 75–80.   George Henry Glasse.

'Peter Pindar's *Nil Admirari* . . .', 80–1.   Anonymous.

'Letter I. To a Predestinarian', 81–3.   William Jones of Nayland.

'Internal Feeling', 84.   William Agutter.

'Strictures on a Paper. . . . [signed "D. W."]', 84–90.   NA.

'Necrology', 90–1.   William Agutter.

'To the Editor [signed "Misospludes"]', 91–4.   John Giffard of Dublin.

'To the Editor [signed "Normannus"]', 94–9.   John Giffard of Dublin.

'To the Editor [signed "C. W. A."]', 99–100.   C. W. Atkinson.

'Observations on Sir Richard Hill's *Apology for Brotherly Love*', 101–6.   John Skinner.

'To the Editor [signed "Ucalagon"]', 106.   NA. [Possibly William Stevens, who used the signature 'Ucalagon' in *AJ*, III, 99.]

'Advertisement: To all Lovers of Modern Philosophy, and Gallican Principles!!! . . . [signed "Sieyes & Co."]', 107–8.   Anonymous.

'To the Editor [signed "West Riding"]', 108–9.   Richard Munkhouse.

'To the Editor [signed "Clericus N."]', 109–10.   Richard Munkhouse.

'To the Editor [signed "Pythias"]', 110–11.   NA.

'Parody on the celebrated Epigram of William Shakspeare, on a notorious Usurer . . .', 111.   Lawrence Hynes O'Halloran.
'Summary of Politics, Foreign and Domestic', 111–18.   John Gifford.
'To Correspondents', 119.   John Gifford.
'Literary Intelligence', 120.   NA.

Volume V, February 1800

'*Memoirs of . . . George Horne . . .*', 121–32.   George Henry Glasse.
'*A Short Commentary . . . on . . . Dr. Paley and Mr. Gisborne*', 132–7.   John Whitaker.
'*An Appendix to the Guide to the Church*', 137–45.   John Skinner.
'*St. Leon . . .*', 145–53.   William Heath.
'*Coup d'Oeil sur le Continent . . .*', 153–62.   Mathieu-Mathurin Tabaraud and John Gifford.
'Bertrand's *Annals of the French Revolution*', 162–72.   [?][British Library copy is signed 'M. de Moleville', but this appears to be an error. See note above (*AJ*, v, 48–56).]
'*Reflections on the Political State of Society . . .*', 172–4.   John Gifford.
'*Copies of Original Letters . . .*', 175–9.   John Gifford.
'*A Charge* [by the Bishop of Exeter] . . .', 179–82.   Richard Polwhele.
'*A second Letter to the Rev. Dr. Hawker. By . . . R. Polwhele . . .*', 183–4.   John Gifford[?].   [British Library copy is signed 'R. Polwhele', but this appears to be an error, unless Polwhele reviewed his own work. Article probably by John Gifford, who reviewed the first and third *Letters to the Rev. Dr. Hawker* [*v. AJ*, IV, 97–102; VI, 440–3).]
'*Report from the Clergy . . .*', 184–90.   John Gifford.
'*Letter . . . to . . . Charles James Fox . . .*', 190–3.   John Gifford.
'*Thoughts on Government . . .*', 193–4.   John Gifford.
'*Observations on the Union . . .*', 194.   John Gifford.
'*Critical Examination of . . . Lavoisier's Elements of Chemistry . . .*', 194–200.   John Barclay.
'*The Influence of Local Attachment . . .*', 200–4.   John Gifford.
'*Grove Hill . . .*', 204–6.   John Gifford.
'*Affectation . . .*', 206–8.   John Gifford.
'*The Poor Man's Moralist . . .*', 208–9.   John Gifford.
'*Advise to Editors of Newspapers . . .*', 210.   John Gifford.

'Dr. Duigenan's *Fair Representation* . . .', 210–15.   John Gifford.
'*Vindiciae Regiae* . . .', 215–17.   John Gifford.
'*A View of the Agriculture of Middlesex* . . .', 217–25.   John Gifford
 (pp. 217–19) and [?] (pp. 219–25). [pp. 219–25 consist of a letter to
 the editor on the subject of tithes (signed 'Academicus') bearing
 no attribution in the British Library copy.]
'To the Editor . . . [signed "Academicus"]', 226.   NA.
'Letter II. To a Predestinarian', 226–9.   William Jones of Nayland.
'To the Editor [signed "S. S. E."]', 229–32.   Anonymous.
'Summary of Politics, Foreign and Domestic', 233–40.   John
 Gifford.
'To Correspondents', 240.   NA. [Possibly by John Gifford, whose
 name was signed to 'Literary Intelligence' farther down the page.]
'To Our Readers', 240.   NA. [Possibly by John Gifford, whose
 name was signed to 'Literary Intelligence' farther down the page.]
'Literary Intelligence', 240.   John Gifford.

Volume V, March 1800

'*T. Lucretii Cari De rerum Naturâ Libros Sex* . . .', 241–58.   Richard
 Polwhele.
'*Gilpin's Observations* . . .', 258–63.   Richard Polwhele.
'*Travels in England, Scotland, and the Hebrides* . . .', 263–9.   John
 Gifford.
'*Douglas* . . .', 269–77.   John Gifford.
'Bertrand's *Annals of the French Revolution*', 277–86.   [?][British
 Library copy is signed 'M. de Moleville', but this appears to be an
 error. See note above (*AJ*, v, 48–56).]
'*A Supplement to the Annals of the French Revolution* . . .', 286–9.   [?]
 [British Library copy is signed 'M. de Moleville', but this appears
 to be an error. See preceding note.]
'*Thoughts on the English Government* . . .', 289–95.   John Gifford.
'*A Letter to the Rev. Dr. Hawker* . . .', 295–7.   Richard Polwhele.
'*Loyalty enforced by Arguments* . . .', 297–300.   George Gleig.
'*A concise Selection of the Divine Excellencies of Revelation* . . .', 300–
 1.   Richard Polwhele.
'*Congress at Rastadt* . . .', 301.   John Gifford.
'*Forethoughts on the General Pacification of Europe* . . .', 301–3.   John
 Gifford [Gifford's name is written over George Gleig's name in the
 British Library copy].

'*Considerations concerning Peace* . . .', 303–4.   John Gifford.
'*The Question Stated* . . .', 304.   John Gifford.
'*A Statement of the Differences* . . . *[at] Covent Garden* . . .', 304–
   8.   John Taylor and John Gifford.
'*Orange* . . .', 308–13.   John Gifford.
'*Peter not infallible!* . . .', 314–15.   John Gifford.
'*The Man of Nature* . . .', 315–16.   John Gifford.
'*Zimao, the African* . . .', 316–18.   John Gifford.
'*Dissertation sur les Dents Artificielles* . . .', 318.   John Gifford.
'*Grammigraphia* . . .', 318–20.   William Agutter.
'Miss More and Mr. Daubeny', 320–32.   Anonymous [pp. 320–6]
   and Jonathan Boucher [pp. 326–32].
'Booker's *Hop-Garden*', 332–8.   Luke Booker [signed letter, pp. 332–
   5] and William Heath [pp. 335–8].
'*Monthly Magazine* . . .', 338–9.   William Agutter.
'To the Editor', 339.   George Gleig [signed letter].
'Exposition of the . . . System of Kant', 339–47.   Jean-Joseph
   Mounier.
'To the Editor', 347–8.   William Stevens [the article consists of an
   introductory paragraph by 'Z.' (p. 347), followed by 'an extract
   from a letter written by a friend' regarding William Jones of
   Nayland].
'German Literature', 348–50.   John Gifford.
'Jeu D'Esprit', 351.   John Gifford.
'Summary of Politics, Foreign and Domestic', 351–60.   John
   Gifford.
'To Correspondents', 360.   John Gifford.

Volume V, April 1800

'*Lucretii Cari de rerum Natura, libros Sex* . . .', 361–4.   Richard
   Polwhele.
'*An Account of an Embassy to* . . . *Ava* . . .', 365–72.   John Gifford.
'*Observations on a Tour* . . .', 372–82.   John Gifford.
'*Remarks on* . . . *"The Age of Reason"* . . .', 382–91.   John Whitaker.
'*The Asiatic Annual Register* . . .', 391–9.   John Gifford.
'*A Narrative of the Expedition to Holland* . . .', 399–400.   John Gifford.
'*Remarks on a Tour to North and South-Wales* . . .', 400–2.   John
   Gifford.

'Braidwood's *Vindication* . . .', 463–4.   William Braidwood [signed letter].
'Marshall's *Union* – Bowles's *Reflections* . . .', 464–6.   John James Watson.
'To the Editor', 467–72.   George Henry Glasse [pp. 467–8 consist of a letter to the editor signed 'Emeritus'; pp. 468–72 consist of 'The Earle of Pembrook's Speech to Nol Cromwell, Lord Deputy of Ireland'].
'To the Editor [signed "G. S. F."]', 472–4.   Anonymous.
'To the Editor [signed "I. Kennedy"]', 474–6.   John Kennedy (pp. 474–6) and John Gifford (editorial comments, p. 476).
'To the Editor [signed "Miso-Satanas"]', 476.   Anonymous.
'Summary of Politics', 477–9.   John Gifford.
'Literary Intelligence', 480.   NA. [Possibly by John Gifford, whose name was signed to 'Correspondence' further down the page.]
'Correspondence', 480.   John Gifford.
'Errata . . .', 480.   NA.

Volume V, Appendix

'*Des anciens Gouvernemens Fédératifs* . . .', 481–4.   G. Lake.
'*Précis [sic] des Operations de L'Armée du Danube* . . .', 484–8.   John Gifford.
'*Anecdotes Secretes de la Revolution* . . .', 489–91.   John Gifford.
'*Nouveaux Principes de Geologie* . . .', 491–502.   NA.
'*Remarks on a Journey* . . .', 502–13.   Anthony Florian Madinger Willich.
'*Lettres D'Un Voyageur* . . .', 513–20.   John Gifford.
'*Le Psalmiste* . . .', 520–1.   John Gifford.
'*Discours pour la bénédiction* . . .', 521–3.   John Gifford.
'*Discours de Mons. l'Archevêque et Primat de Narbonne* . . .', 523–4.   John Gifford.
'*Le Dix-huit Brumaire* . . .', 524–32.   John Gifford.
'*Le petit la Bruyere* . . .', 532–9.   John Gifford.
'*Voyage . . . en Gréce [sic]* . . .', 539–40.   John Gifford.
'*Examen de la Constitution de France* . . .', 540–3.   John Gifford.
'*Essai sur les Fables* . . .', 543–7.   John Gifford.
'*Eulogium on . . . General Washington* . . .', 547–50.   John Gifford.
'*An Oration upon . . . General Washington* . . .', 550–1.   John Gifford.

'Journal of the . . . Protestant Episcopal Church . . .', 551–6. NA.
'The Narrative of Patrick Lyon . . .', 556–7. John Gifford.
'Tabulae Anatomicae . . .', 557–8. Francis William Blagdon.
'Voyage Pittoresque . . .', 558–9. Francis William Blagdon.
'Voyage Pittoresque d'Istrie . . .', 559. Francis William Blagdon.
'Historia Numothecae Gothanae . . .', 559–60. Francis William Blagdon.
'Forsoeg til en Skildring af Quindekioenets' huuslige og borgerlige Kaar hos Skandinaverne . . .', 560. Francis William Blagdon.
'Slavischer Bücherdruck in Würtemberg . . .', 560–1. Francis William Blagdon.
'Theorie de la Musique vocale . . .', 561. Francis William Blagdon.
'Un Mois d'hiver . . .', 562. Francis William Blagdon.
'Correza der Franke . . .', 562–4. Francis William Blagdon.
'Le Chateau Noir . . .', 564. Francis William Blagdon.
'Les Dangers de la Seduction . . .', 564. Francis William Blagdon.
'Consolations de ma Captivité . . .', 564–6. John Gifford.
'Die Branntweinbrennerkunst . . .', 566. Francis William Blagdon.
'Natur und Kunst . . .', 566–7. Francis William Blagdon.
'Versuch einer metrischen Uebersetzung des Propheton Jona . . .', 567. Francis William Blagdon.
'Jesus, wie er lebte und lehrte . . .', 567. Francis William Blagdon.
'Memorias Historicas sobre la Legislacion y Govierno del Commercio de las Espanoles . . .', 567. Francis William Blagdon.
'Compendio de Observationes . . .', 568. Francis William Blagdon.
'The Literati and Literature of Germany . . .', 568–80. James Walker.

Volume VI, May 1800

'The Travels of Antenor . . .', 1–12. Richard Polwhele.
'A Letter to the Earl of Lauderdale . . .', 12–23. John Whitaker.
'Morality united with Policy . . .', 23–7. William Heath.
'Reformation-Truth restored . . .', 27–31. Jonathan Boucher.
'On Dr. Huntingford's Call for Union . . .', 31–3. Jonathan Boucher.
'Munimenta Antiqua . . .', 33–45. John Whitaker.
'M. Musuri carmen in Platonem . . .', 45–7. Richard Polwhele.
'Observations on a Tour through the Highlands . . .', 47–52. John Gifford.
'The Three Spaniards . . .', 52–3. Thomas Harral.

[Probably by John Gifford, whose name was signed to the 'To Correspondents' notice further down the page.]

'To Our Readers', 120. NA. [Probably by John Gifford, whose name was signed to the 'To Correspondents' notice further down the page.]

'To Correspondents', 120. John Gifford.

Volume VI, June 1800

'*Munimenta Antiqua . . .*', 121–32. John Whitaker.

'*T. Lucretii Cari de rerum Naturâ libros Sex . . .*', 132–41. Richard Polwhele.

'*General Biography . . .*', 142–6. John Whitaker.

'*Symes's Account of an Embassy to . . . Ava . . .*', 146–56. John Gifford.

'*Philosophy of Mineralogy . . .*', 156–9. Richard Polwhele.

'*Mordaunt . . .*', 159–65. William Heath.

'*Observations on the . . . Income Tax . . .*', 166–73. John Gifford.

'*Irish Pursuits of Literature . . .*', 173–7. Richard Polwhele.

'*A Treatise on Sugar . . .*', 177–84. John Barclay.

'*Medical Cases and Remarks . . .*', 184–5. John Heath.

'*The Efficacy of . . . Metallic Tractors . . .*', 185–6. John Heath.

'*Tracts and Observations in Natural History . . .*', 186–9. John Heath.

'*The Danger of Lukewarmness in Religion . . .*', 189–90. John Gifford.

'*A Sermon . . .*', 191. John Gifford.

'*The Consolations of pure Christianity . . .*', 191–3. Richard Polwhele.

'*A Sermon* [by Legh Richmond] *. . .*', 193–5. John Gifford.

'*Justification by Works . . .*', 196–7. John Prince.

'*Speech of . . . Lord Yelverton . . .*', 197–9. John Gifford.

'*Speech of Lord Hawkesbury . . .*', 199–200. John Gifford.

'*A Letter to the Farmers . . .*', 200–1. John Gifford.

'*Substance of the Speech of Thomas Jones . . .*', 201–2. John Gifford.

'Adultery', 202–6. John Gifford.

'*Substance of the Speeches of . . . the Duke of Clarence . . .*', 206–10. John Gifford.

'*Substance of the Speeches of Lord Auckland . . .*', 210–11. John Gifford.

'*Substance of the Bishop of Rochester's Speech . . .*', 212–13. John Gifford.

'*Substance of the Speeches of Lord Mulgrave . . .*', 213–14. John Gifford.
'*Thoughts on . . . Marriages founded on Adultery . . .*', 214. John Gifford.
'*A Discourse to unmarried Men . . .*', 214. John Gifford.
'*The Annual Anthology . . .*', 215–16. Richard Polwhele.
'*The English Sailor and French Citizen . . .*', 216–17. John Gifford.
'*Hints for History . . .*', 217. John Gifford.
'*A Letter to . . . William Windham . . .*', 217–18. John Gifford.
'*A Praxis of Logic . . .*', 218–19. Richard Polwhele.
'*Pyrology . . .*', 219—28. George Gleig.
'*The Endeavour Society . . .*', 228–9. John Gifford.
'*The Old English Gentleman . . .*', 230–3. NA.
'Verses . . . [signed "W.___ S.___"]', 233. Anonymous.
'Summary of Politics', 234–9. John Gifford.
'Literary Intelligence', 239–40. NA.
'To Correspondents', 240. John Gifford.

Volume VI, July 1800

'*General Biography . . .*', 241–9. John Whitaker.
'*Sketch of . . . Augustus Von Kotzbue [sic] . . .*', 249–54. William Heath.
'*A Refutation . . .*', 254–65. Charles Pears.
'*An Essay on Military Law . . .*', 265–70. George Gleig.
'*Practical Observations . . .*', 270–4. Francis Randolph.
'*The Satires of Persius . . .*', 274–81. Richard Polwhele.
'*The Miscellaneous Works of Hugh Boyd . . .*', 281–5. John Taylor.
'*An Appendix to the Supplemental Apology . . .*', 285–7. John Taylor.
'*An Account of an Embassy to . . . Tibet . . .*', 287–92. John Gifford.
'*Sans Culotides . . .*', 292–301. John Gifford.
'*The . . . Odes of Horace . . .*', 302–6. Richard Polwhele.
'*Lord Auckland's Triumph . . .*', 306–10. John Gifford.
'*Epistle to Peter Pindar . . .*', 310–15. John Gifford.
'*Christian Institutes . . .*', 315–17. Richard Polwhele.
'*A few plain Reasons . . .*', 317–20. Richard Polwhele.
'*A Sermon* [by J. Brand] *. . .*', 321–4. John Gifford.
'*A Sermon on . . . British Jurisprudence . . .*', 324–5. John Gifford.
'*A Sermon* [by William Foster] *. . .*', 325–6. John Gifford.
'*Narrative of . . . J. J. Job Aimé . . .*', 326–8. John Gifford.

'An Answer to a Pamphlet, entitled the Speech of the Earl of Clare . . .',
   328.   John Gifford.
'The British Garden . . .', 328.   John Gifford.
'Proposals for a Rural Institute . . .', 329.   John Gifford.
'A Meteorological Journal . . .', 329.   John Gifford.
'Sheridan's Pronouncing and Spelling Dictionary . . .', 329.   John
   Gifford.
'To the Editor [signed "Vester et Academicus"]', 329–
   36.   Anonymous.
'To the Editor [signed "Amicus Curiae"]', 336–42.   John Whitaker.
'To the Editor [signed "S. R."]', 342.   John Robison [NA; however,
   internal evidence in this letter and the following one proves the
   author to have been Robison].
'Mr. Walker's Letter . . .', 343–9.   James Walker [signed letter].
'To the Editor [signed "I. S."]', 349–54.   Anonymous.
'Upon the Levelling Society, English Assassins, &c. . . .', 354–
   6.   William Hamilton Reid [signed letter].
'Verses to the memory of Count Suworow', 356–7.   Anonymous.
'Summary of Politics', 357–60.   John Gifford.
'To Correspondents', 360.   NA.
'To Our Readers', 360.   NA.
'Errata', 360.   NA.

Volume VI, August 1800

'The History of the Anglo-Saxons . . .', 361–70.   John Whitaker.
'Tytler's *Essay on Military Law* . . .', 370–80.   George Gleig.
'The . . . *Prose Works of John Dryden* . . .', 381–5.   John Taylor.
'The Essence of Malone . . .', 385–6.   John Taylor.
'Bevan's *Refutation* . . .', 386–98.   Charles Pears.
'Turner's *Embassy to Tibet*', 398–406.   John Gifford.
'Oratio Crewiana . . .', 406–9.   Anonymous.
'A Tour round North Wales . . .', 409–16.   John Gifford.
'A general View of . . . Chemistry . . .', 416–20.   John Barclay.
'An Essay on the Theory . . . of Bleaching . . .', 420–4.   John Barclay.
'Notice of some Observations . . .', 424–8.   John Barclay.
'Medical Jurisprudence. On Madness . . .', 429–30.   Anonymous.
'A Lecture on the Preservation of Health . . .', 430–1.   Charles Pears.
'Pleasures of Solitude . . .', 432–3.   John Gifford.

'*Epistle to Peter Pindar* . . .', 434.   John Gifford.
'*Reflection* . . .', 435.   John Gifford.
'*The Farmer's Boy* . . .', 435–8.   Richard Polwhele.
'*A Sermon* [by C. Daubeny] . . .', 438–40.   John Gifford.
'*A Third Letter, on* . . . [*Dr. Hawker*] . . .', 440–3.   John Gifford.
'*The Duty of not remaining in Debt* . . .', 443–4.   John Gifford.
'*Why are you a Churchman?* . . .', 444.   John Gifford.
'*A Sermon* [by A. Burnaby] . . .', 444–5.   John Prince.
'*Select Sermons* . . . *of Bossuet* . . .', 446–7.   John Gifford.
'*Mr. Pitt's Democracy Manifested* . . .', 447–9.   John Gifford.
'*A Letter from the Rev. Peter Flood* . . .', 449.   John Gifford.
'*Andrew Stuart* . . .', 449–51.   Thomas Harral.
'*Ormond* . . .', 451.   Thomas Harral.
'*Critical Remarks on Pizarro* . . .', 452–4.   John Gifford.
'*The Lisbon Guide* . . .', 454.   John Gifford.
'*Amusing* . . . *Conversations for Children* . . .', 454.   John Gifford.
'*The Art of teaching the* . . . *English Language* . . .', 455.   John Gifford.
'*The Angler's Pocket-Book* . . .', 455.   John Gifford.
'Pratt's *Gleanings in England*', 455–60.   George Henry Glasse and Richard Polwhele.
'*Observations upon* . . . *Letters from the French Army* . . .', 460–4.   John Gifford.
'Jacobin Societies', 464–6.   NA.
'Peter Pindar', 466–8.   William Cobbett.
'Retrospect of the Causes . . . of English Jacobinism . . .', 468–72.   William Hamilton Reid [signed letter].
'*The Old English Gentleman* . . .', 472–5.   [The entire article consists of excerpts from Richard Polwhele's *Old English Gentleman*.]
'To the Author of the *Epistle to Peter Pindar*. [signed "F."]', 475.   William Thomas Fitzgerald. [Name incorrectly listed as 'G. W. Fitzgerald' in British Library copy. See, however, William Thomas Fitzgerald, *Miscellaneous Poems* (London: printed by W. Bulmer, 1801) p. 189, where the poem appears.]
'Summary of Politics', 476–80.   John Gifford[?] [NA. Article undoubtedly written by John Gifford, who is listed as the author of all but one – also unattributed – of the other articles in this series.]
'To Correspondents', 480.   John Gifford.

Volume VI, Appendix

'Arnould's *Systeme Maritime et Politique* . . .', 481–94. John
Andrews.
'Schiller's *Tragedy of Mary Stewart*', 494–8. James Walker.
'*L'Abeille Française* . . .', 498–500. John Gifford.
'*Biographies de Suicides* . . .', 500–4. John Gifford.
'*Les Derniers Adieux à Bonaparte Victorieux* . . .', 504–9. John
Gifford.
'*Voiage* . . .', 510–13. John Gifford.
'*La Foi Couronnée* . . .', 513–16. John Gifford.
'*Ueber den Gang* . . .', 516–17. G. Lake.
'*Reise nach Ostindien* . . .', 517–19. Francis William Blagdon.
'*Reise nach dem Vorgebirge der Guten Hoffnung* . . .', 520. Francis
William Blagdon.
'*ΠΛΟΥΤΑΡΧΟΥ ΤΟΥ ΧΑΙΡΩΝΕΩΣ ΤΑ ΗΘΙΚΑ. Plutarchi
Chaeronensis moralia* . . .', 520. Francis William Blagdon.
'*Astronomisches Jahrbrich* [sic] *füer* [sic] *das Jahr, 1802* . . .', 520–
4. Francis William Blagdon.
'*Beyträge zur Hydraulischen Architecture* . . .', 524. Francis William
Blagdon.
'*Louise, Raugräfinn zu Pfalz* . . .', 524–5. Francis William Blagdon.
'*Lettre.* . . . By Mr. Stockler . . .', 525–9. John Brand.
'*Eulogium on . . . Washington* . . .', 530–1. John Gifford.
'*An Oration upon the Death of . . . Washington* . . .', 531–4. John
Gifford.
'*Desultory Reflections* . . .', 534–43. John Gifford.
'*A Brief Statement of Opinions* . . .', 544–58. John Gifford.
'*Transactions of the American Philosophical Society* . . .', 558. John
Gifford.
'*A Sermon . . .* [on] *the Death of . . . Washington* . . .', 558–60. John
Gifford.
'*A Discourse . . . on . . . Washington* . . .', 560–1. John Gifford.
'*The Scripture Doctrine of Regeneration* . . .', 561. John Gifford.
'The Literati and Literature of Germany . . .', 562–76. James
Walker[?] [NA. Undoubtedly written by Walker (*v. AJ*, v,
568–80).]
'Mr. Boettiger to Mr. Walker . . .', 576–8. Karl Augustus Boettiger
[signed letter].
'Mr. Walker's Reply', 578–80. James Walker [signed letter].

Bibliographical Note

Researchers in late eighteenth-century history are the beneficiaries of a recent surge of interest in Radical and conservative movements in Britain during the 1790s. The publication of E. P. Thompson's *The Making of the English Working Class* (New York: Random House, 1963), with its controversial Marxist explanation of English Radicalism, stimulated a spate of publications, as scholars have increasingly challenged (or rejected outright) Thompson's class-war interpretation of events in the 1790s and his exclusionary preoccupation with the Radical side of English politics and opinion. The result has been a host of new publications distinguished by an even-handed treatment of Radical and conservative elements, a rigorous re-examination of the sources, and a jettisoning of many preconceptions about the period.

For an exhaustive and judiciously written survey of 1790s Radicalism readers can do no beter than Albert Goodwin's *The Friends of Liberty* (Cambridge, MA: Harvard University Press, 1979), which has superseded Carl B. Cone's *The English Jacobins* (New York: Charles Scribner's Sons, 1968), Simon Maccoby's *English Radicalism, 1786–1832* (London: George Allen and Unwin, 1955), and Philip A. Brown's *The French Revolution in English History* (London: Crosby Lockwood, 1918). Henry W. Meikle's *Scotland and the French Revolution* (Edinburgh: James Maclehose and Sons, 1912), while outmoded, is still useful for Scottish Radicalism. For a short textbook approach and up-to-date historiographical survey H. T. Dickinson's *British Radicalism and the French Revolution, 1789–1815* (Oxford: Basil Blackwell, 1985) is excellent, outstripping Clive Emsley's similar *British Society and the French Wars, 1793–1815* (Totowa, NJ: Rowman and Littlefield, 1979). Emsley, a specialist in the Pitt Ministry's responses to Radicalism, has also written several articles debunking the idea of a Pittite 'White Terror', the best of which are 'An Aspect of Pitt's "Terror": Prosecutions for Sedition during the 1790s' (*Social History*, vi [May 1981] 155–84), 'Repression, "Terror" and the Rule of Law in England during the Decade of the French Revolution' (*English Historical Review*, c [October 1985] 801–25), and 'The Home Office and Its Sources of Information and Investigation, 1791–1801' (*English Historical Review*, xciv [July 1979] 532–61). On a related subject Ian R. Christie's *Stress and Stability in*

Late Eighteenth-Century Britain (Oxford: Clarendon Press, 1984) analyses why Britain was able to avoid a revolution during the 1790s, while J. Ann Hone's *For the Cause of Truth: Radicalism in London, 1796–1821* (New York: Oxford University Press, 1982) is particularly useful concerning the government's spy network. Roger Wells's *Insurrection: The British Experience, 1795–1803* (Gloucester: Alan Sutton, 1983) takes exception to Malcolm I. Thomis and Peter Holt, *Threats of Revolution in Britain, 1789–1848* (Hamden, CT: The Shoe String Press, 1977), which, in Wells's opinion, plays down the revolutionary threat in Britain unduly. Students of the period can also find chapters on Radical and conservative movements in the 1790s in Edward Royle and James Walvin, *English Radicals and Reformers, 1760–1848* (Lexington: The University Press of Kentucky, 1982), John Stevenson, *Popular Disturbances in England, 1700–1870* (New York: Longman, 1979), and Colin Jones (ed.), *Britain and Revolutionary France: Conflict, Subversion and Propaganda* (Exeter: University of Exeter, 1983).

For more specialised studies of the political and philosophical background of the 1790s in Britain scholars can turn to Marianne Elliott's *Partners in Revolution: The United Irishmen and France* (New Haven, CT: Yale University Press, 1982) for an exhaustive study of Irish Radicalism; John Ehrman's *The Younger Pitt: The Reluctant Transition* (Stanford, CA: Stanford University Press, 1983), which forms the second volume of Ehrman's definitive biography of Pitt and covers events from 1788 to 1796; and Mary Thale's *Selections from the Papers of the London Corresponding Society, 1792–1799* (Cambridge: Cambridge University Press, 1983), which complements Henry Collins's 'The London Corresponding Society' in John Saville (ed.), *Democracy and the Labour Movement* (London: Lawrence and Wishart, 1954). Robert R. Dozier's *For King, Constitution, and Country* (Lexington: The University Press of Kentucky, 1983) provides a cursory treatment of the Loyalist movement and should be supplemented by Eugene Charlton Black's still useful *The Association* (Cambridge, MA: Harvard University Press, 1963). Readers should also see Austin Mitchell's 'The Association Movement of 1792–3' (*Historical Journal*, IV [1961] 56–77), which claims that John Reeves's Association for Preserving Liberty and Property turned 'the whole country Tory', and Donald E. Ginter's 'The Loyalist Association Movement of 1792–93 and British Public Opinion' (*Historical Journal*, IX [1966] 179–90), which argues that it did not. For excellent analyses of Radical and conservative thought scholars can rely on H. T. Dickinson's *Liberty and Property: Political Ideology in Eighteenth-Century Britain* (New York: Holmes and Meier, 1977), which examines changing Radical and conservative philosophical patterns, and Margaret C. Jacob's *The Radical Enlightenment: Pantheists, Freemasons and Republicans* (London: George Allen and Unwin, 1981).

Very little material exists in print concerning the *Anti-Jacobin Review* (or its weekly predecessor) specifically. Brief references to the *Review* are to be found in Alvin Sullivan (ed.), *British Literary Magazines: The Romantic Age, 1789–1836* (Westport, CT: Greenwood Press, 1983), Walter James Graham's *English Literary Periodicals* (New York: Thomas Nelson and Sons, 1930), John O. Hayden's *The Romantic Reviewers, 1802–1824* (London: Routledge and Kegan Paul, 1969), and Derek Roper's *Reviewing before the 'Edinburgh', 1788–1802* (London: Methuen, 1978), while Arthur Aspinall's *Politics and the Press, c. 1780–1850* (London: Home and Van Thal, 1949) provides a useful background for general press history during the period. A number of brief accounts (most of them old) exist concerning the *Anti-Jacobin; or, Weekly Examiner*. For short histories see W. B. Duffield, 'The Anti-Jacobin. An Anniversary Article', *Cornhill Magazine*, n.s. v (July 1898) 17–32; Charles Edmonds (ed.), 'Editor's Preface', *Poetry of The Anti-Jacobin* (2nd edn; London: G. Willis, 1854) pp. iii–x; H. R. Fox Bourne, 'Anti-Jacobins and Reformers', *GM*, cclxiii (December 1887) 559–84; Josceline Bagot (ed.), 'The "Anti-Jacobin"', *George Canning and His Friends* (London: John Murray, 1909) i, 135–52; plus chapters in the more recent Roy Benjamin Clark, *William Gifford: Tory Satirist, Critic, and Editor* (New York: Columbia University Press, 1930), and Wendy Hinde, *George Canning* (New York: St Martin's Press, 1973). Emory Lee Head's unpublished work, 'A Study of *The Anti-Jacobin; or, Weekly Examiner*' (Ph.D. dissertation, Duke University, NC, 1971), concentrates on an analysis of the newspaper's content. For speculations concerning the identity of contributors see Edward Hawkins, 'Authors of the Poetry of the Anti-Jacobin', *Notes and Queries*, 1st ser., iii (3 May 1851) 348–9; Bolton Corney, [Note on the *Anti-Jacobin*], *Notes and Queries*, 1st ser., iii (3 May 1851) 349; H. W. V. Temperley, 'The "Anti-Jacobin", Gillray, and Canning', *Academy*, lxviii (25 March 1905) 345; Richard H. Perkinson, 'The Anti-Jacobin', *Notes and Queries*, clxxii (6 March 1937) 164; L. W. Hanson, 'Canning's Copy of "The Anti-Jacobin"', *British Museum Quarterly*, xi (October 1936) 19; Emsley, *British Society and the French Wars*, p. 66; and Martin J.

Griffin, [Note on Sir James Mackintosh's Copy of the *Anti-Jacobin*],
Athenaeum, 3268 (14 June 1890) 769–70. In addition, see J. D. C.'s
'The "Anti-Jacobin"', *Athenaeum*, 3268 (14 June 1890) 769, for a
discussion of the demise of the *Anti-Jacobin* newspaper; J. D. C.'s
'Coleridge and the Anti-Jacobins', *Athenaeum*, 3266 (31 May 1890)
703–4, for an account of Coleridge's reply to the 'New Morality'
verses in the *Anti-Jacobin*; and Frederick Greenwood's article,
'Canning's "Anti-Jacobin"' (*Academy*, LXVIII [18 March 1905] 275–6),
describing the physical appearance of the *Anti-Jacobin* newspaper.

   For readers interested in the exciting game of detective work that
is involved in identifying obscure late eighteenth-century parsons,
civil servants, schoolmasters, pamphleteers, and *émigrés*, a brief
introduction to the principal sources and reference material is in
order. A number of useful biographical dictionaries are available,
including Alexander Chalmers's *General Biographical Dictionary*,
William Upcott's *A Biographical Dictionary of the Living Authors of
Great Britain and Ireland* (London: Henry Colburn, 1816), the
indispensable *Biographie Universelle, Ancienne et Moderne* and
Nouvelle Biographie Générale, the *Biographie des Hommes Vivants* (Paris:
L. G. Michaud, Imprimeur-Libraire, 1816–19), and of course the
Dictionary of National Biography. Other basic references include the
Gentleman's Magazine, with its thousands of obituaries; the *Annual
Biography and Obituary*; the *Index Ecclesiasticus* (Oxford: Parker, 1890)
with its list of clerics and their livings in England and Wales before
1840; the *Alumni Oxonienses*, the *Alumni Cantabrigienses*, and similar
matriculation lists for the universities of Edinburgh, Glasgow, and
Dublin; and registers of admission to the Inns of Court (*A Calendar of
the Inner Temple Records*, *Records of the Honorable Society of Lincoln's
Inn*, *The Register of Admissions to Gray's Inn*, and the *Register of
Admissions to the Honourable Society of the Middle Temple*). Assorted
membership lists for learned and professional societies, such as the
Society of Antiquaries of London, the Society of the Antiquaries of
Scotland, the Royal College of Physicians (London and Edinburgh),
the Royal College of Surgeons, the Medical Society (London and
Edinburgh), and the Society of Writers to Her Majesty's Signet, are
also useful, as are the *Transactions* of the Royal Society of London
and the Royal Society of Edinburgh. For publication lists readers
should consult the British Library's *General Catalogue of Printed Books*
and the *Catalogue Général des Livres Imprimés de la Bibliothèque Nationale*
(Paris), plus the *English Catalogue of Books . . . , 1801–1836* and
Robert Watt's *Bibliotheca Britannica* (Edinburgh: Archibald

Constable, 1824). Finally, useful titbits of literary arcana can be found in John Nichols' *Literary Anecdotes of the Eighteenth Century* (London: printed for the author, 1812–15), Nichols's *Illustrations of the Literary History of the Eighteenth Century* (London: printed for the author, 1817–58), David Rivers's *Literary Memoirs of Living Authors of Great Britain* (London: R. Faulder, 1798), and William Beloe's *The Sexagenarian; or, the Recollections of a Literary Life* (2nd edn; London: F. C. and J. Rivington, 1818).

Index

[For a complete listing of each contributor's articles appearing in the *Anti-Jacobin Review* see headnote preceding the relevant biographical entry in the text.]